Śrī Sūrya Sahasranāmam – Explanations & Comments

*

Kamalātmānanda Nāthaḥ @ **Dr. Ramamurthy N.**

M.Sc., B.G.L., CAIIB, CCP, DSADP, CISA, PMP, CGBL, Ph.D.

*

*

Name: *Śrī Sūrya Sahasranāmam* – Explanations & Comments

First Edition: 2024

Author: *Kamalātmānanda Nāthaḥ* @
Dr. Ramamurthy N,
http://ramamurthy.jaagruti.co.in/

ISBN (13): 978-93-341-3790-3

Number of pages: 322

Price: ₹ 450.00

Printed at:

Published by:

*****

Table of Contents

*****

Dedication

|| *Oṃ Chāyā Suvarcalāṃbā Sameta Śrī Sūryanārāyaṇa Svāmine Namaḥ* ||

|| ॐ छाया सुवर्चलांबा समेत श्री सूर्यनारायण स्वामिने नमः ||

This book is dedicated with devotion to all the *upasakas* of Sun God, especially those who belong to *Soura* sub-religion. There cannot be even an iota of doubt that all will be blessed by *Śrī Rudran*.

Kamalātmānanda Nāthaḥ @ Dr. Ramamurthy N

*****

Reg No : 87/2014 BKIV

ARSHA VIDYA VILASAM FOUNDATION

TRICHY - TUTICORIN - THANE

Tasmat Sastram Pramanam Te...

AVVF

Vedanta

Meditation

Yoga

Sanskrit

Blessings

दुर्लभं त्रयमेवैतत् देवानुग्रहहेतुकम्।
मनुष्यत्वं मुमुक्षुत्वं महापुरुषसंश्रय।

Durlabhaṃ Trayamevaitat Devānugrahahetukam ।
Manuṣyatvaṃ Mumukṣutvaṃ Mahāpuruṣasaṃśraya: ॥

As *Shrimad Bhagavad Padal* (Viveka Choodamani – 148) has blessed, it is the rarest of rare to get a human body. Even if one does find one;

शुभैराप्नोति देवत्वं निषिद्धैर्नारकीं तनुम् ।
उभाभ्यां पुण्यपापाभ्यां मानुष्यं लभतेऽवश ॥

Śubhairāpnoti Devatvaṃ Niṣiddhairnārakīṃ Tanum ।
Ubhābhyāṃ Puṇyapāpābhyāṃ Mānuṣyaṃ Labhate'vaśa:॥
(*Naiśkarmya Siddhi*: 1.41)

This verse by Sureshvaracharya, the chief disciple of Shrimad Adi Shankarar, tells us an important truth about our birth – that although human birth is rare, at the time of birth, a human being is born with 50% merit (virtues) and 50% demerit (sins). That is why he experiences happiness as a result of merit and sufferings as a result of sin. Life is a two-pronged struggle, running after happiness and running away from sufferings. Very few people manage to reach the shore from this struggle.

No.30, Linga Receidency, Yours Colony, 1st Main Road, Ramalinga Nagar, Woraiyur, Trichy - 620 003.
Mobile No : 94428 56102 e-mail : avvf.office@gmail.com
web : www.avvf.co.in

But most people's lives are like being caught in the middle of the ocean, caught in the middle of the ocean, caught in the grip of a storm, drowning in the deep sea, unable to recover, being reborn, struggling and dying again and again.

In order to change this situation and enable the common man to attain enlightenment, our ancestors, the Rishis, the sages and the wise, have bestowed upon us a wonderful boon. That is, a way of life called 'Upasana'.

The etymology of Upasana is, *Saguṇabrahma Dhyānarūpa Mānasīka Vyāpāra*: (सगुणब्रह्म ध्यानरूप मानसीक व्यापारः). That is, the Supreme Being, which is present everywhere, is established in a form and is meditated on and worshipped in a proper manner. When we perform the Upasana, that is, the worship, our sins are completely removed and we can attain the blissful great life, even in this body.

Thus, innumerable Upasanas and their methods are found in our Vedas, Agamas and Puranas. Among them, the most important is the worship of the Sun, the Practical Devata.

जन्मना जायते शूद्रः संस्काराद् द्विज उच्यते ।
वेदपाठाद् भवेद् विप्रः ब्रह्म जानाति ब्राह्मण : ॥ *Skanda Purāṇam* 31-34

Janmanā Jāyate Śūdraḥ Saṃskārād Dvija Ucyate ।
Vedapāṭhād Bhaved Vipraḥ Brahma Jānāti Brāhmaṇa: ॥

As stated in this verse, "The worship of the Sun God, called 'Savita' of the Gayatri Mantra, which makes a person a human being, makes him a person who knows the Vedas, makes him a person who is not a garment, realises the Supreme Being, the philosophy of Brahmam, which is everywhere and makes him a supreme sage, is of great importance."

This book makes us understand the above greatness and subtleties very easily. Surya Sahasranamam – The explanations and commentaries of the 1,000 divine names of the Sun God, have been explained in a very simple manner and beautifully by the author, Dr. Ramamurthy, without diminishing its quality.

We are very happy that by the grace of Sri Rajarajeshwari Lalita Maha Tripura Sundari, this book will make us realise the secrets of Sri Surya Sahasranamam and provide us with deeper knowledge and Siddhi.

We offer our full blessings and prayers that this rare book will reach all classes of people, be read and understood by them, and that the entire human society will rise higher and attain paragati Siddhi and that Sanatana Dharma will stand firm forever.

*****

Introduction

Oṃ Śrī Gurubhyo Namaḥ I ॐ श्री गुरुभ्यो नमः I

Gurur Brahmā Gurur Viṣṇur Gururdevo Maheśvaraḥ I
Gurusākshāt Param Brahma Tasmai Śrī Gurave Namaḥ II

गुरुर्ब्रह्मा गुरुर्विष्णुर्गुरुर्देवोमहेश्वरः । गुरुसाक्षात् परं ब्रह्म तस्मै श्रीगुरवे नमः ॥

The force of *Parabrahmam*, without any image, qualities and undefined, which includes a number of morphological, incomprehensible and inexhaustible materials, seems to be limited. The absolute philosophical paradigm is not amorphous.

However, we are not yet mature enough to realise the formless *Parabrahmam* (no need of writing/ reading this book, if we are that much mature). Someone has to hold back or attach side wheels until one learns to drive a bicycle. Once he becomes expert these are not needed. We need a boat to cross a river. Once we have reached the other shore, what is the need of a boat.

Therefore, until we mature, we will try to learn about one or o33ther God.

Śrī Ādi Śaṅkara Bhagwat Pādar, the greatest philosopher and thinker, in a short life span of 32 years, has created a collection of art-essays of Indian culture and the intellectual and emotional integration of this sub-continent.

The supreme beauty of his teachings is that they apply to all human beings irrespective of religion or race, caste or creed or nationality. That is why he is undoubtedly *'Jagadguru'*.

There is one name as *"Śanmada Stāpakar"* in the *ashtotram* of *Adi Shankarar* – the founder of *Shanmada*. He has streamlined six sub-religions of Hinduism.

Worshipping of these Gods were there even before *Sri Adi Shankara*. However, he only structured them, brought a system into play and hence, called as the author of *Shanmada* and Advaita doctrines. According to *Shrimad Devi Bhagavata Maha Purana*, worshipping of deities such as Lord

Shiva, *Viṣṇu*, Shakti, Ganapati and Surya were in vogue. Accordingly, sub-branch religions such as Shaivism, Vaishnavism, Shaktam, Ganapadyam and Souram, though not so named, were prevalent. As Lord Kumara was not born then, Koumaram could not have existed.

Sri Adi Shankara also included one more sub-religion called *Koumaram*. These six religions are considered to be the branches of Hinduism. Hinduism is a conglomeration of these six sub-religions. Hence, the Advaita concepts are common to all the six sub-religions. Later, the *Smārtas*, which is not one of the six branches, appear to be a branch of Hinduism, which in some sense is associated with *Shaivam*. In one perspective, they can be called *smārtas* because all the gods are worshipped in the same sense by them – *sama* + *artha*.

Sauram – Worshipping Sun God primarily as the main deity is called *Sauram*. Sun God is traditionally one of the major five deities, all of whom are considered as equivalent deities in the *Panchayatana puja* and a means to realise *Brahmam*.

Earlier the author of this book has translated the Samskruta Bhashyam of Sri Bhaskararaya on Sri Lalitā Sahasranamaminto English. Also, the Bhashyam of Sri Adi Shankara on Sri Lalitā Triśatī (300 names on Sri Lalitā) both in English and Tamil. He has also written commentaries on Gāyatri Sahasranamam and Rudra Triśatī both in English and Tamil. Similar requests were received to write the comments on the 1,000 names of Lord Suryaa also. No Bhashyam seem to exist for Sri Surya Sahasranamam. Hence an attempt has been made here to give possible comments on the 1,000 names of Lord Sun. Wherever possible comparisons are made with Shiva, Lalitā and *Viṣṇu* Sahasranamams, Lalita and Rudra Trisathee, Srimad Bhagavad Gita and some other Veda sentences. Although there are many Sahasranamams and Trishathi Archanas for all the Gods, the above mentioned ones are taken from the Vedas/ Puranas. Hence, these are very special.

Conventions – Wherever **He** is used to indicates *Lord Shiva*. The transliterated Samskrutam or other language words are written in *italics*. When Samskruta words are transliterated in English diacritical marks are used for proper pronunciation like;

ā – as in *Rama* *ḍ* – as in mud
ḍh – as in godhood *ḥ* – visarga in as in *Rāmaḥ*

ī – as in peel *ṇ* – as in pun
ṛ – as in strewn *ś* – as in Shankar
ṣ – as in fish *ṭ* – as in cut
ṭh – as in anthill *ū* – as in root

Humble pranams to HH *ŚrīŚrī* ***Prnavānanda Swāmijee***, who has blessed me and the readers with his nice introduction and some pleasantries. I am fortunate to have association with people like ***Swāmijees***, who are my *Gurus*. Sincere thanks are due to all who helped me in bringing this book so nicely.

Appreciation and acknowledgements are due to all those who supported in this noble cause.

The readers are requested to feel free in providing feedback. Let all the readers be blessed with glory of Gods.

This book is also being written by the same author in Tamil simultaneously.

Om Tat Sat

Chennai
2024

Dr. *Ramamurthy N*

*****

Śrī Sūrya God

Lord Sun is the only Pratyaksha God – Grossly visible to everyone. The Sun is visible to every being and is the basis of life of all creatures on earth.

Sūrya is the Sun as well as the solar deity in Hinduism. He is traditionally one of the major five deities, all of whom are considered as equivalent in the Panchayatana puja and a mean to realise Brahmam. Other names of Surya in ancient Indian literature include Aditya, Arka, Bhanu, Savitr, Pushan, Ravi, Martanda, Mitra, Bhaskara, Prabhakara, Kathiravan, and Vivasvan. These are a few of one thousand names, we are going to understand in the later chapters.

Lord Surya has lots of connection with number seven. The iconography of Surya is often depicted riding a chariot harnessed by seven horses, which represent the seven colours of visible light and the seven days of the week. During Makara month (January-February), seventh day (Saptami) bright lunar fortnight, the day is called *"Ratha Saptami"* – the day Bheeshma attained moksha. On that day *argyam* and *tarpanam* are done for Bheeshma and Lord Surya.

During the medieval period, Surya was worshipped in tandem with Brahma during the day, Shiva at noon, and *Viṣṇu* in the evening. In some ancient texts and art, Surya is presented syncretical with Indra, Ganesha, and others. Surya as a deity is also found in the arts and literature of Buddhism and Jainism. In the Mahabharata and Ramayana, Surya is represented as the spiritual father of Rama and Karna (protagonists of the Ramayana and the Mahabharata, respectively). Surya was a primary deity in veneration by the characters of the Mahabharata and Ramayana, along with Shiva. In fact, Lord Rama was born in Surya race.

Shrimad Devi Bhagavata and Devi related texts mention that Sun, Moon and Agni (fire god) are the three eyes of Sri Devi. In some texts it is mentioned that Sun and Moon are the breasts of Sri Devi.

Surya's chariot is normally depicted with only one wheel, also interpreted as Dharmachakra. Surya is the lord of Siṃha (Leo), one of the twelve constellations in the zodiac system of Hindu astrology. He moves from one zodiac sign to the next, once a month. In that way he will go around all the 12 signs, once in a year. Surya or Ravi is the basis of Ravivara or Sunday, in the Hindu calendar.

Having survived as a primary deity in Hinduism longer than any most of the original Vedic deities, the worship of Surya declined greatly around the 13th century, perhaps as a result of the Muslim destruction of Sun temples in North India. New Sun temples virtually ceased to be built, and some were later repurposed to a different deity. A number of important Surya temples remain, but most are no longer in worship. In certain aspects, Surya has tended to be merged with the prominent deities of *Viṣṇu* or Shiva, or seen as subsidiary to them.

Though as per Astronomy Sun is considered as one of the Stars. But as per Astrology, he is the most important planet in Navagraha. We used to call *Ādityāti Navagraham*. The colour pertaining to him is red. He is facing East direction. Sage Kashyapa and Athiti are his parents. Chaya and Usha Devi are his two wives. In some places it is mentioned as *Chaya* and *Swarchalamba*. Planet Saturn (*Sanīśwaran*) is a son born to him and Chaya. Vaivashvata Manu, Yama, Yami, Ashvins, Revanta, Tapati, Savarni Manu, Sugriva and Karna are his other children.

According to astrology, Sun, lord of Leo, ascends in Aries. He is the lord of the Magam, Pooram and Uttaram (first part) stars. He is friendly with Mars and Jupitar. Venus is his enemy. Wheat is his favorite grain. Among the nine gems the ruby stone belongs to Surya. He is generally referred to as *Pitru Karagan* (meant for ancestors).

In Mahabharata he is the father of Karna. In Ramayana, Sun is the father of Sugrivan. He is the *guru* (teacher) of Anjaneya and taught him all the Vedas, Eight great siddhis. The story goes this way – Vayu (Air god) father of Anjaneya requested Sun God to be the Guru of his son. But Sun said his chariot is always – 24 x 7 – moving and he cannot stop and teach. Anjaneya ran backwards in front of the chariot of Sun with the same speed and learnt from Sun God.

During the battle with Ravana, sage Agastya taught *Aditya Hrudayam* (30 verses praying the Sun God – *Valmiki Ramayanam* 6-107) to Rama and asked to chant this and pray to Sun God just before the last fight. Rama also prayed Sun God and won the battle.

According to the verse of Srimad Vishnu Bhagavatam (12.11.32), Lord Suryanarayana, who is in the form of time, travels around the world with his 12 separate Ganas, each month starting from Chitrai (April-May), in order to ensure that the world's affairs run smoothly. As per *Rig Veda*, there are 12 Adityas, who are personified deities representing different aspects of the Sun as experienced in the 12 months of the Hindu calendar. They are all offsprings of Aditi Devi and sage Kashyapa. They have been seen as upholding the movables and immovable Dharma. Adityas are beneficent gods who act as protectors of all beings, who are provident and guard the world of spirits and protect this world. In the form of Mitra-Varuna, the Adityas are true to the eternal Law and act as the exactors of debt. The names of the 12 Adityas are – 12 verses of Srimad Vishnu Bhagavatam (12.11.33 – 44) describe the the names of Sun God for each month in a different way;

- Vivasvan (Surya)
- Aryaman
- Tvashta
- Savitr
- Bhaga
- Dhata
- Mitra
- Varuna
- Amsa
- Pushan
- Indra
- Vishnu (in the form of Vamana)

Srimad Vishnu Bhagavatam (12.11.46 - 49) 4 verses say;

1. These twelve Gandharvas first roam everywhere with their six Ganas in the 12 months and spread goodness in this world and in heaven.

2. The great sages praise the Lord Sun with all their heart through the three Vedas, namely Rig, Yajur and Sama, which highly talk about the Sun. The Gandharvas sing about him. The Apsara women dance before him.
3. The Nagas tie the Sun's chariot tightly. The Yakshas decorate it. The strong demons push it from behind.
4. The 60,000 Brahma Rishis, called Valakillis, who are holy, go in front of the Sun, facing Him, praising Him with many hymns.

According to the verse of Srimad Vishnu Bhagavatam (12.11.30), the Lord Sri Hari, who is actually the soul and creator of all the worlds, becomes the Sun in the form of Antaryama. Although He is the one, the Rishis describe Him in many forms. This is because He is the root cause of all the actions mentioned in the Vedas, that is, there is no difference in nature except for the difference in action.

There are 132 *Panjātis,* in 32 *Anuvākas* called "*Aruŋa Praśnam*" in *Taitrīya Āraŋyakam* of *Krishna Yajur Veda*. In this, the structure of the universe, time chronology and human anatomy have been discussed in detail. Reciting it on Sundays for physical health and doing 183 (*Pūrvānga* 42, *Panjatis* 132, *Navagraham* 9) prostrations is not uncommon. Those who are unable to do so, perform 83 (*Pūrvānga* 42, Anuvākas 32, Navagraham 9) prostrations. Those who are still unable to do that will simply recite.

Reciting this, there will be no shortage of physical health. Mainly, it is believed that if the husband chants the 13th *Anuvaka,* while the wife is in the labour ward, the delivery will be smooth.

In a non-religious perspective, Surya Namaskar is a powerful yoga pose. Besides being a great cardiovascular workout, Surya Namaskar is also known to have an immensely positive impact on the body and mind.

Practicing Surya Namaskar steps is best done early morning on an empty stomach. Each round of Sun Salutation consists of two sets, and each set is composed of 12 yoga poses. There are several versions on how to practice Sun Salutation. Besides good health, Surya Namaskar also provides an opportunity to express gratitude to the Sun for sustaining life on this planet.

Greek mythology had two sun gods – Helios, the God Sun and Apollo, the god of light and justice, who was often conflated with Helios. Roman mythology worshipped Helios as Sol and the later Roman Empire even crafted a cult of that god, naming him Sol Invictus.

There are two versions of Surya Sahasranama Stotram and naturally the 1,000 names derived from the stotrams. One is from Bhavishya Puranam and the other one is from Skanda Puranam. However, majority follow the one from Bhavishya Puranam and hence, the same is followed in this book.

As the Sunrise dispels that darkness of the worlds, Surya also removes the darkness of ignorance and bestows wisdom. Sun is said to be the embodiment of all knowledge. The worship of the Sun increases the brightness, strength, age and light of the eyes of man. Human beings have longevity. Surya is the deity to remove all eye diseases and skin diseases. The best time to chant Surya Mantra is early morning during Sunrise.

Normally during any arcana, be it, *sahasranama*, *ashtotra* or anything else, the names are prefixed with ' *Oṃ*' and suffixed with '*Namaḥ*'. *Oṃ* is *Pranava mantra* and prefixed with all the mantras. *Namaḥ*, in general means "I bow". But, '*Namaḥ*' is one of the Seven crores great mantras. Its fruit will bring wealth. "*Vayam Namaḥ Sampatkaram Tatā*". Hence the deva who is said with '*Namaḥ*' in the end (in Tamil koti means end) will give us all wealth. Hence the result of worshiping the Lord is getting wealth.

*****

Souram (Worship of *Sūrya*)

The sub-religions of Hinduism (*Şaŋmadas*) founded by Sri Adi Shankara – *Gāŋapadyam, Koumāram, Śaivam, Vaişŋavam, Śāktam* and *Souram*. Those who treat the Sun predominantly and worship him are called Souras.

Our forefathers, Vedic Rishis, were great sages who lived in harmony with nature. They are real scientists who discovered the true power and utility of each of the five primary elements[1] – earth, fire, water, ether and wind – through their subtle spiritual intelligence. Because of that, they did not ignore the forces of nature as immaterial objects like today's scientific geniuses, but had a systematic relationship with them. Finding each of these natural forces as the source of life in this world, they used to worship them as deity forms. Among such natural forces, the Sun was worshiped primarily by our Maharishis. This is evidenced by the numerous mantras found in the Vedas regarding Surya. Several *sooktas* in the Rig Veda, the section Aruna *Kātakam* in the Yajur veda and the sixth musical samas of the Samaveda, called Sukriyam, explain the scientific aspects of the Sun and the divine power. Our rishis saw the Sun not only as an ordinary rising and setting star in the sky, but also as the source of life, the giver of energy and food, the creator of the universe and even the giver of salvation.

This *soura* religion practiced by the rishis of our Vedic period is the origin of the principle of Monotheism, which many religions of the world today celebrate as their specialty. The source of all energy, the one who gives us knowledge, health and spiritual prosperity is the one and only Sun. Sauram stresses us that He is the manifest to us.

The 50th sooktam of the first mandala of the Rig Veda – "*Druśe Viśvāya Sūryam*" – the Sun, who imparts the knowledge of their duty to all and exhorts them to do it without fail.

---

[1] Later in this Sahasranama, different names refer to Lord Surya as the form of each of these five primary elements.

The 4th rig of this *Sookta* expounds some more important principles of the Soura religion;

Taranirviśwadarśito Jyotiśkrudasi |
Sūrya Viśwamabhāsi Rocanam ||

The term *Taraniḥ* describes the Sun God as one who travels through a difficult path that no one can cross. Two types of *Bhashyas* are provided for this;

1. One who enables his devotees to cross the difficult path of birth.
2. He who resolves any incurable deadly diseases. And when any karma is performed according to the Vedic rules, some unknown errors creep in. This creates a sin in the karta's name. He removes the disease of that sin.

Sapta Yuñjanti Rathamēkacakrō Aśvō Vahati Saptaṉāmā |
Triṉābhi Cakramajaramaṉarvam Yatrēmā Viśvā Bhuvaṉādhi Tasthuḥ ||

This *rig* describes the Sun's chariot as having one wheel and seven well-drawn horses. The wheel of this chariot ' *Triṉābhi*' – wheel of time with three yoked holes representing the three time periods (past, present, future). It is *Ajaram* = imperishable, *Anarvam* = non-hanging. It is the source for all the worlds.

The seven horses harnessed to this chariot are the seven gases called *Sapta Maruts* and his seven bright rays are the seven aspects of time namely *Ayanam*, *Rtu*, Month, *Paksham*, Day, Night and Muhurtham. Thus, Surya God is understood to be the creator of this world, the source that sustains it and stabilises it in action and the eternal deity.

Apart from this, there is a sooktam called "*Rogagna Upanishat*", consists of three rigs and is made available to us by sage *Prashkanva*. Soura religion tells us that it is like shield from Sun God protecting especially from heart and skin diseases and fear of poison.

Na Gayatriya Param Jabyam – Gayatri[2] is the best among all the mantras. The holy torch of the Sun God, called Savitru, is meditated upon as the inner Devata form of the supremely holy Gayatri Mantra. An explanation given by Swami Vivekananda in this regard;

[2] A separate chapter detailing the glory of Gayatri mantra is included in this book.

The Deva *Savitru*, the creator of the universe, inspires our intellect and stimulates us to perform our divine and holy duties. His glorious effulgence will destroy all our sins.

Apart from the *Vedas, Bhavishya Purana, Brahma Purana, Varaha Purana, Matsya Purana, Bhavishyottara Purana, Kālikā Purana, Mārkandeya Purana*, etc., explain Surya worship in detail.

In the Srimad Bhagavad Gita, the essence of all the Upanishats, Lord Krishna declares – *Ādityānām Aham Viṣṇuḥ, Jyotiṣām* Raviramśuman – I am the Sun in all that shines.

The majesty of *Āditya Hrudaya Stotram* preached by Sage Agastya to Lord Rama in Ramayana is very famous.

Above all these, the Saura religion shows a superior prayer mantra of the best quality;

Devam Devatrā Sūryamaganma Jyotirutham |

Above all the Devass, Suryan is the bestower of bountiful resources to worshippers. This mantra is prayed daily by all during the three-times *Sandyavantanam*.

Major festivals and pilgrimages in reverence for Surya include Makar Sankranti, Pongal, Samba Dashami, Ratha Saptami, Chath puja, and Kumbha Mela.

He is particularly venerated in the Saura tradition found in Indian states such as Rajasthan, Gujarat, Madhya Pradesh, Bihar, Maharashtra, Uttar Pradesh, Jharkhand, and Odisha.

There are lot many temples exclusively meant for Sun God. The main among them is Konark. A world heritage site, Konark Sun Temple of Odisha is also listed as one of the Seven Wonders of India. Other major temples are;

- Sun Temple, Modhera.
- Sun Temple, Martand.
- Sun Temple, Gwalior.
- Balaji Sun Temple, Unao.
- Sun Temple, Ranchi.

- Sun Temple, Katarmal.
- Surya Pahar Temple, Assam.

Apart from these, among the Navagraha temples around Kumbakonam in Tamil Nadu, Suryanar Temple, Thirumangalakudi is the most famous.

May this Sun God, who has been worshiped by our Vedic Rishis for ages, bless us all with health, knowledge, energy and spiritual wealth.

*****

Śrī Sūrya Sahasranāma Mantras

Each name on Sun God is a mantra. Let us try to understand them to an extent.

1. *Oṃ Viśvavide Namaḥ* I ॐ विश्वविदे नमः ।

I bow the विश्वविदे नमः God of this universe.

Viśva = Universe. He is the creator of this universe. My salutations to him.

2. *Oṃ Viśvajite Namaḥ* I ॐ विश्वजिते नमः ।

My salutations to the conqueror of this universe.

3. *Oṃ Viśvakartre Namaḥ* I ॐ विश्वकर्त्रे नमः ।

My salutations to the creator of this universe.

Viśva = universe. *Kartre* = to make. He only made this universe – i.e. created this universe.

4. *Oṃ Viśvātmane Namaḥ* I ॐ विश्वात्मने नमः ।

I bow to the atma of this universe.

Viśva = Universe. *Ātmane* = soul. He is the soul of this entire universe.

225th name in *Viṣṇu* Sahasranamam is *Viśvātmā* – the universal soul. He spreads energy to the Universe.

Purusha Sooktam says "He covers the Earth, etc.".

5. *Oṃ Viśvatomukhāya Namaḥ* I ॐ विश्वतोमुखाय नमः ।

He is the mouth of this entire universe. I bow him.

Shrimad Bhagavat Gita (10-11) says having – He having eyes, heads and faces on all sides.

6. *Oṃ Viśveśvarāya Namaḥ* I ॐ विश्वेश्वराय नमः ।

I bow the Lord of this entire universe.

7. *Oṃ Viśvayonaye Namaḥ* I ॐ विश्वयोनये नमः ।

I bow the creator of this entire universe.

He is the source of this entire universe.

8. *Oṃ Niyatātmane Namaḥ* I ॐ नियतात्मने नमः ।

He is self-restrained or self-controlled. I bow him.

Niyama and Yama are the two means of acquiring Yoga. He can be reached only by these two methods.

865th name in *Viṣṇu* Sahasranamamam is *Aniyamaḥ* – Being himself the all-ordained, he knows no restraint.

69th name below may also be referred.

9. *Oṃ Jitendriyāya Namaḥ* I ॐ जितेन्द्रियाय नमः ।

I bow him, who has subjugated his senses.

Since he has controlled all his senses, he can be called as an ascetic or Yogi.

10. *Oṃ Kālāśrayāya Namaḥ* I ॐ कालाश्रयाय नमः ।

He is the controller of time. I bow him.

He controls the wheel of time. Normally the day-time starts when Sun rises and ends when Sun sets. In some countries like Australia, USA and all they adjust the clock for different seasons depending on the Sun rise and set.

11. *Oṃ Kālakartre Namaḥ* I ॐ कालकर्त्रे नमः ।

In continuation of previous name, he is the maker of Time. I bow him.

Shrimad Bhagavad Gita (7-9 & 10-30) says – I am the time of counting.

12. *Oṃ Kālaghne Namaḥ* I ॐ कालघ्ने नमः ।

He is death personified for the enemies. I bow him.

He is the destroyer of time (*Mrutyu*)

Svetasvatara Upanishad VI-2, says – Omniscient, time of time, possessed of all qualities, all knowing – *Brahmam* is the *Kāla* (death) for *Yama* (God of death) himself –

"Gnaḥ Kālakālo Guṇī Sarva Vidyāḥ".

13. *Oṃ Kālanāśanāya Namaḥ* I ॐ कालनाशनाय नमः ।

One who can overcome time. I bow him.

In the form of Lord Shiva, as Samhara Murthy, to protect Markandeyan, he killed Yama (Kalan) and of course gave him re-birth also.

642nd name in *Viṣṇu* Sahasranamam is *Kālanemi* – slayer of demon called Kalanemi.

138th name in Gāyatri Sahasranamam is – *Kālarūpiṇī* – She is in the form of time (*kalam*).

She only decides/ controls the time.

Devi Upanishat mentions that **She** is in the form of a minute time period.

14. *Oṃ Mahāyogine Namaḥ* I ॐ महायोगिने नमः ।

He is a great Yogi. I bow him.

Yoga is a group of physical, mental and spiritual practices or disciplines and aim to control (yoke) and still the mind. one who practices this is a yogi. But Sun God is a Mahayogi – great Yogi.

Integrating those that are differentiated is called *Yoga*. What is differentiated from us is the *Eshvara's* quality. The tool to integrate is *Yoga*. *Yogis* are those who got this *Eshvara's* quality through this. The experts among those are called *Mahāyogis*.

225th name in Sri Lalitā Sahasranamamis *Mahāyogeśvareśvarī*. Sri Bhaskararaya comments this name as;

(i) One who is worshipped by all spiritual adepts – who is *Eshvaree* of all *Yogeshvaras*.
(ii) *Mahāyogas* are the best in yoga methods. The experts in this are called *Mahāyogeeshvaras*. **She** is the head of all those.

33rd, 64th & 964th names below may also be referred.

15. *Oṃ Mahāsiddhaye Namaḥ* I ॐ महासिद्धये नमः ।

I bow to Mahasiddha.

The heaven etc., are useless, since they are perishable and the only imperishable thing is He, who is the wisdom in all substances and who has transcendental form. He is Mahasiddha.

Eight (*ashtama*) great siddhis;

1. *Aṇimā* – moving around without being seen by others by reducing the body to the atomic level.
2. *Mahimā* – Making the body very big.
3. *Lakimā* – To lighten the body even though it is large in size.
4. *Karimā* – Making the body small yet very heavy.
5. *Prapti* – Attainment of desired.
6. *Prākāmyam* – Unhindered fulfillment of desires.
7. *Eeshitvam* – Making the body and the soul transgress the order.
8. *Vashitvam* – Conduct according to one's own will without depending on others. Or conquering everyone/ everything.

In *Valmiki Ramayana* we read about Anjaneya manifesting all these eight siddhis.

One who has the capacity of any one or more of the above Siddhis is a Siddha. Lord Sun has all the Siddhis and he is the one who bestows these siddhis to his devotees.

473rd name in Sri Lalitā Sahasranamamis *Siddhamātā* – mother and guard of *Siddhas* (aspirants).

979th name in Sri Gāyatri Sahasranamamis *Siddhīḥ* – She is the manifestation of all Siddhis. She is the accomplishments like of Ashta Siddhis. She bestows Ashtamaa Siddhis to all.

16. *Oṃ Mahātmane Namaḥ* I ॐ महात्मने नमः ।

I bow the great soul *Mahātma*.

Ātma is any general soul like us. *Mahātma* is a great soul. Lord Sun is a *Mahātma*.

The word *Ātmā* has several meanings – body, mind, *Brahmam*, nature, firmness and intelligence. All these names apt for Sun God.

617th name in Sri Lalitā Sahasranamamis *Atmā* and 618th name is *Paramā*. She is in the form of *Ātman* or *Jeeva* (soul) and also in the form of *Paramatma*.

We used to call Gandhiji as *Mahātma*.

17. *Oṃ Sumahābalāya Namaḥ* I ॐ सुमहाबलाय नमः ।

Balā means strong.

Mahābalā means very powerful.

Sumahābalā means good and very powerful. I worship such a God.

847th name below may also be referred.

18. *Oṃ Prabhave Namaḥ* I ॐ प्रभवे नमः ।

He in the one from whom all things were born. I bow Him.

Among the 60 years in Tamil, the first year is Prabhava. He rules that year.

35th name in *Viṣṇu* Sahasranamam is *Prabhavaḥ* – the superior of origin.

540th name below may also be referred.

19. *Oṃ Vibhave Namaḥ* I ॐ विभवे नमः ।

He is the bestower of all wealth. I bow him.

Among the 60 years in Tamil, the second year is Vibhava. He rules that year.

693rd name below may also be referred.

20. *Oṃ Bhūtanāthāya Namaḥ* I ॐ भूतनाथाय नमः ।

I bow that Lord who is the evolver of all beings.

He creates, supports or protects and destroys all beings.

21. *Oṃ Bhūtātmane Namaḥ* I ॐ भूतात्मने नमः ।

I bow that Lord who is the Atma in all beings.

He lives in the heart of all beings.

8th name in *Viṣṇu* Sahasranamam is *Bhūtātmā* – the Bhatta inner ruler of all beings.

Brahadaranyaka Upanishat (5-7-4) says – this is thy self, the inner ruler and immortal being.

22. *Oṃ Bhuvaneśvarāya Namaḥ* I ॐ भुवनेश्वराय नमः ।

He is the Lord of the entire world. I bow him.

The word *Bhuvanā* has many meanings – earth, heaven, water, etc. **He** is the head of all these.

294th name in Sri Lalitā Sahasranamamis *Bhuvaneśvarī*. She is the sovereign ruler of the universe comprising of fourteen worlds – seven worlds beneath this earth viz., *Athalam, Vitalam, Sutalam, Talātalam, Mahātalam, Rasātalam* and *Patālam*. Six worlds above the earth viz., *Bhuvarloka, Suvarloka, Mahālokā, Janolokā, Tapo Lokā* and *Sathya Loka*. These 13 alongwith our Earth are the 14 worlds. **She** steers these 14 worlds as per **Her** wish.

767th name in Sri Gāyatri Sahasranamamis *Bhuvaneśvarī* – The Shakti due to whom the Universal evolution is made possible and the various Beings are sustained without hassles.

23. *Oṃ Bhūtabhavyāya Namaḥ* I ॐ भूतभव्याय नमः ।

His greatness consists in His having an absolute existence unassociated with any iota of time. I bow him.

4th name in *Viṣṇu* Sahasranamam is *Bhūta Bhavya Bhavat Prabhuḥ* – the lord of the past, present and future.

24. *Oṃ Bhāvitātmane Namaḥ* I ॐ भावितात्मने नमः ।

He can be realised only through deep meditation. I bow him.

The soul is purified by meditating on the universal soul or whose thoughts are fixed on the Supreme Spirit.

25. *Oṃ Bhūtāntaḥkaraṇāya Namaḥ* I ॐ भूतान्तःकरणाय नमः ।

He is the conscience of all the living beings. I bow him.

He only causes end of all beings.

26. *Oṃ Śivāya Namaḥ* I ॐ शिवाय नमः ।

Salutations to him who is in the form of all auspicious things.

In *Śiva* sahasranamam – 614th name – *Śivaḥ* – Blemish-less pure and auspicious form – *Śuddhaḥ Nirūpātiridyarttaḥ* ।

Viśuddhiḥ Śivatā Svataḥ Iti Vāyusam Hitāyām ।

The *Pancākṣara mantra,* as popularly known, is the holy five syllables/ letters that is the supreme *mantra* of all devotees of Lord *Śiva*. This great *mantra* is *Oṃ Namaḥ Śivāya*. The five syllables in this mantra are *na - maḥ - śi - vā - ya* (*Oṃ* is the *praṇava* prefixed to any mantra and not accounted for).

This mantra is the heart of *Vedas*. It is the core of the very famous chapter of Vedas that stands in the middle of the Vedas – the *Śatarudrīyam*. This great *mantra* of *Veda Samhita* while hailing the God as the Lord of everything in the world, salutes the God as *Namaḥ Śivāya Ca Śivatarāya Ca*.

The subtle meaning of this very holy *mantra* is – *namama* – not mine; *Śivāya* – belongs to *Śiva*. It is negating the *ahankara* (ego) and realising everything to belong to Lord *Śiva* only.

Vedas are the best of *Vidyas*. Among the Vedas, *Sri Rudra Namakam* which has eleven *anuvakas* is the best. Among them *Namaḥ Shivaya* is the best *panchakshara* (5 lettered phrase). Among them, especially the two letters *Shiva* are the best.

Sri Rudra Namakam (10.10) – Oh giver of all that is required by worshippers, be a bestower of auspiciousness and good thoughts.

Mīḍhuṣṭama Śivatama Śivo Naḥ Sumanā Bhava I

The statement in the *Vedas* – *Yāte Rudra Sivāthanūḥ* may be referred in this place.

In *Lalitā* sahasranamam – 53rd & 998th – *Shivā* & – *Śrīśivā* – *Śiva*'s consort and hence *Śiva* – inseparable from *Śiva*. Embodiment of auspiciousness, bestower of auspiciousness – The *Icchā Śakti* of the Supreme Being – Liberation personified. Everything ultimately rests with *Śrī Devī*. Hence *Śivā*.

Lord *Parameswara* has eight forms, viz. Earth, Water, Fire, Wind, Space, Sun, Moon and Jiva. *Śiva* in the form wind is called *Isana*. **His** consort is *Śivā*.

She is *Śivā* with *Śrī* (wealth). Since **She** is the sacred consort of *Śiva* and since **She** is an integral part of *Śiva*, **she** got the name as *Śiva*. Hence whatever meaning applicable to *Śiva* is applicable to **Her** also.

In *Viṣṇu* sahasranamam – 27th & 600th names – *Śivaḥ* – One who is eternally pure. In Him can never be any contamination of the imperfection of *Rajas* and *Tamas*. "Non-apprehension of Reality" is *Tamas* and "mis-apprehensions of Reality" constitute *Rajas*. In the Reality itself there can be neither of them "He is *Brahmam*; He is *Śiva*", hence the *Upaniṣat* declares of the Absolute Oneness, which is *Vishnu*.

Śrī Ādi Śaṇkara in his commentary mentions; since he is pure and not influenced by the three qualities, he is called as *Śiva*. *Nārāyaŋopanişat* advises the integrated form, *Vişŋu* only is being worshipped as *Śivā*;

Nistraiguŋyatayā Śuddhatvāt Śiva: I *"Sa Brahma Sa Śivaḥ"*
Ityabhedopadeśāt Śivādināmabhiḥ Harireva Stūyate II

Lord *Nārāyaṇa* is adored here as *Śivaḥ* and, at the same time, everyone whether Śaivites or Vaişṇavites repeat *Vişṇu Sahasranāma*. Human prejudices have no logic or reason. *Śrī Nārāyaṇa* is *Śiva* (auspiciousness) and there is no difference between the two. "I am the dweller of Vaikuṇṭa, *Vişṇu*. Between us there is no difference", so says Lord *Śiva* Himself. *Vişṇu* is the 'Purifier' (*Śiva*), as his names, when chant and his form-divine, when meditated upon, become a means of quietening the mind and sharpening our perceptions of the subtler and the transcendental.

Colloquially *Śivaḥ* indicates Lord *Śiva* only. But here we see that it indicates *Vişṇu* also. Even in *Śiva Sahasranāma* the name occurs once only, but in *Vişṇu Sahasranāma* it occurs twice, indicating no difference between them.

The Vedic phrase *Śiva Ekotyeyaś Śivankaraḥ* – The word Shiva means the giver of greatness and fame. Anywhere else like Puranas if any other meaning is given that is included in the meaning given by Vedas.

In the Agama Shastras the word Shiva is said to be *Jeevaratnam* (gem of jeevas). The Shiva Puranas describe its glories in great detail.

Thus, it has been again and again stressed that Lord Shiva, *Vişṇu* and Surya are all one and the same. There is only one God – that is Brahmam.

27. *Oṃ Śaraṇyāya Namaḥ* I ॐ शरण्याय नमः ।

He is the God with whom everyone seeks refuge with. I bow him.

316th & 390th names below may also be referred.

28. *Oṃ Kamalānandāya Namaḥ* I ॐ कमलानन्दाय नमः ।

He feels happy by sitting on a Lotus flower. I bow him.

He makes the lotus flower joyful, by sitting on it.

29. *Oṃ Nandanāya Namaḥ* I ॐ नन्दनाय नमः ।

He is the source of happiness for all beings. I bow him.

In *Viṣṇu* sahasranamam – 527th name – *Nandanaḥ* – conveying the same meaning.

599th name below may also be referred.

30. *Oṃ Nandavardhanāya Namaḥ* I ॐ नन्दवर्धनाय नमः ।

Nanda – Ananda – bliss – He bestows bliss to all. I bow him.

He takes his devotees towards bliss.

31. *Oṃ Vareṇyāya Namaḥ* I ॐ वरेण्याय नमः ।

Supreme bliss to bow with.

In *Śiva* sahasranamam – 881st name – *Vareṇyaḥ* – conveying the same meaning.

32. *Oṃ Varadāya Namaḥ* I ॐ वरदाय नमः ।

I bow him, who bestows all the boons to his devotees.

Any legal desire asked for will be satisfied by Him.

In *Viṣṇu* sahasranamam – 330th name – *Varadaḥ* – Sri Adi Shankarar comments for this name as – He gives the boons desired by the devotees in their minds. He becomes the doer of sacrificial fire and gives the boons i.e. the cow as a price. "*Gourvai Varaḥ*" is the *Veda* saying quoted for this.

In *Gāyatri* sahasranamam – 896th name – *Varadā* – She grants boons to *Brahma, Viṣṇu* and other devotees. *Narada* says in *Matsya* and *Padma Puranas* – *Sri Devi*'s uplifted hand (*varada mudra*) ever confers boons. She will give boons to all *Devas, daityas* and ascetics. It has to be understood that the word *varada* indicate that the hand is the instrument of giving, here the hand of *Sri Devi*, is said to confer boons. In reality, the expression means simply to fulfill the desire of the *Devas* – not having the emblem of granting boons.

In *Lalitā* sahasranamam – 331st name – *Varadā* – conveying the same message.

Sri Adi Shankara says in his commentary to *Soundaryalaharee* (4th verse) – without even the emblem of boons in hands, *Sri Devi* provides the boons more than expected to her devotees.

Sri Devi Puranam also says – **She** fulfills the desires of the *Devas* who seek boons. From the root *'Vr'* to choose, **she** is called *Varadā*, conferrer of boons, i.e. giver of the things chosen.

In the *Varaha Purana* also in the chapter on the *Vetrāsuravadha, Sri Devi* is always to be worshipped, by concentration on the ninth day of the lunar fortnight; **She** will certainly become the giver of boons to all worlds.

In *Śiva* sahasranamam – 6th name – *Varadaḥ* – conveying the same meaning.

134th and 961st names names below may also be referred.

33. *Oṃ Yogine Namaḥ* । ॐ योगिने नमः ।

He has a *Yoga* form. I bow him.

The most significant Yoga is that of Ashtanga Yoga is not only a Physical Exercise but a Spiritual Experience and Discipline comprising;

- *Yama* comprises Ahimsa or Non-Violence, Satya or Truthfulness, Asteya or non-stealing, Brahmacharya or celibacy, and Aparigraha or non- greediness;
- *Niyama* comprising Shoucha or Purity, Santosha or Contentment, Tapas or austerity, Swadhyaya or Self-Teaching or Introspection and Ishwara Pranidhana or inquisitiveness of Divinity;

- *Asana* or the sitting posture of a yogi which serves five purposes viz. normal activity of limbs, exercise of limbs, mental energy, intellectual enhancement and Spiritual Awareness. There could be many postures of Asanas while standing, forward bending, supine or prostrate, inverted, abdominal or lumbar, twisting, back bending, balancing and so on. But the Padmasana is the most popular of Ashtanga yoga;
- *Pranayama* or control of breathing – the methods being Sahita Kumbhaka or retention techniques for physical and mental soundness, Surya Bhedi Pranayama or inhalation (Pooraka) through right nostril and exhalation (Rechaka) through the right nostril for good digestion and removing impurities of body and mind, Ujjayi Pranayama or travel of breathing between nose and heart to control cough and cold besides removal of impurities, Bhraamari or concentrated and fixed pattern of breathing to improve concentration and will power, Murccha Pranayama is an extreme form of breath retention which only yogis could perform as it would be a near unconscious state and finally Kewali Pranayama is temporary stoppage of breath;
- *Pratyahara* is extraction and suppression of senses from karmendriyas and Jnanendriyas;
- *Dharana* or retention of that stage for long durations;
- *Dhyana* or immersion of the Self in deep meditation and Samadhi or the climactic stage of trance;

In *Lalitā* sahasranamam – 654th name – *Yogadā* – She bestows Yoga to her devotees.

In *Vişņu* sahasranamam – 18th name – *Yogaḥ* – Lord *Vişņu* is in Yoga form.

In *Śiva* sahasranamam – 79th & 782nd names – *Yogiḥ* – Lord Shiva himself is a Yogi.

In *Gāyatri* sahasranamam – 828th name – *Yogā* – She is what Yoga is all about.

14th above and 64th & 964th names below may also be referred.

34. *Oṃ Susaṃyuktāya Namaḥ* । ॐ सुसंयुक्तायनमः ।

He is the paramatma integrating with other jeevatmas. I bow him.

Saṃyukta means joining or integrating. *Susaṃyukta* is well integrating. That is mainly for assuring.

35. *Oṃ Prakāśakāya Namaḥ* I ॐ प्रकाशकाय नमः ।

He is an illuminator. I bow him.

He reveals his form to his devotees.

As per astronomy, stars are self-illuminating bodies. Sun is a star and hence self-illuminating.

In *Viṣṇu* sahasranamam – 274th name – *Prakaṣanaḥ* – conveying the same message.

In *Śiva* sahasranamam – 508th name – *Prakhaśaḥ* – Lord Shiva is illuminating.

In *Gāyatri* sahasranamam – 861st name – *Prakāśin* – She shines like anything. *Sri Devi*, who is in the form of Brahmam, resides within the Sun also. *Sri Devi* shines as the only brilliant ruler of the universe. One who shines with all divine qualities.

36. *Oṃ Prāptayānāya Namaḥ* I ॐ प्राप्तयानाय नमः ।

He is always young and I bow him.

37. *Oṃ Paraprāṇāya Namaḥ* I ॐ परप्राणाय नमः ।

The individual self or supreme self. He is the breath of others. I bow him.

The word *Prāŋan* (life) indicates the five breaths viz., *Prāŋa, Apāna, Samāna, Udāna & Vyāna* and again the 11 organs (5 organs of action, 5 organs of knowledge and mind).

In *Viṣṇu* sahasranamam – 67th, 320th and 407th names – *Prāṇaḥ* – and again 65th, 321st, 408th and 956th names – *Prāṇadaḥ* – He is life breath and he only gives life breath to all beings.

In *Lalitā* sahasranamam – 783rd name – *Prāŋadā* – **She** gives the life to all. It can also be split as – *Prānān* + *Dyati* – *Gandayati* – to obliterate. That is, it means that **She** wipes out the above said *Prāŋan*.

In *Śiva* sahasranamam – 695th name – *Prāṇadhāraṇaḥ* – **He** gives the life to all living beings.

38. *Oṃ Pūtātmane Namaḥ* । ॐ पूतात्मने नमः ।

He is the pure atma. I bow him. Any thought that he is attached to Sattva and other gunas is by his own wish or the devotees' wish.

Svetashwara Upanishat (6-11) says – He is pure and devoid of qualities.

In *Vişṇu* sahasranamam – 10th name – *Pūtātmā* – He is Nirguna atma.

611st name below may also be referred.

39. *Oṃ Prayatāya Namaḥ* । ॐ प्रयताय नमः ।

He is ritually pure and I bow him. He is purified by rituals and karmas.

40. *Oṃ Priyāya Namaḥ* । ॐ प्रियाय नमः ।

He loves all and is loved by all.

In *Śiva* sahasranamam – 797th name – *Priyaḥ* – **He** is a loving God.

467th name below may also be referred.

41. *Oṃ Nayāya Namaḥ* । ॐ नयाय नमः ।

He is the leader of all beings. I bow him.

In *Vişṇu* sahasranamam – 399th name – *Nayaḥ* – conveying the same meaning.

42. *Oṃ Sahasrapāde Namaḥ* । ॐ सहस्रपदे नमः ।

He has a thousand feet. I bow him. Thousand here means thousands of and not mere exact 1,000 in number.

Puruṣa Sūktam starts with

Oṃ Sahasrásīrṣā Purúṣaḥ I *Sahasrākṣaḥ Sahasrápāt* I

The *Virat Purush* – *Parabrahmam* (universal being) has thousand heads, thousand eyes and thousand feet. Thousand signifies innumerable.

In *Viṣṇu* sahasranamam – 227th name – *Sahasrapāt* – One who has thousand feet.

In *Śiva* sahasranamam – 797th name – *Sahasrapāt* – Conveying the same meaning.

In *Lalitā* sahasranamam – 284th name – *Sahasrapāt* – **She** has countless feet.

43. *Oṃ Sādhave Namaḥ* I ॐ साधवे नमः ।

He is a righteous one. I bow him.

He accomplishes everything without the help of any external requirements.

In practice the word *Sādhu* means – one who tolerates the troubles done by others and habitually does only good to others (even for those who has done bad to them). In this sense also it can be taken as Lord *Surya* does good to others.

In *Viṣṇu* sahasranamam – 243rd name – *Sādhuḥ* – He helps the good as the case may demand.

In *Lalitā* sahasranamam – 711th name – *Sādhu* – She is the most suitable.

44. *Oṃ Divyakuṇḍalamaṇḍitāya Namaḥ* I
ॐ दिव्यकुण्डलमण्डिताय नमः ।

He is adorned with a splendorous ear-ornament. I bow him.

In *Lalitā* sahasranamam – 22nd name – *Tāṭanka Yugalī Bhūta Tapanodupa Maṇḍalā* – One type of ornament worn by ladies in their ears is called *Tāṭanka* (palm-leaf). She shines wearing such an ornament. The Sun and the Moon take the form of this *Tāṭankas* to beautify *Śrī Devī*'s face.

45. *Oṃ Avyaṅgadhāriṇe Namaḥ* । ॐ अव्यङ्गधारिणे नमः ।

He is unmanifested perfect Lord, who cannot be visibly seen. I bow him.

Avyakta is a category along with *Mahat* (Cosmic Intelligence) and *Purusha*.

In *Gāyatri* sahasranamam – 2nd name – *Avyaktā* – She is in an unmanifested or devoid of form.

In *Viṣṇu* sahasranamam – 129th name – *Avyaṅgaḥ* – conveys the same meaning.

Shrimad Bhagavad Gita (2-15) also affirms that he is unmanifested.

46. *Oṃ Dhīrātmane Namaḥ* । ॐ धीरात्मने नमः ।

One who has courage. I bow him.

One who bestows the non-dual intellect.

In *Lalitā* sahasranamam – 916th name – *Dhīrā* – She is learned and knowledgeable.

Again, in *Lalitā* sahasranamam – 917th name – *Dhīrasamarchitā* – She is well worshipped by the clever and learned.

47. *Oṃ Savitre Namaḥ* । ॐ सवित्रे नमः ।

One who is full of rays. I bow him.

In *Viṣṇu* sahasranamam – 884th name – *Savitā* – he brings forth all the beings. He produces all beings.

In *Śiva* sahasranamam – 626th name – *Savitraḥ* – for which the interpreted meaning – equating Lord Shiva to Sun God. This is one of the very famous names of Sun God.

121st, 334th & 895th names below may also be referred.

48. *Oṃ Vāyuvāhanāya Namaḥ* | ॐ वायुवाहनाय नमः ।

He travels with air his vehicle. I bow him.

In *Viṣṇu* sahasranamam – 414th name – *Vāyuḥ* – he himself approaches all the places irrespectively as odour.

Again, in *Viṣṇu* sahasranamam – 331st and 856th names – *Vāyuvāhanaḥ* – conveying the same meaning.

In *Śiva* sahasranamam – 624th name – *Vāyuḥ* – conveys the same meaning.

In *Shrimad Bhagavad Gita* (7-9), Lord Krishna says I am the agreeable odour on the Earth.

Taitreeya Upanishat (2-8) says – the wind blows through the fear of him.

Vayu's son Hanuman is the vehicle for Sri Rama.

328th, 340th & 723rd names below may also be referred.

49. *Oṃ Samāhitamataye Namaḥ* | ॐ समाहितमतये नमः ।

He has a mind or thoughts collected or composed. I bow him.

50. *Oṃ Dātre Namaḥ* | ॐ दात्रे नमः ।

In the form of Brahma, he conceives all.

In *Viṣṇu* sahasranamam – 44th name – *Dātā* – In the form of Ananta (Adishesha) he supports this world.

51. *Oṃ Vidhātre Namaḥ* | ॐ विधात्रे नमः ।

He is dispenser of fruits of action and inducer of actions. I bow him.

In *Viṣṇu* sahasranamam – 45th and 484th names – *Vidhātā* – conveying the same meaning.

52. *Oṃ Kṛtamaṅgalāya Namaḥ* | ॐ कृतमङ्गलाय नमः ।

He does auspicious tasks only. I bow him.

He has a beneficent form.

In *Lalitā* sahasranamam – 933rd name – *Mangalākruti*: – She has a beneficent form.

53. *Oṃ Kapardine Namaḥ* I ॐ कपर्दिने नमः ।

He wears a braided or knotted hair. I bow him.

Usually only Lord Shiva is said to have knotted hair. But here Lord Sun also is said to have knotted hair. This emphasises the oneness of Lord Sun and shiva.

147th name in Rudra Trishati is – *Namáḥ Kapa̱rdinė Ca̱ Namáḥ* – Salutations to the one who has knotted hair.

54. *Oṃ Kalpapāde Namaḥ* I ॐ कल्पपादे नमः ।

Kalpataru bestows anything sought for. Similarly, the lotus feet of Lord Sun will provide whatever asked for. I bow him.

55. *Oṃ Rudrāya Namaḥ* I ॐ रुद्राय नमः ।

Salutations to him who removes all types of sorrows.

Generally, the name Rudran conjures up a terrifying image. People think the Lord in the form with anger. But not really.

The name Rudra can usually be a bit intimidating. But it means destroyer of *samsara* sorrow. If this is understood, the fear will go away.

Lord Sun is called as *Rudra*. During great dissolution Sun rises and burns the entire world. On account of this, torridly rains and world submerges in the waters. To start with he originated from the forehead of Brahma. He wept loudly and fearfully; because he wept, he is called the weeper (*Rudra*).

This is an important name about Lord Shiva in Sri Rudra Prashna. In many places this name occurs during recitation.

From the word *'Rudra'* the meaning that Lord alone is qualified to relieve the sorrow of samsara can be got. *Shvedashvara Upanishat* says that the sorrows of this world get removed only through the knowledge of the Lord;

Rutaṃ Saṃsāraduḥ Khaṃ Drāvayatīti Rudraḥ

Oṃ Namo Bhagavate Rudrāya Viṣṇave Mṛtyurme Pāhi – Our salutations to Lord Rudra in the form of *Viṣṇu* also.

In *Śiva* sahasranamam – 143rd name – *Rudraḥ* – One who removes all sorrows. *Ṛt – Rodhana Hetur Dhuḥkkham Tat Drāvayati Vināśayati Iti Rudraḥ – Ṛt* means dreadful distress. He removes all those types of sorrows. Or during the period of great dissolution (*pralaya*) he makes every living being cry. Or he is in the form of *prāṇa* to everyone – *Prāṇā Vāva Rudraḥ*.

In *Lalitā* sahasranamam – 269th name – *Rudrarūpā* – One who is the in the form of *Rudra*. The form of *Śrī Devī* when the *tamas* quality dominates is called *Rudra*. In this form **She** destroys the world. *Rudra*, who drives away sorrows; because of the *samsārā* cycle. *Rujam* – sorrow, *Drāvayati* – removes, *Rotayati* – make another cry. The separation on account of destruction makes others cry. Hence *Rudra*.

In *Viṣṇu* sahasranamam – 114th name – *Rudraḥ* – One who makes all people weep, at the time of death or during the total dissolution. One who makes all weep is *Rudraḥ*. From a devotee's standpoint the same term is interpreted as the one who liquidated all sorrows is *Rudraḥ*. *Bhagavān* declares Himself to be "Among the *Rudras*, I am *Śaṅkara* – (*Gīta* X-23). According to *purāṇas* there are 11 *Rudras*; the eleventh *'Rudra'* is called as *Śaṅkaraḥ – Sam Karoti Iti = Śaṅkaraḥ* – One who blesses all with Auspiciousness (*Sam*) is *Śaṅkara*. In the normal sense (colloquially) the word *Rudra* will mean lord *Śiva*. But here it specifies Lord *Viṣṇu* – indicating the oneness.

18th, 142nd & 234th names in Rudra Trishati can also be referred.

56. *Oṃ Sumanāya Namaḥ* I ॐ सुमनाय नमः ।

Salutations to the good hearted.

57. *Oṃ Dharmavatsalāya Namaḥ* I ॐ धर्मवत्सलाय नमः ।

I bow to the loving piety. He is so much dedicated to his duty that he works 24 x 7.

58. *Oṃ Samāyuktāya Namaḥ* I ॐ समायुक्ताय नमः ।

I bow to that Lord who is committed and always prepared for his work.

320th name below may also be referred.

59. *Oṃ Vimuktātmane Namaḥ* I ॐ विमुक्तात्मने नमः ।

I bow the emancipated self.

Katopanishad (5.1) says "He is liberated".

In *Viṣṇu* sahasranamam – 452nd name – *Vimuktātmā* – conveying the same message.

In *Śiva* sahasranamam – 1,004th name – *Vimuktaḥ* – He is the one freed from this world.

60. *Oṃ Kṛtātmane Namaḥ* I ॐ कृतात्मने नमः ।

I bow that disciplined Atma.

61. *Oṃ Kṛtināṃ Varāya Namaḥ* I ॐ कृतिनां वराय नमः ।

He is the cause of every activity of all beings. I bow him.

In *Viṣṇu* sahasranamam – 83rd name – *Kṛtiḥ* – he is every act of all beings.

62. *Oṃ Avicintyavapave Namaḥ* I ॐ अविचिन्त्यवपवे नमः ।

He cannot be imagined or reflected. I bow him.

In other words, he can be imagined only upon deep concentrated meditation.

63. *Oṃ Śreṣṭhāya Namaḥ* । ॐ श्रेष्ठाय नमः ।

He is the greatest.

In *Viṣṇu* sahasranamam – 68th name – *Śreṣṭaḥ* – he is the eldest and excellent.

Brahadāraŋyaka Upanishat (8-1-1) says – The *prānan* is the eldest and excellent.

Brahma Sūtram (2-4-8) says – He is the excellent. The chief prana or being the universal cause, it is above all.

The second of the five-brahma aspect of Lord Shiva is *Vāmadevā*. The corresponding mantra says – he is the *Jyeṣṭha* and *Śreṣṭha*.

315th & 506th names below may also be referred.

64. *Oṃ Mahāyogine Namaḥ* । ॐ महायोगिने नमः ।

He is a great Yogi. I bow him.

14th, 33rd above & 964th below names may also be seen.

65. *Oṃ Maheśvarāya Namaḥ* । ॐ महेश्वराय नमः ।

He is the supreme sovereign. I bow him.

The three gods *Brahma, Vishnu* and *Rudra* do three main functions of creation, protection and destruction. *Maheshvara* is above these three and is transcending the three characteristics (*Gunas – Rajas, Tamas* and *Sattva*) in equal proposition. He is *Maheshwara*.

As per *Veda, Maheshvara* is devoid of the three *gunas* (*nirguna*).

The word *Maheshvara* means – one who is the head of all the *Boota Ganas* or by all the great practicing celibacies.

Linga Purāṇā says –

Tamasā Kālardrākyo Rajasā Kanakāṇṭa Jaḥ ।
Satvena Sarvako Viṣhṇuḥ Nairguṇyena <u>Maheshwaraḥ</u> ॥

In *Lalitā* sahasranamam – 750th name – *Maheśvarī* – One who is the supreme sovereign.

Again, in *Lalitā* sahasranamam – 208th name – *Māheśvarī* – conveying the same meaning.

In *Gāyatri* sahasranamam – 798th name – *Maheśvari* – One who is the consort of Lord *Maheshvara* (*Paramashiva*). Gāyatri Devi assumes the premier forms of Devis representing Prosperity, Destruction, Virginity and Might respectively.

In *Śiva* sahasranamam – 164th name – *Maheśvaraḥ* – One who is the great leader.

679th name below may also be referred.

66. *Oṃ Kāntāya Namaḥ* । ॐ कान्ताय नमः ।

Since He is effulgent, he looks like the Ultimate beauty. The luster is the beauty and brightness of the body. I bow him.

Kam – Brahmam. Anta - final. Unconditioned *Brahmam* is his final form. This is the last philosophy of *Sun*'s form without any quality (*nirguṇā*). To start as a teacher, followed by *saguṇā* form and *nirguṇā* form is made perceived by him.

Or he is the cause of end of (anta) of Brahma at the close of second half of the yug.

In *Lalitā* sahasranamam – 329th name – *Kāntā* – One who is most beautiful.

In *Gāyatri* sahasranamam – 124th name – *Kāntā* – One who is most beautiful.

In *Viṣṇu* sahasranamam – 654th name – *Kāntaḥ* – he is so handsome – in all his incarnations he assumes most handsome forms.

772nd name below may also be referred.

67. *Oṃ Kāmāraye Namaḥ* । ॐ कामारये नमः ।

He is very versatile and gorgeous. I bow him.

He is desired by all those who seek the four kinds of human aspirations.

In *Vişņu* sahasranamam – 651st name – *Kāmadevaḥ* and again 297th & 653rd name – *Kāmaḥ*. He possesses all good qualities.

68. *Oṃ Ādityāya Namaḥ* I ॐ आदित्याय नमः ।

He is the golden person in the disc of solar system. I bow him.

He is the consort of Aditi, the undifferentiated mother Earth. The Sun reflects himself as many in several vessels of water, hence, the one Atman shows as many in the various bodies.

Taitreeya Samhitai (5-1-7) says "the mother Earth is Aditi"

Taitreeya Brahmanam (3-1-2) says "the divine earth is the wife of Vishnu.

In *Vişņu* sahasranamam – 39th & 563rd name – *Ādiṭyaḥ*. Lord *Vişņu* is one of the twelve *Ādityas*.

Shrimad Bhagwat Gita (10-21) – I am the *Vişņu* among the *Ādityas*.

In *Gāyatri* sahasranamam –20th name – *Aditi* – *Aditi* is one of the wives of sage *Kashyapa* and she is the mother of all the Devas.

Again, In *Gāyatri* sahasranamam – 56th name – *Āditya Maṇḍala Gatāyai* – she is in the midst of the solar orbit.

In *Śiva* sahasranamam – 565th name – *Aditiḥ* – and again 310th name – *Ādityaḥ* – Lord Shiva and Sun are one and the same.

211th name below may also be referred.

69. *Oṃ Niyatātmane Namaḥ* I ॐ नियतात्मने नमः ।

He is self-restrained or self-controlled. I bow him.

8th name above may also be referred.

70. *Oṃ Nirākulāya Namaḥ* I ॐ निराकुलाय नमः ।

He is the obviously visible Lord and I bow him.

Among all the Gods he is the one immediately visible to all – pratyaksha Lord.

71. *Oṃ Kāmāya Namaḥ* | ॐ कामाय नमः ।

He is so beautiful like *Kāman* (*Manmathan* = Cupid).

He satisfies all the *Kāmās* – wishes of all his devotees.

In *Viṣṇu* sahasranamam – 297th & 653rd names – *Kāmaḥ* and again 294th name – *Kāmāḥ*. He is desired by all, since he possess all good qualities.

In *Lalitā* sahasranamam – 796th name – *Kāmarūpiŋī* – One who is in the form of *Kāma*, the supreme *Shiva*. **She** is in the form of *Kāmeshvara*. *Śreedevee* and *Kāmeshvara* have the same forms, decorations, weapons, etc., **She** is in his form.

Again, in *Lalitā* sahasranamam – 63rd name – *Kāmadāyinī* – One who bestows all the desires and wishes.

Again, in *Lalitā* sahasranamam – 795th name – *Kāmadhuk* – One who fulfills all the desires.

4th verse of *Soundaryalaharee* says that **She** bestows more than what was asked or desired; *Tvadanya Panibhyām*.

In *Śiva* sahasranamam – 100th & 331st names – *Kāmaḥ* – conveying the same meaning.

72. *Oṃ Kāruṇikāya Namaḥ* | ॐ कारुणिकाय नमः ।

The most compassionate and merciful lord.

73. *Oṃ Kartre Namaḥ* | ॐ कर्त्रे नमः ।

He is the doer of all activities.

He is the doer, the beneficiary and the task itself.

74. *Oṃ Kamalākarabodhanāya Namaḥ* | ॐ कमलाकरबोधनाय नमः ।

He holds a lotus flower in his hand causing forth a perfume.

75. *Oṃ Saptasaptaye Namaḥ* I ॐ सप्तसप्तये नमः ।

The number seven is associated with Lord Sun in many a way;

- He rides in a chariot driven by 7 horses, which run swiftly.
- He causes the week containing 7 days and he is the first day.
- He is said to have seven tongues.
- He brightens 7 worlds and worshipped by all in the 7 worlds.
- He is fond of Saptami (seventh day of lunar fortnight).
- He creates seven colours though his rays.
- Seven solar forms like Arogan.
- For each manvantara, different seven main rishis are appointed by Surya to create the world.
- There are seven pranas in the seven holes in the head. The seven Ritviks Hotha, Prasastha, Brahmana, Bodha, Neshta, Achavan and Agneetharan as aspects of the seven Suns. Each of these seven is said to be in-charges of each of the pranas. These seven are the lords of the seven directions.
- At the command of the Sun, seven types of air masses form seven types of clouds are created.
- Aruna Prashnam (73) states that Lord Surya saves us from seven types of hells.

188th, 686th, 747th, 748th, 749th, 757th, 758th & 854th names below may also be referred.

76. *Oṃ Acintyātmane Namaḥ* I ॐ अचिन्त्यात्मने नमः ।

He is incomprehensible, because he is *Niroopa* and *Nirguna*.

He is free from all worries.

In *Vişṇu* sahasranamam – 832nd name – *Acintyaḥ*. By any means he cannot be thought of in particular form separate from this universe.

In *Lalitā* sahasranamam – 554th name – *Achintyarūpā* – One who is of unthinkable form or inaccessible to mind.

In *Gāyatri* sahasranamam – the very first name – *Acintyalakṣaṇā* – she is *Nirguna*, but her main quality is unthinkable form.

In *Śiva* sahasranamam – 997th name – *Acintyaḥ* – conveying the same meaning.

77. *Oṃ Mahākāruṇikottamāya Namaḥ* I ॐ महाकारुणिकोत्तमाय नमः ।

Kāruṇikaḥ – He is compassionate on his devotees.

Mahākāruṇikaḥ – He is great in compassionate on his devotees.

Mahākāruṇikottama – He is par excellent among all those who are great in compassionate.

Shrimad Bhagavatam says – the good dispositions are of four types;

- Friendship with those who are happy without being envious (*maitree* or friendship),
- Compassion for those who are suffering (*karuna*),
- Gladness to see the righteous (*muditā*) and
- Overlooking or not mindful of the sinful (*upekshā*).

These four tendencies contribute to clarity of mind and purify it.

In *Lalitā* sahasranamam – 326th name – *Karuŋārasa Sāgarā* – One who is the ocean of compassion.

In the meditation verse of Sri Lalitā Sahasranamam also it has been mentioned as; *Aruṇām Karuṇā Tarangidākshim* – stressing *Karuṇā*, the compassion.

In *Lalitā Trishati* also the compassion of *Sri Devi* is described in various names like, 9th name *Karuṇāmruta Sāgarā*, 151st name *Kaṭākshasyandi Karuṇā* and 153rd name *Kārunya Vigraha*.

In *Gāyatri* sahasranamam – 147th name – *Karuṇāpāṅg* – One who embodiment of pity, compassion, empathy, merci and what not.

78. *Oṃ Sañjīvanāya Namaḥ* I ॐ सञ्जीवनाय नमः ।

He makes his devotees alive. Alive here does not mean being alive (without dying). But it means leading a fruitful life by being alive.

That is the reason, it has been mentioned as *Sañjīvana* and not mere *Jīvana*.

79. *Oṃ Jīvanāthāya Namaḥ* I ॐ जीवनाथाय नमः ।

He is the supporter of all beings (*jeevas*). When he is there no one is an orphan.

80. *Oṃ Jayāya Namaḥ* I ॐ जयाय नमः ।

He is always victorious over all beings. He conquers his devotees to bestow his blessings.

In *Viṣṇu* sahasranamam – 509th name – *Jayaḥ* – one who is victorious of all the living beings.

Again, in *Viṣṇu* sahasranamam – 798th name – *Jayantaḥ* – victorious over enemies. For protecting Devas, in every incarnation, he was victorious over the enemies.

In *Lalitā* sahasranamam – 377th name – *Jayā* – She is in the form of victory.

In *Gāyatri* sahasranamam – 332nd name – *Jayā* – she is always victorious.

81. *Oṃ Jīvāya Namaḥ* I ॐ जीवाय नमः ।

The 78th name above was *Sañjīvanāya* and now it is *Jīvāya*. But do convey the same meaning as he is in the form jeevas in all beings.

Again, in the 79th name above he was addressed as *Jīvanāṭhāya*.

In *Viṣṇu* sahasranamam – 513th name – *Jīvaḥ* and again 930th name – *Jīvanaḥ*. He supports the *prana* and senses. He enlivens his devotees.

82. *Oṃ Jagatpataye Namaḥ* I ॐ जगत्पतये नमः ।

He is the leader of this world. He is the leader of all the seven worlds.

He is the chief of the entire universe.

83. *Oṃ Ayuktāya Namaḥ* I ॐ अयुक्ताय नमः ।

He is merged and unsplittable with everything. He is very careful.

84. *Oṃ Viśvanilayāya Namaḥ* I ॐ विश्वनिलयाय नमः ।

He is the abode of this entire universe.

85. *Oṃ Saṃvibhāgine Namaḥ* I ॐ संविभागिने नमः ।

He is the one who cannot be divided.

86. *Oṃ Vṛṣadhvajāya Namaḥ* I ॐ वृषध्वजाय नमः ।

One who has a bull in his flag.

87. *Oṃ Vṛṣākapaye Namaḥ* I ॐ वृषाकपये नमः ।

He Is the controller of all the demi-gods like Indra.

88. *Oṃ Kalpakartre Namaḥ* I ॐ कल्पकर्त्रे नमः ।

He is the author of rules on rituals or ceremonies.

Kalpa shastram defines the procedures for all rituals like pujas, yagnas, etc. He is the author of the same.

89. *Oṃ Kalpāntakaraṇāya Namaḥ* I ॐ कल्पान्तकरणाय नमः ।

He is the only person surviving during the great dissolution.

Kalpāntam means the great dissolution (*pralayā*) of this universe – the entire universe sub-merged with Lord himself. This is the fourth task called *Thirodana*. Lord *Sun* was pleased by sub-merging within him all that was created.

In *Lalitā* sahasranamam – 232nd name – *Maheśvara Mahākalpa Mahā Tāṇḍava Sākṣiṇī* – One who is the witness to the great awesome destructive cosmic dance of Lord *Maheshvarā* at the end of creative cycle.

90. *Oṃ Ravaye Namaḥ* । ॐ रवये नमः ।

He takes away – absorbs – all the juices.

Only when he absorbs water from the sea, we get rain from the clouds.

In *Viṣṇu* sahasranamam – 881st name – *Raviḥ* – He is the Sun God.

In *Śiva* sahasranamam – 627th name – *Raviḥ* – He is the Sun God.

91. *Oṃ Ekacakrarathāya Namaḥ* । ॐ एकचक्ररथाय नमः ।

He rides in a chariot[3] with a single wheel.

With a single wheel chariot, it is very easy for him to turn in all directions.

973rd name below may also be referred.

92. *Oṃ Maunine Namaḥ* । ॐ मौनिने नमः ।

He is so silent. He silently taught everything to Hanuman.

93. *Oṃ Surathāya Namaḥ* । ॐ सुरथाय नमः ।

He has yoked to an excellent chariot.

589th & 653rd names below may also be referred.

94. *Oṃ Rathināṃ Varāya Namaḥ* । ॐ रथिनां वराय नमः ।

Manmatha (Cupid) was burnt by Lord Shiva through his third eye. At the request of his wife Rathi, Lord Sun gave rebirth to Manmatha.

He is always riding in a chariot and bestows boons to his devotees.

95. *Oṃ Sakrodhanāya Namaḥ* । ॐ सक्रोधनाय नमः ।

He is passionate towards his devotees.

---

[3] The chariot of Sun God has been described in detail earlier in a chapter.

At the outset this name may mean that he is very much angry. But with deeper knowledge we will get the above meaning.

96. *Oṃ Raśmimāline Namaḥ* I ॐ रश्मिमालिने नमः ।

He wears a garland of rays.

He is the one who radiates rays on all sides. It is poetic metamorphically referred to as a garland.

97. *Oṃ Tejorāśaye Namaḥ* I ॐ तेजोराशये नमः ।

He has splendorous energy.

He is full of energy, so that he keeps on travelling without stopping.

98. *Oṃ Vibhāvasave Namaḥ* I ॐ विभावसवे नमः ।

He creates a condition that excites the state mind in the human body.

Our mind becomes dull in the dark and happy when there is a bright Sun. This is very general to all human beings. But individual persons may get affected differently, depending on the Sun's rays.

99. *Oṃ Divyakṛte Namaḥ* I ॐ दिव्यकृते नमः ।

He has a beautiful divine form. With a naked we are not able to see the Sun directly. But with telescope and other instruments, when we him, he is so attractive.

100. *Oṃ Dinakṛte Namaḥ* I ॐ दिनकृते नमः ।

He is the maker of day, i.e. day and night.

Throughout the world the daytime is calculated from Sunrise to Sunset. It is 6 months daytime and 6 months night in South Pole and North Pole based on the presence or otherwise of the Sun.

706th name below may also be referred.

Thus ends 100 divine names on Lord *Sūrya* from 1 to 100.

*****

101. *Oṃ Devāya Namaḥ* । ॐ देवाय नमः ।

Since, he sports with tasks of creation, etc., he is a *Devan*. He protects all beings including Devas.

Shvetashvatara Upanishat (6-11) says there is only one Deva.

In *Viṣṇu* sahasranamam – 375th name – *Devaḥ* – Conveying the same meaning.

In *Śiva* sahasranamam – 570th, 742nd & 937th names – *Devaḥ* – Conveying the same meaning.

960th name below may also be referred.

102. *Oṃ Devadevāya Namaḥ* । ॐ देवदेवाय नमः ।

The previous name called him as Devan. In this name he is called *Devadevan* – head of all Devas.

In *Lalitā* sahasranamam – 607th name – *Deveśī* – she is the head of all divine forces like *Brahma*, *Viṣhṇu*, *Shiva* and others.

103. *Oṃ Divaspataye Namaḥ* । ॐ दिवस्पतये नमः ।

Undoubtedly, he is the lord of the sky.

The Indra of the 13th Manvantara (Rauchya or Deva Savarni) is called *Divaspati.* Lord Sun is in his form.

According to the Padma Purana, Nahusha married Ashokasundari, the daughter of Shiva and Parvati. They are said to have given birth to Yayati and a hundred daughters. That Nahusha is also called as Vishnu or Divaspati.

104. *Oṃ Dīnanāthāya Namaḥ* । ॐ दीननाथाय नमः ।

He is the Lord or master of poor.

105. *Oṃ Harāya Namaḥ* । ॐ हराय नमः ।

One who holds a triad as a weapon –

Hantītī Hā Sūlastamrāti Ādatte Sa Haraḥ.

In *Sri Rudra Laghunyasam* we read – *Hastayor Harastiṣṭhatu* – let *Haraḥ* be in my hands.

In *Śiva* sahasranamam – 13th, 105nd & 748th names – *Haraḥ* – conveying the same meaning.

339th name below may also be referred.

106. *Oṃ Hotre Namaḥ* | ॐ होत्रे नमः ।

One who accepts all the sacrifices offered by devotees.

203rd, 391st and 714th names below may also be referred.

107. *Oṃ Divyabāhave Namaḥ* | ॐ दिव्यबाहवे नमः ।

He has splendorous shoulders.

The shoulders of every Deva/ God have been described in every purana and other texts. In Ramayana, Sri Rama is addressed as *Mahabāhu* – having great shoulders. Similarly, Lord Krishna addresses Arjuna as *Mahabāhu* in Shrimad Bhagavad Gita.

108. *Oṃ Divākarāya Namaḥ* | ॐ दिवाकराय नमः ।

He is the day maker. He is like a crown flower.

265th name below may also be referred.

109. *Oṃ Yajñāya Namaḥ* | ॐ यज्ञाय नमः ।

He is worship or sacrifice. He is in the form of all sacrifices. All Vedic sacrifices are his powers.

Taitrīya Samhita (2-5-5) says – Sacrifice is indeed his form.

In *Viṣṇu* sahasranamam – 445th and 971st names – *Yagnaḥ* – he is in the form of all sacrifices.

110. *Oṃ Yajñapataye Namaḥ* | ॐ यज्ञपतये नमः ।

He is the lord of worship or sacrifice.

In *Viṣṇu* sahasranamam – 972nd name – *Yagnapatiḥ* – he is the lord or protector of all sacrifices.

Shrimad Bhagawad Gita (9-24) – Bhagawan Krishna says – I am the enjoyer of all the sacrifices and also the lord of them.

111. *Oṃ Pūṣṇe Namaḥ* I ॐ पूष्णे नमः ।

He is the one who nourishes and fulfills the desires of his devotees.

Pūṣā is the name of one of the twelve Adityas – the offspring of Sage Kashyapa and Aditi. He is in that form.

112. *Oṃ Svarṇaretase Namaḥ* I ॐ स्वर्णरेतसे नमः ।

He has golden seeds (testicles). His energy has gold like sperms.

In Shrimad Bhagavata, the Devas are called Urdvaredhas. Because their energy is directed upwards.

187th and 366th names below may also be referred.

113. *Oṃ Parāvarāya Namaḥ* I ॐ परावराय नमः ।

A traditional leader of the whole universe.

114. *Oṃ Parāparajñāya Namaḥ* I ॐ परापरज्ञाय नमः ।

Brahmam is called *Parā* (absolute), *Aparā* (relative) and *Parāparā* (both absolute and relative). He is the one who provides this knowledge of Brahmam.

Parā – the other person, *Aparā* – dependent on self, i.e., it respectively means an enemy and a friend.

Śreemad Bhagavad Geeta (IX-29) says that the *Brahmam* is of these two types; *Na Me Dveshyosti Na Priya*: - I have neither foe nor friend.

Parā - superior and *Aparā* - inferior. *Sruti* says, "*Brahmam* is the servant. *Brahmam* is ferry-men; and Brahmam is these gamblers";

Brahmadāsā Brahmadāshā Brahmameme Kitavā Uta.

Parā - he who is far off, *Aparā* he who is near. *Śreemad Bhagavad Geeta* (XIII-15) - "I am far and near".

In general, the *Brahmam* is said to be two types viz., pure form and an adulterated form. *Parāparam* is of third type.

The *Prashno Upanishad* (V-2) says - "This is indeed, Oh *Satyakāma*, *para* and *apara*"; *Etadvai Satyakāma Param Chāparam Cha*".

The *Smruti* also says, "Two Brahmams are to be known, one is *Parā* and the other is *Aparā*";

Dve Brahmaŋee Veditavye Param Chāparameva Cha.

Parā - posterior; *Aparā* - anterior. *Shiva* with the unified form of *Shakti* is *Parāparam or Parabrahmam.* To give such meanings for the words *Para* or *Apara* there are enough evidences in *Vedas*;

"*Yuje Vām Brahma Poorvyam Namobhi*:" or

"*Esho Ushā Apoorvyā Vyachchati Priyā Diva*: II".

Parā and *Aparā* are the twofold ether.

The twofold knowledge, as described in the *Muŋḍaka Upanishad* (I-1-4) *Parā Vidyā* and *Aparā Vidya*.

The *Linga Purāŋa* also says, "Two kinds of knowledge should be known, *parā* and *aparā*; the *Vedas* are *Para* and the *Vedāngās* are *Apara*.

Skānda Purāŋa (*Yagna Vaibhava Kānḍa*, 6th chapter) says two types of the *Praŋava* are *Parā* and *Apara*. *Parā* has the qualities of *Sachitānanda* and *Aparā* is pure form, in the form of sound. Since it prays *Parabrahmam*, it is called as *Praŋava* (the word *nava* has such a meaning). Since it is a tool to reach *Parabrahmam*, it is called as *Praŋavam*.

There itself, the interpretation of *Vedas* is of two types – the Supreme Being is *Param* and the tool to reach it is called *Aparam*.

In the *Yoga Sāstra* also knowledge is divided into three - *Parā, Aparā* and *Parāpara*. For it is said, "Knowledge is said to be threefold by the division of *para, apara* and *parāpara*. Of these, the first is the supreme knowledge and is the cause of cognizing the Lord, the bondage and the Self. The second, *aparā* knowledge, is simply the cause of cognising the bondage. The *parāparā* knowledge is, just as the change of the sight between a man and cat in the night, it does not distinguish the marks *vilakshaṇā*".

In *Lalitā* sahasranamam – 790th name – *Parāparā – Śrī Devī*'s *pooja* is of three types – *Parā, Aparā and Parāpara. Para* is worshipping with non-duality in mind (however it is done). *Apara* is worshipping *Śree Chakra,* imagining it as Sri Devi. *Parāpara* is worshipping different types of idols.

The speech is of two types – *Parā* and *Apara. Aparā* includes *Pashyantee, Madyamā* and *Vaikharee.*

Para is the fourth state. *Aparā* is the three states awaken (*Jāgrath*), dream (*Swapna*) and deep sleep (*Sushupti*).

The *homa* (sacrificial fire) is of two types *Parā* and *Apara*. The *Parā* is the state after the destruction of all dualistic interpretations respecting the known, the knower and knowledge. The *Parā homa* is said to be that which being absorbed, does not arise again, in the blaze of the great eternal fire of own Self, which burns forever without fuel. This is done in an imaginative way.

Varāha Purāṇa says when speaking about the *Trimoortis* - The creative energy is said to be *Para* which is the white colour. *Vaishnavee*, which is red and long-eyed is *Apara*. The *Raudri* energy is called *parāpara*.

In *Gāyatri* sahasranamam – 12th name – *Aparā* – Nobody is there other than herself.

In *Śiva* sahasranamam – 562nd & 1,001st names – *Paraḥ* – conveying the same meaning.

115. *Oṃ Taraṇaye Namaḥ* I ॐ तरणये नमः I

He makes his devotees to swim across the ocean of samsara.

563rd name below may also be referred.

116. *Oṃ Aṃśumāline Namaḥ* I ॐ अंशुमालिनेनमः ।

Aṃśu means ray. *Mālin* means a garland. He wears a garland of rays.

Earlier in 96th name itself the same meaning was conveying.

117. *Oṃ Manoharāya Namaḥ* I ॐ मनोहराय नमः ।

He is an appealing/ enchanting/ attractive lord.

In *Viṣṇu* sahasranamam – 461st name – *Manoharaḥ* – Being the unlimited bliss, he is charming.

336th name below may also be referred.

118. *Oṃ Prājñāya Namaḥ* I ॐ प्राज्ञाय नमः ।

He is a wise and intelligent lord.

119. *Oṃ Prājñapataye Namaḥ* I ॐ प्राज्ञपतये नमः ।

He is the leader of wise and intelligent.

120. *Oṃ Sūryāya Namaḥ* I ॐ सूर्याय नमः ।

He is the star around which all the planets revolve.

121. *Oṃ Savitre Namaḥ* I ॐ सवित्रे नमः ।

47th above and 334th & 895th names below may also be referred.

122. *Oṃ Viṣṇave Namaḥ* I ॐ विष्णवे नमः ।

The all-pervading lord. His nature is omni-presence, or his rays are spread everywhere or he after creating entered into them.

Śreemad Bhagavat Geeta (VII – 14) – this is my divine illusion, consisting of *Guṇas* is hard to surmount;

Daiveehyeshā Guṇamayee Mama Māyā Duratyayā ।

In *Durga Saptashatee* also we read;

Yādevī Sarvabhūteśu Viṣṇu Mayeti Śabtitā I
Namastasyai Namastasyai Namastasyai Namo Namaḥ I

Rig Veda (1-156-3) says – cognizant of his greatness, celebrate his name; Oh Vishnu! Enjoy thy favour.

The word *Vishnu* is derived from the root *Vish* – to pervade.

Narayana Upanishat (1-13) says – Narayana pervades the whole universe both externally and internally.

It can also be construed as to mean to enter or permeate.

Vishnu Puranam (3-1) says – because this whole world has been pervaded by the energy of the great soul, he is name as *Vishnu*.

Mahabharata (Shanti Parva 342) Lord Krishna Says – Oh Partha, as I have pervaded the horizons, my glory stands foremost and as I have measured the three worlds with three steps, I am named *Vishnu*.

In *Vişṇu* sahasranamam – 2nd, 258th & 657th names – *Viṣṇuḥ* – He is omnipresent. In the Vamana incarnation, he measured the three worlds with his 3 steps.

Brahmam is the only one that is all pervading.

In *Lalitā* sahasranamam – 339th name *Vişŋumāyā* & 893rd name *Vişŋurūpiŋī* – She is the *Vişhŋu Māyā Shakti*. **She** is the *Māyā* of Universal Absolute. The *Shakti*, which limits this Absolute is illusion. She is in the form of *Vişhŋu*.

The *Kālikā Purāŋā* also says *Vişhŋumāyā* is that which differentiates, everything, into manifested and un-manifested according to the *tamas*, *rajas* and *satva* qualities.

In *Gāyatri* sahasranamam – 930th name – *Vişŋurūpāyai* – She is in the form of *Vişŋu*.

In *Śiva* sahasranamam – 617th name – *Vişhŋuḥ* – he is omnipresent.

123. *Oṃ Aṃśumate Namaḥ* I ॐ अंशुमतेनमः I

Moon and other celestial bodies are part of Lord Sun. He is the super set of all celestial bodies.

124. *Oṃ Sadāgataye Namaḥ* | ॐ सदागतये नमः ।

He is in the form of Universal sprit or wind, always in motion.

125. *Oṃ Gandhavahāya Namaḥ* | ॐ गन्धवहाय नमः ।

He in the form wind, bears fragrances to the whole world.

126. *Oṃ Vihitāya Namaḥ* | ॐ विहिताय नमः ।

He strictly follows all that prescribed by the scriptures. If he follows, surely his devotees will follow.

127. *Oṃ Vidhaye Namaḥ* | ॐ विधये नमः ।

He is the creator of rules in the scriptures.

In the previous name it was mentioned as he follows the rules. Here it is mentioned that he only created the rules.

128. *Oṃ Āśugāya Namaḥ* | ॐ आशुगाय नमः ।

He moves swiftly as a wind.

It is worth connecting that it was earlier mentioned that he himself is in the form of wind and also, he uses the wind as vehicle.

129. *Oṃ Pataṅgāya Namaḥ* | ॐ पतङ्गाय नमः ।

Like a bird he is always flying.

130. *Oṃ Patagāya Namaḥ* | ॐ पतगाय नमः ।

He is like sky flying luminary.

The previous name and this name can be conjointly read.

131. *Oṃ Sthāṇave Namaḥ* | ॐ स्थाणवे नमः ।

He is so static and constant like a trunk of a tree.

Our Astrology says that Sun is moving from one sign to another. That is what so far, the previous names were also mentioning. But our Astronomy says that he is constant and static. All the other celestial bodies in the solar system move around him.

In *Viṣṇu* sahasranamam – 8th name – *Sthāṇuḥ* – He is constant.

Again, in *Viṣṇu* sahasranamam – 120th name – *Śaśvatasthānuḥ* – He is eternal and firm.

Again, in *Viṣṇu* sahasranamam – 427th name – *Sthāvarasthāṇuḥ* – He is firm and motionless.

132. *Oṃ Vihaṅgāya Namaḥ* I ॐ विहङ्गाय नमः ।

He ensures that the configuration of stars is stable and constant. He is constant and ensures other celestial bodies also to be constant.

133. *Oṃ Vihagāya Namaḥ* I ॐ विहगाय नमः ।

In contrast to the previous name this name says that he is flying like birds.

134. *Oṃ Varāya Namaḥ* I ॐ वराय नमः ।

He bestows all the boons to his devotees.

32nd above and 961st below names may also be referred.

135. *Oṃ Haryaśvāya Namaḥ* I ॐ हर्यश्वाय नमः ।

He is the king of solar dynasty.

The word *Haryaśva* has lots of meanings. Some of them are;

Bhāgavata Purāṇa (9.6.23-24) – Haryaśva is one of the sons of *Dṛḍhāśva* (one of the three remaining sons of *Kuvalayāśva*). He had a son named *Nikumbha*.

Bhāgavata Purāṇam (9.7.4) – Haryaśva is one of the sons of *Anaraṇya* (son of *Trasaddasyu*, who was the son of *Purukutsa*). He had a son named *Prāruṇa*.

Again, *Bhāgavata Purāṇam* (9.13.15) – *Haryaśva* is one of the sons of *Dhṛṣṭaketu* (son of *Sudhṛti*). He had a son named *Maru*.

Śiva Purāṇa (2.2.13) – Haryaśva – The five thousand sons born to Dakṣa through his wife Asiknī are known as Haryaśvas. As Brahmā said to Nārada — In his wife Vīriṇī, Dakṣa Prajāpati begot sons named Haryaśvas. All those sons were devoted to their father and followed the Vedic path. They did not have separate virtues and practices. Advised by their father, the sons of Dakṣa went in the western direction for penance in order to create subjects (progeny).

Haryaśva – A King of the solar dynasty.

- He was king of Ayodhyā. A Powerful ruler, he had a fully equipped army. (Udyoga Parva, Chapter 115. Verse 18).
- He took Mādhavī, daughter of Yayāti as his wife and thus solved the problem of gurudaksiṇā for Gālava.
- Never in life did he eat flesh. (Anuśāsana Parva, Chapter 11, Verse 67).

Haryaśva – Father of Sudeva, King of Kāśī. He was killed by the sons of Vītahavya. (Anuśāsana Parva, Chapter 30, Verse 10).

136. *Oṃ Haritāśvāya Namaḥ* । ॐ हरिताश्वाय नमः ।

He has reddish horses for his chariot.

137. *Oṃ Haridaśvāya Namaḥ* । ॐ हरिदश्वाय नमः ।

He has fallow horses in his chariot.

138. *Oṃ Jagatpriyāya Namaḥ* । ॐ जगत्प्रियाय नमः ।

He loves all the seven worlds.

He is treasured by all those in the seven worlds.

139. *Oṃ Tryambakāya Namaḥ* । ॐ त्र्यम्बकाय नमः ।

One who is three-eyed.

It can also be considered as – **he** is in the form of father of the three gods – *Brahma, Vișhṇu* and *Rudra*.

The same meaning is conveyed in Sri Lalitā Sahasranamam – 453rd – *Trinayanā*, 477th – *Trilocanā* and 762nd – *Tryambakā*, names.

In the dhyana verses about almost all the Gods, especially about Lord Shiva and Sri Devi, it has been mentioned as having three eyes.

In Śiva Sahasranamam – 799th name – *Trilocanaḥ* – three eyed.

140. *Oṃ Sarvadamanāya Namaḥ* । ॐ सर्वदमनाय नमः ।

He is all-subduing or all-taming.

The name of the son of Shakuntala (Bharath) is *Sarvadaman*.

141. *Oṃ Bhāvitātmane Namaḥ* । ॐ भावितात्मने नमः ।

He creates, protects and destructs the whole world.

He is like a saint, with a purified universal soul.

142. *Oṃ Bhiṣagvarāya Namaḥ* । ॐ भिषग्वराय नमः ।

He is an excellent physician.

Earlier also it has been mentioned that he is worshipped for health and long life. In that angle he is a physician.

Generally, we all know, taking Sun bath increases inter alia, Vitamin D contents in the body.

143. *Oṃ Ālokakṛte Namaḥ* । ॐ आलोककृते नमः ।

He causes and spreads light to the entire world with his lustre.

He is a spectator for all the tasks of the world. Nothing can be missed from his sight.

144. *Oṃ Lokanāthāya Namaḥ* I ॐ लोकनाथाय नमः ।

He is the Lord of all the seven worlds.

In *Vişṇu* sahasranamam – 734th name – *Lokanāthaḥ* – conveying the same message.

145. *Oṃ Lokālokanamaskṛtāya Namaḥ* I ॐ लोकालोकनमस्कृताय नमः ।

He is worshiped by all in all the world – human and devas alike.

We have already seen the specialties of Surya Namaskar.

146. *Oṃ Kālāya Namaḥ* I ॐ कालाय नमः ।

He is in the form of time. He causes the calculation of time.

He is death personified for enemies.

Svetasvatara Upanishad (VI-2) says, omniscient, time of time, possessed of all qualities, all knowing – *Brahmam* is the *Kāla* (death) himself - *Gnaḥ Kālakālo Guṇī Sarva Vidyāḥ*

In *Vişṇu* sahasranamam – 418th name – *Kālaḥ* – conveying the same message.

In *Shrimad Bhagavad Gita* (7-9 & 10-30), Lord Krishna says "I am the time of counting".

In *Lalitā* sahasranamam – 557th name – *Kālahantrī* – She is the destroyer of time (*Mrutyu*).

In *Gāyatri* sahasranamam – 138th name – *Kālarūpiṇyai* – She is in the form of time or death.

In *Śiva* sahasranamam – 152nd, 368th, 382nd, 531st & 910th names – *Kālaḥ* – He is in the form of time.

894th name below may also be referred.

147. *Oṃ Kalpāntakāya Namaḥ* I ॐ कल्पान्तकाय नमः ।

Kalpa = *yug*. *Anta* = end. He causes the end of the yug.

It was earlier mentioned that he is the cause of and calculation of time. The maximum period of time calculation is yug. He is causing the end of it.

In *Śiva* sahasranamam – 397th name – *Kalpaḥ* – He is in the form of yug.

Again, in *Śiva* sahasranamam – 615th name – *Mahākalpaḥ* – He is the cause for the great conception.

148. *Oṃ Vahnaye Namaḥ* I ॐ वह्नये नमः ।

He causes the fire. In lots of places, we have seen, fire being created focusing the rays of the Sun through convex lens.

He arranges to take the oblations offered in the holy fire to the concerned.

Vahni means fire or number three. Hence three *maṇḍalās* (fire, Sun and Moon). These are respectively in *Mūlādhāra*, *Anāhata* and *Sahasrāra* chakras.

Purusha Sooktam (4) says that one portion of his has become the universe.

In *Viṣṇu* sahasranamam – 233rd name – *Vahniḥ* – he is the space.

In *Lalitā* sahasranamam – 352nd name – *Vahnimaṇḍalavāsinī* – She resides in the circle of fire.

202nd name below may also be referred.

149. *Oṃ Tapanāya Namaḥ* I ॐ तपनाय नमः ।

He is in the form of *Araṇi* tree.

The word *Tapan* means *Araṇi* tree. In olden days, even nowadays in some places, by churning the *Araṇi* tree, fire is created.

In *Śiva* sahasranamam – 397th name – *Tapanaḥ* – He is in the form of Sun.

293rd name below may also be referred.

150. *Oṃ Saṃpratāpanāya Namaḥ* I ॐ संप्रतापनाय नमः ।

He is so warm and make everything also to be warm.

In *Viṣṇu* sahasranamam – 277th name – *Pratāpanaḥ* – the burner of the cosmos by his manifestations.

151. *Oṃ Virocanāya Namaḥ* I ॐ विरोचनाय नमः ।

The only god shining with luster.

Based upon him only the year is calculated.

In *Viṣṇu* sahasranamam – 882nd name – *Virocanaḥ* – of various tastes.

152. *Oṃ Virūpākṣāya Namaḥ* I ॐ विरूपाक्षाय नमः ।

He has various occupations or diversely-eyed.

Brahmam has no specific form. He is the Brahmam. Hence, he does not have any form (*viroopi*). On account of ignorance of devotees like us, he appears to be *saroopa* – with different forms.

Śvētāśvatara Upanishat (IV-19) advises as – No one is equal to him – *Na Tasya Pratimā Asti*.

In *Gāyatri* sahasranamam – 912th name – *Virūpiṇyai* – She is without any form. One who is peerless or without any comparable person.

In *Viṣṇu* sahasranamam – 882nd name – *Virocanaḥ* – of various tastes.

153. *Oṃ Sahasrākṣāya Namaḥ* I ॐ सहस्राक्षाय नमः ।

He has thousands of eyes. Hence, he is witness to every task in the world.

A thousand should not be literally taken as a thousand. It has to be considered as countless.

Puruṣa Sūktam starts with – The *Virat Purush* – *Parabrahmam* (universal being) has thousand heads, thousand eyes and thousand feet – *Oṃ Sahasráśīrṣā Purúṣaḥ* I *Sahasrākṣaḥ Sahasrápāt* I

In *Viṣṇu* sahasranamam – 226th name – *Sahasrākṣaḥ* – having thousands of eyes.

In *Lalitā* sahasranamam – 283rd name – *Sahasrākṣī* – She has countless eyes.

In *Śiva* sahasranamam – 55th name – *Sahasrākṣaḥ* – He has a thousand eyes.

In Sri Rudra Namakam (1.9), Rudra Trishati 149th name and in many other places, it has been mentioned Lord Shiva has thousands of eyes.

In Sri Rudra Namakam (1.11) – Thousands of Eyed One! He who has many quivers.

154. *Oṃ Purandaraya Namaḥ* I ॐ पुरन्दराय नमः ।

He is the destroyer of enemies. He is in-charge of East direction, the king of Devas (Indra). He is the lord of fire (Agni).

In *Viṣṇu* sahasranamam – 335th name – *Purandaraḥ* – destroyer of enemies of Devas. Destroyer of cities.

155. *Oṃ Sahasraraśmaye Namaḥ* I ॐ सहस्ररश्मये नमः ।

He has thousands of rays. Number of his rays cannot be counted. Hence mentioned as thousands.

156. *Oṃ Mihirāya Namaḥ* I ॐ मिहिराय नमः ।

One who is affected by eclipses.

157. *Oṃ Vividhāmbarabhūṣaṇāya Namaḥ* ।
ॐ विविधाम्बरभूषणाय नमः ।

One who is adorned with variety of jewels.

There are different types of jewels worn in every organ of the body. He has all those jewels.

158. *Oṃ Khagāya Namaḥ* । ॐ खगाय नमः ।

He is the wind god. He flies like a bird.

In *Śiva* sahasranamam – 308th name – *Khagaḥ* – He is the Sun God.

431st & 880th names below may also be referred.

159. *Oṃ Pratardanāya Namaḥ* । ॐ प्रतर्दनाय नमः ।

He is the destroyer of everything during great dissolution.

Katopanishat (2-24) says "For him the Brahmins and the Kshatriya classes are the food.

Vedantra Sutra (1-2-9) says "He is the eater of movable and immovable ones".

In *Viṣṇu* sahasranamam – 59th name – *Pratardanaḥ* – destroyer of beings during pralaya.

160. *Oṃ Dhanyāya Namaḥ* । ॐ धन्याय नमः ।

His devotees are very much thankful to him. Makara Sankarathi and other festivals are basically a thanks giving to Sun God.

Kubera and others became wealthy because of him.

As means of expressing gratitude to the devotees who worship **him**, **he** bestows the results.

He bestows wealth. It can also be taken that **he** has wealth.

Shrimad Bhagavad Gita (VIII-6) says – whatever a man thinks of at the last moment when he leaves his body, that alone does he attain, Oh Kaunteya, being ever absorbed in the thought thereof.

In *Viṣṇu* sahasranamam – 754th name – *Dhanyaḥ* – Bestower of fortunes.

In *Lalitā* sahasranamam – 957th name – *Dhanyā* – also conveys the same meaning.

In *Gāyatri* sahasranamam – 485th name – *Dhanyā* – One who is grateful.

161. *Oṃ Hayagāya Namaḥ* I ॐ हयगाय नमः ।

He is very much related to number seven. This has been mentioned earlier also in detail.

162. *Oṃ Vāgviśāradāya Namaḥ* I ॐ वाग्विशारदाय नमः ।

He is an eloquent in speech.

In *Viṣṇu* sahasranamam – 267th name – *Vāgmiḥ* – He from whom speech begins.

Śrī Ādi Śaṇkara says, in his 100th verse of *Soundaryalaharī* that all types of letters, words and speeches belong to *Śrī Devī* only;

Tvadeeyābhir Vākbhis Tava Janani Vācham Stutiriyam.

In *Lalitā* sahasranamam – 640th name – *Vāgadhīśvarī* – She is the head of speech. **She** is the head of the eight *Vasinee* and other *Vāg Devees*. That is the reason, they could write this *Sahasranāma*, by **Her** order. **She** has *Vāgvādinee*, who is the head of speech and letters, as her part.

The words, which are the physical forms of speech (*Vaikharee*) only express or identify the physical form of *Brahmam* (the *Virāt*) and do not correspond to the pure unconditioned *Brahmam*, the speech is divided into four stages; *Parā*, *Pashyantee*, *Madyamā* and *Vaikharee*. All these four are different names of Sri Lalitā.

277th, 500th and 626th names below may also be referred.

163. *Oṃ Śrīmate Namaḥ* I ॐ श्रीमते नमः ।

He is so splendorous.

In *Vişṇu* sahasranamam – 22nd, 178th, 220th, & 613th names – *Śrīmān* – He is united with Goddess Lakshmi. Sri eternally abides on his chest. Even in the incarnation of Narasimhan – man-lion body, there is no diminution of beauty.

In *Śiva* sahasranamam – 1,006th name – *Śrīmān* – He is eternally beautiful.

In *Gāyatri* sahasranamam – 957th name – *Śrīmatī* – Devi Gayatri the Signage of womanhood with brightness and happiness.

170th & 649th names below may also be referred.

164. *Oṃ Aśiśirāya Namaḥ* I ॐ अशिशिराय नमः ।

He with his hot rays so scorching.

165. *Oṃ Vāgmine Namaḥ* I ॐ वाग्मिने नमः ।

In the 162nd name above his eloquence in speech has been discussed in detail.

311th name below may also be referred.

166. *Oṃ Śrīpataye Namaḥ* I ॐ श्रीपतये नमः ।

Lord of 'Sri' – i.e. Lord of Goddess Lakshmi.

Obviously, all of us are aware that Lord of Goddess Lakshmi is God Vishnu. But here it is mentioned that Sun God is *Śrīpati.* This implies that Vishnu and Sun are one and the same.

Śrī also means Para Shakti. He is the Lord of Para Shakti.

In *Vişṇu* sahasranamam – 603th name – *Śrīpatiḥ* – When she came out of Milky Ocean, Lakshmi has chosen Lord Vishnu as her husband rejecting all the devas, asuras and others during the churning of the ocean for nectar.

Svetashvatara Upanishat (6-8) says "the supreme shakti of Him is declared to be various.

167. *Oṃ Śrīniketanāya Namaḥ* I ॐ श्रीनिकेतनाय नमः ।

He dwells with *'Sri'*, Goddess Lakshmi.

168. *Oṃ Śrīkaṇṭhāya Namaḥ* I ॐ श्रीकण्ठाय नमः ।

He is the one with a black neck.

Normally Lord Shiva is used to be called as *Śrīkaṇṭhan* – blue necked. Here Sun is termed as blue necked. This clearly indicates that Lord Shiva and Sun are one and the same.

Earlier in the 166th name above, it was made clear that Lord Vishnu and Sun are one and the same.

Putting these two names together, Lords Vishnu, Shiva and Sun are same. The concept that Brahmam is only one is reiterated.

In Sri Lalitā Sahasranamam – 392nd name – *Śrīkanṭhārdha Śarīriṇī* – The meaning of the word *Shree* is venom. Since Lord *Paramashiva* has venom in his neck, he got the name as *Śrıkanṭhan* (*Kantam* – neck). **She** has *Paramashiva as* **Her** half body or **She** has in-differentiable half body with *Paramashiva*.

169. *Oṃ Śrīdharāya Namaḥ* I ॐ श्रीधराय नमः ।

The bearer of 'Sri' – Goddess Lakshmi.

He supports the prosperities.

In *Viṣṇu* sahasranamam – 610th name – *Śrīdharaḥ* – He keeps Lakshmi in his chest.

170. *Oṃ Śrīmate Namaḥ* I ॐ श्रीमते नमः ।

He is so beautiful.

163rd above & 649th below names may also be referred.

171. *Oṃ Śrīnivāsāya Namaḥ* | ॐ श्रीनिवासाय नमः ।

He is the abode of 'Sri' – Goddess Lakshmi.

Śrīnivasa is the presiding deity at Thirumala. Lord Sun is in that form.

163rd and 6 names from 166th talk about the connection between 'Sri' and Sun God.

In *Viṣṇu* sahasranamam – 607th name – *Śrīnivasaḥ* – abiding always with wealth.

172. *Oṃ Vasupradāya Namaḥ* | ॐ वसुप्रदाय नमः ।

He is the conferrer of salvation.

Brahadaranyaka Upanishat (5-9-28) says – it is Brahmam, who is wisdom and bliss, the highest aim of any being.

In *Viṣṇu* sahasranamam – 694th name – *Vasupradaḥ* – giver of moksha or he who deprives the demons of their wealth.

699th name below may also be referred.

173. *Oṃ Kāmacāriṇe Namaḥ* | ॐ कामचारिणे नमः ।

He is devoid of any desires.

He moves or acts at his pleasure. Nobody can control him or no one need to guide him.

Kāma indicates Cupid. Lord Shiva killed him. Sun is in that form.

174. *Oṃ Mahāmāyāya Namaḥ* | ॐ महामायाय नमः ।

Māyā is illusion. *Mahāmāyā* is great illusion. He is in that form.

In Shrimad Bhagavad Gita (7-14), Lord Krishna says "My maya is very difficult to cross".

Again, in Shrimad Bhagavad Gita (7-25), I am veiled by the *yogamaya*.

In Devi Mahatmyam and Devi Bhagavatam, Sri Devi has been described as appearing as *yogamaya*.

In *Vişṇu* sahasranamam – 170th name – *Mahāmāyaḥ* – the great illusionist.

871st name below may also be referred.

175. *Oṃ Mahogrāya Namaḥ* । ॐ महोग्राय नमः ।

He is in the form of a great serpent.

Sesha and other serpents are his manifestations.

In Shrimad Bhagavad Gita (10-21), Lord Krishna says "of serpents I am Vasuki".

176. *Oṃ Aviditāmayāya Namaḥ* । ॐ अविदितामयाय नमः ।

Sun Lord is beyond any rule to control or monitor.

Every being should follow one or other rules. For human beings the fundamental rule is Manu Dharma Shastram. But for Sun Lord there cannot be any rule. He is beyond all these.

177. *Oṃ Tīrthakriyāvate Namaḥ* । ॐ तीर्थक्रियावते नमः ।

He makes everyone to perform the ceremonies in a perfect manner in the holy rivers.

178. *Oṃ Sunayāya Namaḥ* । ॐ सुनयाय नमः ।

He has beautiful eyes. Earlier itself it was mentioned that he has thousands of eyes. All those are so beautiful and active so that no activity is missed out of his eyes.

179. *Oṃ Vibhaktāya Namaḥ* । ॐ विभक्ताय नमः ।

He is separated from his devotees. He is at a distance from his devotees.

In reality, seemingly he is separated from his devotees. But when concentrated puja is performed a devotee can always merge with him.

180. *Oṃ Bhaktavatsalāya Namaḥ* | ॐ भक्तवत्सलाय नमः ।

He destroys the sins of his devotees. He keeps them under control.

In *Viṣṇu* sahasranamam – 736th name – *Bhaktavatsalaḥ* – he is merciful to his devotees.

181. *Oṃ Kīrtaye Namaḥ* | ॐ कीर्तये नमः ।

He is famous so that he is known to all.

182. *Oṃ Kīrtikarāya Namaḥ* | ॐ कीर्तिकराय नमः ।

He confers fame to his devotees. He is famous and hence he can confer fame to all.

183. *Oṃ Nityāya Namaḥ* | ॐ नित्याय नमः ।

He is eternal. The soul is eternal.

Brahdāraṇya Upanishat (IV-5-14) says *Avinānāshi Vā Areyamātmā*.

In Sri Lalitā Sahasranamam – 136th name – *Nityā* – She is eternal. There are 16 Thithi Nitya Devis[4] in-charge of the thithis. She is in those forms.

210th & 883th name below mạy also be referred.

184. *Oṃ Kuṇḍaline Namaḥ* | ॐ कुण्डलिने नमः ।

He wears whale-shaped pendants representing Sankhya and Yoga Shastras.

He is in the form of the *Kuṇḍalinī* energy.

---

[4] This author has written separate book both in English and Tamil detailing Thithi Nitya Devis.

Kundalinee energy resides in the bottom tip of the backbone of a human being. It is in the form of a snake coiled in 3.5 rounds with head inside.

The three rounds respectively represent the letters *A*, *Oo* and *Ma*. The half round is the half scale. That implies *Kunḍalinee* corresponds to *Oṃ* – the *Praŋava Mantra*.

The method of awakening the sleeping *Kunḍalinee* energy (snake) and taking it to *Brahmarandhram* has been described in the *Yoga Sāstra*. The *Kunḍalinee* energy wakes up, reaches the *Brahmarandhram* and rains the nectar by ardent devotion, the results of adoration and the blessings of the teacher in addition to the *Haṭayoga* methods.

The form of *Kunḍalinī* is explained in detail in the 10th *verse* of *Soundaryalaharī*.

In *Viṣṇu* sahasranamam – 907th name – *Kuṇḍalī* –*Śree Ādi Śaṇkara* in his commentary of *Vişhŋu Sahasranāma* mentions – *Vişhŋu* is in the form of *Ādi Sesha* – a snake. *Vişhŋu* wears the earrings similar to the Sun's galaxy.

185. *Oṃ Kavacine Namaḥ* I ॐ कवचिने नमः I

He wears a body shield always.

He is like a warrior king and hence he needs to wear a shield.

In Mahabharata, his son Karna born with a kavaca and kundela (shield and ear rings).

186. *Oṃ Rathine Namaḥ* I ॐ रथिने नमः I

He always travels in chariot.

In any puja, there are many upacarams. Among them one upacaram is *Rathān Arohayāmi*. It means ascending the God on a chariot.

In Rudra Trishatee there are lots of names connecting Lord Shiva and Chariot. Some examples are;

- 21st name – *Namȧḥ Sūtāyạ Namȧḥ* – Salutations to the one who drives the world in the form of a chariot.
- 111th name – *Namȯ Rạthibhyọ Namȧḥ* – Salutations to the one who is in the form of riding in a chariot.
- 114th name – *Namọ Rathĕ̈bhyọ Namȧḥ* Salutations to Him, who is in the form of a Chariot.
- 115th name – *Rathȧpatibhyaścạ Namȧḥ – Salutations* to Him who is in the form of Lord seated in the chariot.

187. *Oṃ Hiraṇyaretase Namaḥ* । ॐ हिरण्यरेतसे नमः ।

He has golden seeds.

In 112th name above it was mentioned as *Svarṇaretase* – which has the same meaning.

366th name below may also be referred.

188. *Oṃ Saptāśvāya Namaḥ* । ॐ सप्ताश्वाय नमः ।

He rides in a chariot with seven horses.

Above 75th name and 686th, 747th, 748th, 749th, 757th, 758th & 854th names below may also be referred.

189. *Oṃ Prayatātmane Namaḥ* । ॐ प्रयतात्मने नमः ।

He is so pure and hence holy.

In *Śiva* sahasranamam – 889th name – *Prayatātmāḥ* – He is the holy Lord.

634th name below may also be referred.

190. *Oṃ Parantapāya Namaḥ* । ॐ परन्तपाय नमः ।

He destroys the enemies. When it is said as enemies, it need not be human outside enemies. It is internal enemies of the mind like *kama* (desire), *krodha* (anger), *lobha* (greed), *mada* (Sense of I), *moha* (attachment) and *matsarya* (partiality). Ananya Bhakti with focused mindedness can be achieved only by destroying these enemies. Lord

Surya is the one who destroys those enemies and conquers the devotees.

To protect the Devas and his devotees he harasses the enemies.

In Rudra Trishatee – 34th name – *Ākrandayate* – Destroyer of enemies.

191. *Oṃ Buddhimate Namaḥ* I ॐ बुद्धिमते नमः ।

Most intelligent Lord.

A verse on Lord Anjaneya goes – "*Bhuddhimatām Varişţam*". Most excellently intelligent. It is not a surprise that Lord Anjaneya is intelligent, since he is the disciple of Lord Sun.

192. *Oṃ Amaraśreṣṭhāya Namaḥ* I ॐ अमरश्रेष्ठाय नमः ।

He is the best of the Devas. *Amara* – Immortal Devas. *Śreṣṭha* – the best.

193. *Oṃ Rociṣṇave Namaḥ* I ॐ रोचिष्णवे नमः ।

He shines with Luster. No need to explain the shine of Lord Sun.

194. *Oṃ Pākaśāsanāya Namaḥ* I ॐ पाकशासनाय नमः ।

He demolished a demon called *Pāka*.

He teaches the ignorant devotee and brings him up.

195. *Oṃ Samudrāya Namaḥ* I ॐ समुद्राय नमः ।

He is in the form of ocean.

The water from the ocean evaporates, comes down again as rain and joins the ocean. He is the maker of this cycle.

196. *Oṃ Dhanadāya Namaḥ* I ॐ धनदाय नमः ।

He gives booty or treasures to the needy.

In *Gāyatri* sahasranamam – 480th name – *Dhanadā* – She in the form of Goddess Lakshmi is in-charge of wealth and she bestows the wealth to all.

938th name below may also be referred.

197. *Oṃ Dhātre Namaḥ* I ॐ धात्रे नमः ।

He is very receptive to his devotees.

In the form of Lord Brahma, he conceives all.

In *Viṣṇu* sahasranamam – 44th name – *Dhātā* – He supports the entire world.

In *Śiva* sahasranamam – 615th name – *Dhātraḥ* – conveying the same meaning.

198. *Oṃ Māndhātre Namaḥ* I ॐ मान्धात्रे नमः ।

He is in the form of Mandhatra.

Mandhatra was a legendary pre-historic king of the Raghuvaṃśa branch of the Suryavamsha (Rama's ancestors) or Solar dynasty. He was said to have conquered the entire world and composed Hymn 134 of Mandala 10 in the Rig Veda.

The Mahabharata calls him the son of Yuvanashva. Yuvanashva wanted a child. But he consumed the magic potion that was meant to make his wife pregnant. As a result, it was he who became pregnant.

199. *Oṃ Kaśmalāpahāya Namaḥ* I ॐ कश्मलापहाय नमः ।

He is devoid of all impurities.

He is *nirgunan* – without any qualities or characters.

200. *Oṃ Tamoghnāya Namaḥ* I ॐ तमोघ्नाय नमः ।

He is the remover of darkness.

It is needless to say Sun only removes the darkness. It is obviously known to all.

Darkness is not only without light. It also means illusion in the form ignorance, covering the knowledge of Brahmam. He removes this also.

The *Íshāvāsya* Upanishat (9th verse) says, they who worship ignorance enter blind darkness;

Andham Tamaḥ Pravishanti Y'vidyā Mupāsate.

In Sri Lalitā Sahasranamam – 361st name – *Tamopahā* – Remover of the darkness called ignorance from the devotees.

Thus ends 100 divine names on Lord *Sūrya* from 101 to 200.

*****

201. *Oṃ Dhvāntaghne Namaḥ* | ॐ ध्वान्तघ्ने नमः ।

He is self-illuminating body.

35th name above may also be referred.

202. *Oṃ Vahnaye Namaḥ* | ॐ वह्नये नमः ।

He is in the form of fire.

148th name above may also be referred.

203. *Oṃ Hotre Namaḥ* | ॐ होत्रे नमः ।

He happily accepts the sacrifices offered through homas (havans).

106th name above and 391st & 714th names below may also be referred.

204. *Oṃ Antaḥkaraṇāya Namaḥ* | ॐ अन्तःकरणाय नमः ।

He is always a conscientious Lord. He neither has sleep nor rest.

205. *Oṃ Guhāya Namaḥ* | ॐ गुहाय नमः ।

He is concealed, in the cave called the heart of the devotees.

Guhyā means one who dwells in a cave, i.e. heart.

The word *Guhyā* can be considered to mean *Jeevātma* (soul), *Paramātmā* (supreme) and the union of both. The presiding deity who can bestow these results is called *Guhya.*

Kaṭopanishad (I-2-12) says;
Ȅśa Sarveśu Bhūteśu Kūṭātmā Na Prakāśate.

In *Viṣṇu* sahasranamam – 383rd name – *Guhaḥ* – He is reclining in the heart. One who can be understood by the secret *Upanishads* or one who dwells in the secret cavity viz., heart.

In Sri Lalitā Sahasranamam – 624th name – *Guhyā* – She is most secretive both in form and meanings.

In *Gāyatri* sahasranamam – 222nd name – *Guhyāyai* – she is most secretive and can be seen or attained only through focused devotion.

In *Śiva* sahasranamam – 261st & 974th names – *Guhaḥ* – again 260th name – *Guhāvāsī* – he lives in a cave, which is the heart of devotees.

Again, in *Śiva* sahasranamam – 507th name – *Guhyaḥ* – He is secretive and cannot be attained easily.

792nd name below may also be referred.

206. *Oṃ Paśumate Namaḥ* I ॐ पशुमते नमः ।

He is a blemishless and error free God.

Paśu = (literal meaning is cattle) are those who are devoid of the conviction of non-separation (*abhedajnāna*).

The *Brahādāraŋya Upanishad* (I-4-10) says, now, he who worships another deity, thinking the deity is one and himself another individual, he does not know. He is like a *pashu*. Here the word *yo'nyām* (*yah* – one and *anyam* – another) means the triangular *Śree Chakra*;

"Yo'nyām Devatāmupāste'nyo'sā Vanyo'hama Smeeti Na Sa Veda Yathā Pashuḥ".

In *Taitreeya Upanishad* it is mentioned as; in the golden three-petalled bud three (syllabled *mantra*, i.e. of *Śreedevee*) is established.

Pa – thirst, *Asha* – hunger. Hence *Pasha* indicates these two. These two – hunger and thirst are due to five types of afflictions (bondages or bindings). These afflictions themselves are bindings only; hence on the whole there are seven bondages. Lord *Surya* releases the ignorant, who get satisfied from these bondings.

He releases such *pashus* from the bondings.

Note: *Pashu, Pāsam* and *Pathi* have been explained in the 88th and 89th chapters of *Upadesa Kāṇḍa, Shiva rahasya Kāṇḍa, Śaṇkara Samhita* in *Skāṇḍam, Śree Anantharāma Deekshatar*'s edition may be referred.

The five types of afflictions referred to are;

(1) Nescience, ignorance or *Avidyā* – the absence of discrimination between the self and the not-self.
(2) Egoism or *Asmitā* – thinking the body, mind and organs as 'I', on account of ignorance and thinking that I am in that form (for instance eyes) - assumption of that body, etc., which are not-self as self.
(3) Strong desire for worldly things or *rāgā* due to *Asmitā* – having interest on the things, which are perceived by the organs and self-involvement in it. Desire is the craving for flowers, scents, etc., which are the means of bodily enjoyment.
(4) Anger, hatred or *Dwesham* on account of *rāgā*; when the interest is affected or if one does not get the things of interest, it results in anger and consequent hatred. Even if the interested things are got, but not the expected results, frustration is created. This is *dwesham* (created on account of *rāgā*).
(5) Ardent attachment is not renouncing a thing even though one knows it is no beneficial. The *dwesha* discussed above is temporary; however, the affect in the mind on account of it is a long standing one. Even if the person knows that this is not good or not a suggested one, he cannot leave it. This is *Abhinivesam*.

These are explained in detail in the *Yoga Sūtra* (III.3-9). But in *Devee Bhāgavatam* these are explained under different names. This is explained in *Linga Purāŋa* also under different names. Again, each of these has many sub- divisions.

The list goes;

Affliction	**Alternate name in *Linga Purāŋā***	**Number of sub-divisions**
Nescience	*Tamas*	8
Egoism (*asmitā*)	Bewilderment (*moha*)	8
Desire (*rāgā*)	Great bewilderment (*mahāmoha*)	10
Hatred (*dwesham*)	*Tāmisram*	8 (18 as per some schools)

Affliction	Alternate name in *Linga Purāṇā*	Number of sub-divisions
Ardent Attachment (*apinivesam*)	*Andatāmisram*	18
Total		52
If *Tāmisram* is considered as 18 then the total		62

As per *Kulārnava Tantra*, there are eight afflictions. They are; *kruṇā*, *shankā*, fear, shyness, *jugupsā*, race, fame and caste. These eight and the above 52 (or 62 as the case may be) are created by compiling the sub-divisions in various forms. By the fear that the size of the explanation will be uncontrollable, *Śree Bhāskararāya* has not explained further sub-divisions of each of these eight.

Pashu means complete – without any balance. In *Vedas* in the statement; *"Lodham Nayanti Pashumanyamānāḥ"* – this has been interpreted as indeclinable word with complete as its meaning.

Pashupa – protector of cattle, lord. *Āsha* – those who are interested in reaching Lord *Surya*. **He** completely releases those people.

From *Brahma* to the most inert everything has the character of *Pashu* (animal). The tool that binds them is ignorance. The various methods of these are called *Pāshās*. **He** releases them through devotion to Lord *Surya*.

In *Gāyatri* sahasranamam – 584th name – *Paśupāśavinirmuktāyai* – She releases her devotees from all the attachments.

In *Śiva* sahasranamam – 865th name – *Paśupatiḥ* – head of all living beings.

696th name below may also be referred.

207. *Oṃ Prayatānandāya Namaḥ* I ॐ प्रयतानन्दाय नमः ।

He has a pure mind and hence always happy.

He gets much happiness in well preparing and planning for all the activities.

In *Śiva* sahasranamam – 889th name – *Prayatātmāḥ* – One who has a purest mind.

208. *Oṃ Bhūteśāya Namaḥ* I ॐ भूतेशाय नमः ।

He is the lord of all living beings.

Brahadaranyaka Upanishat (5-7-4) says, "this is thy self – the inner ruler and immortal being".

In *Viṣṇu* sahasranamam – 8th name – *Bhūtātmā* – He is the self in all beings. Inner of beings.

209. *Oṃ Śrīmatāṃ Varāya Namaḥ* I ॐ श्रीमतां वराय नमः ।

Śrīmat = wealth, *Varāya* = who gives boon

Bestower of all wealth (to all his devotees).

In Samskrutam, the word *Śrīmat* has lots of meanings. The main being auspicious/ wealth.

Śrī = Goddess Lakshmi. *Vara* = husband.

Lord Surya is Lord Vishnu himself and hence husband of Goddess Lakshmi.

In *Śiva* sahasranamam – 1,006th name – *Śrīmān* – One who is richly intelligent.

In Shrimad Bhagavatam (11-16-17) – Bhagavan inter-alia says – I am the Sun among all that gives warmth and light.

210. *Oṃ Nityāya Namaḥ* I ॐ नित्याय नमः ।

183rd name above & 883rd name below may be referred.

211. *Oṃ Aditāya Namaḥ* I ॐ अदिताय नमः ।

Son of Aditi Devi.

Aditi is one of the wives of sage *Kashyapa* and she is the mother of all the Devas. During Vamana incarnation of Lord Vishnu, *Aditi* was his mother.

68th name above may also be referred.

212. *Oṃ Nityarathāya Namaḥ* I ॐ नित्यरथाय नमः ।

He is travelling in a chariot permanently without any gap or break.

213. *Oṃ Sureśāya Namaḥ* I ॐ सुरेशाय नमः ।

He is the lord of all lords.

He is the lord of those who confer good.

In *Viṣṇu* sahasranamam – 85th name – *Sureśaḥ* – Lord of all Devas.

In *Śiva* sahasranamam – 389th name – *Surādhyakṣaḥ* – Lord of Devas.

498th name below may also be referred.

214. *Oṃ Surapūjitāya Namaḥ* I ॐ सुरपूजिताय नमः ।

One, who is worshipped by all Devas.

In the previous name, it was mentioned that he is the lord of all Devas. Hence, he is worshipped by all Devas.

215. *Oṃ Ajitāya Namaḥ* I ॐ अजिताय नमः ।

He cannot be won by anyone.

He can be conquered only through yoga and devotion.

The literature *Kāmikā* describes each of *Tantras* to the organs of **His** body. Here the *Tantra* called *Ajitā* is mapped to his knees.

In *Viṣṇu* sahasranamam – 549th name – *Ajitaḥ* – unconquered in all his incarnations.

In *Gāyatri* sahasranamam – 6th name – *Ajitā* – One, who cannot be conquered.

216. *Oṃ Vijitāya Namaḥ* I ॐ विजिताय नमः ।

One, who has conquered everybody else.

He has conquered not only his enemies in the battles, but also the minds of his devotees.

In the previous name it was mentioned that he cannot be won by anyone. Here it is stressed that he has conquered all.

217. *Oṃ Jetre Namaḥ* I ॐ जेत्रे नमः ।

He is always triumphant.

One who is the conqueror of ignorance (*Avidyā*).

He helps the devotees to win over it. **He** in the form of knowledge himself, bestows knowledge and wins over ignorance.

In *Gāyatri* sahasranamam – 318th name – *Jetrī* – One, who is always triumphant.

218. *Oṃ Jaṅgama Sthāvarātmakāya Namaḥ* I
ॐ जङ्गम स्थावरात्मकाय नमः ।

He is in the form of all both movable and immovable objects in this universe.

219. *Oṃ Jīvānandāya Namaḥ* I ॐ जीवानन्दाय नमः ।

He is the bliss of all the souls.

He is the life-pranan of all

220. *Oṃ Nityagāmine Namaḥ* I ॐ नित्यगामिने नमः ।

He is constantly doing some work without any rest.

It is impossible to imagine what this world would become if the Sun takes a break.

221. *Oṃ Vijetre Namaḥ* I ॐ विजेत्रे नमः ।

He is the vanquisher of bad elements and champion.

222. *Oṃ Vijayapradāya Namaḥ* I ॐ विजयप्रदाय नमः ।

He bestows success to his devotees in all the endeavours.

223. *Oṃ Parjanyāya Namaḥ* | ॐ पर्जन्याय नमः ।

Rain personified or lord of rain.

Sun is lord of Devas like *Varuna* (water), *Agni* (fire), *Vayu* (air) and so on. Hence is God of rain.

He extinguishes the three kinds of miseries concerning the body and the rest, even as the rain God that cools the earth by its downpour.

He showers down all the desired objects like rain.

In *Viṣṇu* sahasranamam – 810th name – *Parjanyaḥ* – he is in the form of rain charged cloud.

224. *Oṃ Agnaye Namaḥ* | ॐ अग्नये नमः ।

He is in the form of fire god *Agni*.

In the previous name it was mentioned that he is in the form of water god Varunan. Here it is stated that he is in the form of fire god Agni.

In *Śiva* sahasranamam – 432nd name – *Agnijvālaḥ* – he is like the flame of the fire.

225. *Oṃ Sthitaye Namaḥ* | ॐ स्थितये नमः ।

He is stable and permanent.

He is eternally staying/ being in his chariot.

He is constant in his distribution of blessings even to the irreligious.

In *Viṣṇu* sahasranamam – 203rd name – *Sthiraḥ* – being always the same without any change.

In *Śiva* sahasranamam – 1 & 524th names – *Sthiraḥ* – he is stable or perennial.

647th & 932nd names below may also be referred.

226. *Oṃ Stheyāya Namaḥ* I ॐ स्थेयाय नमः ।

He is stationed fixed.

Actually, we feel and say that Sun rises in the East and sets in the West. But, in reality the rising and setting of Sun is on account of rotation of Earth. Sun is always stationary.

227. *Oṃ Sthavirāya Namaḥ* I ॐ स्थविराय नमः ।

He is the oldest or eldest.

No where the origin of Lord Sun is mentioned. Hence, he should be the eldest.

In Sri Rudram we chant Lord Rudra is *Jyeshta* – eldest.

Sthavira means age. A man aged 70 and more is called *Sthavira.*

The Rig Veda (7-100-3) says – for illustrious is the name of the old one.

228. *Oṃ Nirañjanāya Namaḥ* I ॐ निरञ्जनाय नमः ।

He is free from any stain.

Anjana means black collegium used for eyes. Though it is used for beautification, still it is a stain. In this context *Anjana* implies ignorance or illusion. The knowledge disappears due to ignorance (owing to its quality of darkness in mind). It has to be construed that Lord Sun has no relevance to ignorance or illusion.

Swetashvatara Upanishad (VI-19) indicates *Brahmam* as "*Niravatyam Niranjanam*".

One who is – *Ni* (more) – *Ranjanam* (happiness/ delight).

In *Lalit*ā sahasranamam – 133rd name – *Niranjanā* – One who is free from any stain.

In *Gāyatri* sahasranamam – 510th name – *Nirañjanā* – conveying the same sense.

229. *Oṃ Pradyotanāya Namaḥ* I ॐ प्रद्योतनाय नमः ।

He radiates the world with his blazing light.

230. *Oṃ Rathārūḍhāya Namaḥ* I ॐ रथारूढाय नमः ।

He is always mounted on a chariot.

In *Rudra Trishatee*, in lot many places Lord Rudra is mapped to a chariot as – He is the chariot, owner of the chariot, the driver of the chariot, the controller of the chariot and the person who builds the chariot too. He is also the owner of the chariot.

In the Mahabharata war Arjuna's chariot was driven by Lord Surya in the form of Krishna.

231. *Oṃ Sarvalokaprakaśakaya Namaḥ* I ॐ सर्वलोकप्रकाशकाय नमः ।

He illuminates the entire world. He reveals his form to his devotees.

This is very obvious. Other than the Sun God, who else can brighten the world.

In *Vişṇu* sahasranamam – 274th name – *Prakaṣanaḥ* – he brightens the world.

In *Śiva* sahasranamam – 508th name – *Prakaśaḥ* – he shines like anything.

441st name below may also be referred.

232. *Oṃ Dhruvāya Namaḥ* I ॐ ध्रुवाय नमः ।

He is there forever eternally. He does not take a break.

In *Śiva* sahasranamam – 620th name – *Druvaḥ* – he is in the form of *Druva* star.

233. *Oṃ Meṣine Namaḥ* I ॐ मेषिने नमः ।

Our of the 12 rashis (astrological signs), Sun is most powerful in Mesha (Aries).

234. *Oṃ Mahāvīryāya Namaḥ* I ॐ महावीर्याय नमः ।

Mahāvīra – He is a great warrior.

Mahāvīrya – He is with great energy.

The word *veeryā* in Samskrutam means – semen, might, glory and strength. Sun has all these in a great way.

He possesses the energy of the nature of *Avidya*, which generates '*Mahat*'. His strength is never changed.

In *Gāyatri* sahasranamam – 814th name – *Mahāvīryā* – She is supreme in valour.

In *Lalitā* sahasranamam – 221st name – *Mahāvīryā* – conveying the same sense.

235. *Oṃ Haṃsāya Namaḥ* I ॐ हंसाय नमः ।

The root '*Han*' means to go or to move. He is always on the move.

He is moving in the bodies of all.

Hamsa (Swan) birds are famous for their beauty in walking.

A type of *sanyāsins* called *Paramahamsā* is indifferent to **Him** (i.e. those great *sanyāsins* are always meditating upon **Him**).

The exhale and inhale of breath together is called *Hamsa Mantra* or *Ajapā Mantra*.

Katopanishad (4-6) says "He is *Hamsa* dwelling in heaven".

In *Viṣṇu* sahasranamam – 191st name – *Hamsaḥ* – as he removes the fear of Samsara of those who meditates upon Him as "*Aham Brahmāsmi* – I am He" or "*Śivoham* – I am that Lord *Śiva*".

In *Lalitā* sahasranamam – 456th name – *Hamsinī* – One who is alongwith swans.

236. *Oṃ Saṃsāratārakāya Namaḥ* I ॐ संसारतारकाय नमः ।

He is the protector of his devotees from *Saṃsāra* – The circuit of mundane existence.

In *Lalitā* sahasranamam – 880th name – *Samsāra Panka Nirmagna Samuddharaṇa Paṇḍitā* – One who is skilled in bringing out those sunk in the mire of the trans-migratory life.

Koorma Purāṇa says, "Those who once remember him invoking **His** protection do not fall into the endless ocean of *Samsāra*, which is difficult to be crossed";

Ye Manāgapi Śarvānīm Smaranti Śaranārdinaḥ I
Dustarāpāra Samsārasagare Na Patanti Te II

852nd & 853rd names below may also be referred.

237. *Oṃ Sṛṣṭikartre Namaḥ* I ॐ सृष्टिकर्त्रे नमः ।

One who does the task of creation.

Creation is the function of *Brahma* when the rajas quality predominates. To distinguish the forms like *Brahma* from supreme-being is an illusion (*Māyā*).

In *Lalitā* sahasranamam – 264th name – *Srushṭikartrī* – She does the task of creation.

238. *Oṃ Kriyāhetave Namaḥ* I ॐ क्रियाहेतवे नमः ।

He is the cause of every activity/ task/ ritual.

In *Śiva* sahasranamam – 550th name – *Kriyāvasthaḥ* – he is in the form of all rituals like yaga and all.

478th name below may also be referred.

239. *Oṃ Mārtaṇḍāya Namaḥ* I ॐ मार्तण्डाय नमः ।

He is seen as a bird/ fruit in the sky.

We all know the story of *Anjaneya*, as a child, flew to pluck Sun god thinking it as a fruit.

Similar is the story of *Jatayu*, as a child, flew to pluck Sun god and his elder brother Sambaathi protected him. In this process the wings of Sambaathi were burnt.

240. *Oṃ Marutāṃ Namaḥ* I ॐ मरुतां नमः ।

He is the vital air for all the souls.

241. *Oṃ Pataye Namaḥ* I ॐ पतये नमः ।

The word *'pati'* in Samskrutam has lots of meanings like – husband, leader, chief, etc. He is in the form of all these.

242. *Oṃ Marutvate Namaḥ* I ॐ मरुत्वते नमः ।

He is the container and controller of cloud.

Clouds need to be controlled so that it is raining adequately and no heavily. He is the controller. In fact, he is forming clouds itself through evaporation of water from the oceans.

243. *Oṃ Dahanāya Namaḥ* I ॐ दहनाय नमः ।

Dahana is one of the 5 forms of *Agni* used in yagnas. He is in that form.

He is capable reducing everything and anything into ashes.

244. *Oṃ Tvaṣṭre Namaḥ* I ॐ त्वष्ट्रे नमः ।

He eradicates every living being during dissolution.

This was hinted in the previous name itself, that he is capable of reducing everything into ashes.

In *Viṣṇu* sahasranamam – 72nd name – *Tvaṣṭaḥ* – The reducer.

In *Śiva* sahasranamam – 619th name – *Tvaṣṭā* – He is the Vishwakarma, the architect of Devas.

245. *Oṃ Bhagāya Namaḥ* I ॐ भगाय नमः ।

One who gets a share in every yagna.

One who gives shares to other Devas in every yaga.

Whatever be the *yagna* intended to, there will be at least one offering for Lord Surya – "*Sūryāya Swāhaḥ*".

In *Śiva* sahasranamam – 447th name – *Bhāgaḥ* – and 448th name – *Bhagakaraya* – conveying the same meaning.

246. *Oṃ Bhargāya Namaḥ* I ॐ भर्गाय नमः ।

He is a person of splendorous effulgence.

267th name below may also be referred.

247. *Oṃ Aryamṇe Namaḥ* I ॐ अर्यम्णे नमः ।

He is in the form of *Aryamṇan*, who is the God of manes.

As mentioned earlier, *Aryaman* is one of the 12 *Adityas*.

In *Śiva* sahasranamam – 625th name – *Aryamaḥ* – conveying the same meaning.

248. *Oṃ Kapaye Namaḥ* I ॐ कपये नमः ।

He dries up (*pi*) the water (*ka*) with his rays.

He is the Guru of Lord Anjaneya, an ape (*kapi*).

In *Vişṇu* sahasranamam – 899th name – *Kapiḥ* – Varaha or boar incarnation.

249. *Oṃ Varuṇeśāya Namaḥ* I ॐ वरुणेशाय नमः ।

The setting Sun is called *Varuṇa*, as he withdraws his rays within himself.

He is the lord of *Varuna*, the water god.

Taitreeya Samhita (2-10-11) says – "Oh *Varuṇā*! Listen to our hymns".

In *Viṣṇu* sahasranamam – 553rd name – *Varuṇaḥ* – He is in the form *Varuṇan*, the water God.

250. *Oṃ Jagannāthāya Namaḥ* I ॐ जगन्नाथाय नमः ।

The lord of this whole world.

Usually, Lord *Viṣṇu* is called as *Jagannāthan*. Since Lords Sun and *Viṣṇu* are one and the same, the name is very apt here.

751st name below may also be referred.

251. *Oṃ Kṛtakṛtyāya Namaḥ* I ॐ कृतकृत्याय नमः ।

He is the one who has accomplished his past and present duties. And he will also accomplish his future duties and be contented.

He has nothing to achieve as he has performed all virtuous deeds.

In *Viṣṇu* sahasranamam – 788th name – *Kṛthakarmā* – He has fulfilled all his achievements.

629th name below may also be referred.

252. *Oṃ Sulocanāya Namaḥ* I ॐ सुलोचनाय नमः ।

He has beautiful eyes.

He has superior wisdom and his wisdom to deceive the Daityas/ monsters.

In *Viṣṇu* sahasranamam – 794th name – *Sulocanaḥ* – He has charming eyes.

253. *Oṃ Vivasvate Namaḥ* I ॐ विवस्वते नमः ।

He arises every morning with diffusing light.

In *Śiva* sahasranamam – 899th name – *Vivasvān* – He drenches the world by his nectar like rays.

254. *Oṃ Bhānumate Namaḥ* । ॐ भानुमते नमः ।

His splendid rays are so beautifully luminous.

Katopanishad (4-15) says – "when he shines".

It is also described that *Bhānumaŋḍala* is the *Anāhatachakra*. He is in the form of *Kunḍalinee* there.

In *Viṣṇu* sahasranamam – 284th name – *Bhānuḥ* – He shines.

255. *Oṃ Kāryāya Namaḥ* । ॐ कार्याय नमः ।

He is always acting without any rest.

He makes others to act.

256. *Oṃ Kāraṇāya Namaḥ* । ॐ कारणाय नमः ।

There is no act without cause and effect. He is the one who causes the acts.

In *Lalitā* sahasranamam – 862nd name – *Kāryakāraŋanirmuktā* – she is free from cause and effect.

257. *Oṃ Tejasāṃ Nidhaye Namaḥ* । ॐ तेजसां निधये नमः ।

He is a self-illuminating body. His brightness is reflected by others.

Present day Astronomy also accepts that stars are self-illuminating. Planets, natural satellites, Moons, etc., are reflecting the brightness from Sun.

In *Viṣṇu* sahasranamam – 757th name – *Tejovṛṣaḥ* – He showers his effulgence.

258. *Oṃ Asaṅgagāmine Namaḥ* । ॐ असङ्गगामिने नमः ।

He keeps on going or moving on or in or towards or in any peculiar Manner in an uninterrupted or allighned way.

259. *Oṃ Tigmāṃśave Namaḥ* । ॐ तिग्मांशवे नमः ।

Severe hot and fire person.

260. *Oṃ Dharmāṃśave Namaḥ* I ॐ धर्मांशवे नमः I

He is Dharma personified.

He is the best of all the knowers of Manu Dharma, etc.

He is with the experience of righteousness like bliss and eternity.

Righteousness indicates everything visible, for which *Brahmam* is the basis.

The word *Dharma* has lot of meanings. (The dictionary called *Amara Kosham* gives 42 meanings for the word *dharma*). In general, it indicates virtues. The opposite *Adharma* indicates vices. In this context *dharma* cannot be taken only as virtues. Because something good for one person or in one state could be bad for other person or in other state. The ultimate decision here is only *Veda*. These are rules or laws to conduct the human in virtuous path. These will never bind *Lord Surya*. **He** only created all these rules.

Dharma indicates a sort of limit or restrains. That is, the controls for the caste, religion and other *āshramās* respectively are called *dharma*. If these are broken, it is *adharma*. In this context also, **He** is not bound by these distinctions. Hence, he is beyond *dharma* and *adharma*.

Dharma is a quality or character. For instance, to be hot is a character, hence *dharma*. One who has a character is called *dharmee*. If the fire loses its character of heat, then it is *adharma* (In *Rāmāyana*, Sita requests [not orders] fire to be cool with *Hanumān* – *Śīto Bhava Hanumataḥ* – hence it was cool). If one loses its character, it is *adharma*.

Dharma also means bondage. The soul is bound by various bondages like husband, wife, son, friend, etc. Each relationship is cramming the soul with different bondages. Being without these bondages or getting relieved of them is called liberation, hence it is *adharma*. He is beyond bondages or relief from them.

Righteousness can be defined as the mode of life laid down in each country, by the tradition of the wise and not contrary to the *Vedas.*

In entire *Shrimad Bhagawad Gita*, Lord *Krishna* talks *Dharma* and *Adharma* only.

In *Vişṇu* sahasranamam – 404th name – *Dharma Viduttamaḥ* – The best of the knowers of Dharma.

In *Lalitā* sahasranamam – 255th name – *Dharmādharmavivarjitā* – She is with righteousness by distinguishing *Dharma* and *Adharma.*

Again, in *Lalitā* sahasranamam – 884th name – *Dharmādhārā* – She is a support for *Dharma* (righteousness).

Again, in *Lalitā* sahasranamam – 958th name – *Dharmiṇī* – She promotes righteousness.

Again, in *Lalitā* sahasranamam – 959th name – *Dharmavardhinī* – She is devoid of both virtues and vices.

261. *Oṃ Dīptadīdhitaye Namaḥ* | ॐ दीप्तदीधितये नमः ।

He shines like a very big huge lamp.

262. *Oṃ Sahasradīdhitaye Namaḥ* | ॐ सहस्रदीधितये नमः ।

He shines like thousands of huge lamps lit at a time.

263. *Oṃ Bradhnāya Namaḥ* | ॐ ब्रध्नाय नमः ।

He is Yellow in colour.

Sun will be seen in different colours depending on the weather conditions and also the time of day. But colors are only a perception. In reality Sun is colourless.

337th & 369th names below may also be referred.

264. *Oṃ Sahasrāṃśave Namaḥ* | ॐ सहस्रांशवे नमः ।

He is with thousand rays.

When it is said as thousand, it should not be construed as exact number thousand. It should be construed as thousands of rays.

Taitreeya Brahmanam (3-12-9) says "Kindled by that Light the Sun shines".

Shrimad Bhagawad Gita (15-12) says "the light which is in the Sun...".

In *Vişņu* sahasranamam – 483rd name – *Sahasrāmśuḥ* – with thousand rays.

622nd & 780th names below may also be referred.

265. *Oṃ Divākarāya Namaḥ* I ॐ दिवाकराय नमः ।

108th name above may be referred.

266. *Oṃ Gabhastimate Namaḥ* I ॐ गभस्तिमते नमः ।

He wears a garland of rays.

In *Śiva* sahasranamam – 857th name – *Gabhastiḥ* – He has drenches of light.

267. *Oṃ Dīdhitimate Namaḥ* I ॐ दीधितिमते नमः ।

He shines splendourously.

246th name above may also be referred.

268. *Oṃ Sragviṇe Namaḥ* I ॐ स्रग्विणे नमः ।

He always wears a garland.

In *Vişņu* sahasranamam – 216th name – *Sragviḥ* – He wears a garland called *Vaijayanti*, the symbol of *Tanmātras*, rudimental of the elements.

269. *Oṃ Maṇikuladyutaye Namaḥ* I ॐ मणिकुलद्युतये नमः ।

Born in *Maṇi* clan.

Lord Surya has no birth. Yet here it is said that he was born in *Maṇi* clan, just to make us, common people happy.

270. *Oṃ Bhāskarāya Namaḥ* I ॐ भास्कराय नमः ।

No one is so bright as Lord Sun.

In *Viṣṇu* sahasranamam – 282nd name – *Bhāskaradyutiḥ* – He is bright like Sun.

597th name below may also be referred.

271. *Oṃ Surakāryajñāya Namaḥ* I ॐ सुरकार्यज्ञाय नमः ।

In *Yagnas*, the offerings are offered intended to different Devas. Surya is the person who carries the offerings to the concerned Devas.

272. *Oṃ Sarvajñāya Namaḥ* I ॐ सर्वज्ञाय नमः ।

He is omniscient.

He knows everything.

He is the witness of all happenings.

Brahadaranyaka Upanishat (6-5-7) says "All this is the self....".

In *Viṣṇu* sahasranamam – 453rd name – *Sarvagnaḥ* – All knowing. He recognises all his manifestations.

624th name below may also be referred.

273. *Oṃ Tīkṣṇadīdhitaye Namaḥ* I ॐ तीक्ष्णदीधितये नमः ।

He shines sharply.

266th & 267th names above also describe the shining of Sun.

274. *Oṃ Surajyeṣṭhāya Namaḥ* I ॐ सुरज्येष्ठाय नमः ।

He is the senior most among the Devas.

He is in a great form.

171st name in *Rudra Trishatī* – *Namő Jyẹṣṭhāyả Cą Namảḥ* – Salutations to the one who is in the form of an elder.

In *Camakam*, 2nd Anuvakam also – *Jyaiṣṭhyaṃ Ca Ma"* – the devotees pray to make them as great in all respects.

275. *Oṃ Surapataye Namaḥ* I ॐ सुरपतये नमः ।

Head of all Devas.

276. *Oṃ Bahujñāya Namaḥ* I ॐ बहुज्ञाय नमः ।

He is possessed with great knowledge.

He is the Guru of Lord Hanuman.

277. *Oṃ Vacasāṃ Pataye Namaḥ* I ॐ वचसां पतये नमः ।

He is an expert in speech.

He is the leaders of all speakers.

His disciple Hanuman is an unparalleled maestro of communication.

In *Viṣṇu* sahasranamam – 217th name – *Vācaspati* – Lord of all *Vidyas*.

Again, in *Viṣṇu* sahasranamam – 573rd name – *Vacaspatirayonijaḥ* – Lord of *Vidyas*.

In *Śiva* sahasranamam – 359th name – *Vacaspatiḥ* – Lord of Vidyas.

278. *Oṃ Tejonidhaye Namaḥ* I ॐ तेजोनिधये नमः ।

He is an abounding treasury of glory.

He showers his effulgence in universal form.

In *Viṣṇu* sahasranamam – 757th name – *Tejovṛṣaḥ* – he showers radiance.

424th name below may also be referred.

279. *Oṃ Bṛhattejase Namaḥ* I ॐ बृहत्तेजसे नमः ।

He has great energy. That is the reason, he could continuously act without rest.

Planet Jupiter is also called as *Bṛhattejas*. Lord Sun and Jupiter are one and the same.

280. *Oṃ Bṛhatkīrtaye Namaḥ* I ॐ बृहत्कीर्तये नमः ।

He is far-famed.

281. *Oṃ Bṛhaspataye Namaḥ* I ॐ बृहस्पतये नमः ।

He is *Bṛhaspati*, the Deva Guru.

In 279th name above itself it was mentioned Lord Sun and Planet Jupiter are one the same. Here it is being openly revealed. Brahaspati is Deva Guru, planet Jupiter and in-charge of Thursday.

365th name below may also be referred.

282. *Oṃ Ahimate Namaḥ* I ॐ अहिमते नमः ।

He is possessed of abounding of snakes.

Lord of snakes is Sun God.

283. *Oṃ Ūrjitāya Namaḥ* I ॐ ऊर्जिताय नमः ।

He is with immense strength.

In *Viṣṇu* sahasranamam – 156th name – *Ūrjitaḥ* – he is firm.

284. *Oṃ Dhīmate Namaḥ* I ॐ धीमते नमः ।

He is very learned/ knowledgeable.

285. *Oṃ Āmuktāya Namaḥ* I ॐ आमुक्ताय नमः ।

He is armoured.

He travels in a chariot like a king and necessarily he has dress like a king with necessary armours.

286. *Oṃ Kīrtivardhanāya Namaḥ* I ॐ कीर्तिवर्धनाय नमः ।

His fame is increasing day by day.

More and more people are realising the importance of worshipping Sun God.

Even writing books like this on Him, propagates his fame.

287. *Oṃ Mahāvaidyāya Namaḥ* । ॐ महावैद्याय नमः ।

He is great doctor curing all the diseases of his devotees, both physical and mental worries.

Vaidya is a doctor. *Mahāvaidya* is a great doctor.

In *Viṣṇu* sahasranamam – 164th name – *Vaidhyaḥ* – he is a doctor.

In *Śiva* sahasranamam – 955th name – *Vaidhyaḥ* – conveying the same meaning.

288. *Oṃ Gaṇapataye Namaḥ* । ॐ गणपतये नमः ।

He is head of all groups.

One of the primary meanings of the word *Gaṇa* in Samskrutam is group. In Modern Algebra section of Mathematics also we have something called 'Set', which is a collection of objects. This is called as *Gaṇam* in most of the languages like Tamil, Hindi, Samskrutam, etc. Hence, *Gaṇapati* is leader or head of group(s).

11th Anuvakam of Sri Rudra Namakam says there are thousands of Rudra *Gaṇas*. For all those *Gaṇas* the leader is the *Gaṇapati*.

The word '*Gaṇa*' has lots of meanings. There is one related to language. All the words that come under the same root are grouped together as a '*Gaṇam*' says Samskruta grammer (*Vyakarana*). Ganapati is the lord of all these *Gaṇams*.

But, in practice the word *Gaṇapati* has started to mean by default, Lord *Vinayaka*. Because he is the leader of Deva *Gaṇas* – all the groups of Devas.

In *Śiva* sahasranamam – 96th name – *Gaṇaḥ* – He is in the form of various groups.

Again, in *Śiva* sahasranamam – 98th name – *Gaṇapatiḥ* – Leader of all groups.

289. *Oṃ Dhaneśāya Namaḥ* I ॐ धनेशाय नमः ।

He is the lord of wealth.

In general, in-charge of wealth is said to be Goddess Lakshmi.

Normally, *Kubera Deva* is said to be the presiding deity of wealth. He is one of the famous worshippers of Sun God. The scriptures say that there is no distinction between the worshipper and the worshipped deity. In that fashion Sun is in the form of *Kubera*. Hence, **He** is the head of wealth.

In *Viṣṇu* sahasranamam – 474th name – *Dhaneśvaraḥ* – Lord of wealth.

In *Lalita* sahasranamam – 885th name – *Dhanādhyakshā* – Head of wealth.

Again, in *Lalita* sahasranamam – 886th name – *Dhanadhānya Vivardhinī* – she is increasing the wealth and grain.

290. *Oṃ Gaṇanāyakāya Namaḥ* I ॐ गणनायकाय नमः ।

He is head of all groups of Devas like Kinnara, Ghandarva, etc.

One of the primary meanings of the word *Gaṇa* in Samskrutam is group. In Modern Algebra section of Mathematics also we have something called 'Set', which is a collection of objects. This is called as *Gaṇam*. Hence, *Gaṇanāyakā* is leader or head of that group.

Normally, in practice the word *Gaṇapati* has started to mean by default, Lord *Vinayaka*. Because he is the leader of Deva *Gaṇas* – all the groups of Devas he is called as *Gaṇanāyakā*, here.

288th name above can also be referred.

291. *Oṃ Tīvrapratāpanāya Namaḥ* I ॐ तीव्रप्रतापनाय नमः ।

He is most intensively warm.

It is a known fact that Sun is so hot that no living thing can survive. It is hell like hot. The stories of Hanuman and Jatayu went to catch Sun and were prohibited, not to get burned by heat, were known to all.

292. *Oṃ Tāpine Namaḥ* । ॐ तापिने नमः ।

He is oppressed with heat.

293. *Oṃ Tāpanāya Namaḥ* । ॐ तापनाय नमः ।

He is in the form of *Araṇi* wood, which is used to create fire.

149th name above may also be referred.

294. *Oṃ Viśvatāpanāya Namaḥ* । ॐ विश्वतापनाय नमः ।

He is burning the entire world during great dissolution.

He is worshipped by ascetics of the entire universe. The only request of ascetics is liberation. He is capable of bestowing this wish.

In *Lalita* sahasranamam – 359th name – *Tāpasārādhyā* – worshipped by ascetics.

295. *Oṃ Kārtasvarāya Namaḥ* । ॐ कार्तस्वराय नमः ।

He shines like a gold.

Especially during Sun rise and Sun set, Sun's colour will be like a gold.

296. *Oṃ Hṛṣīkeśāya Namaḥ* । ॐ हृषीकेशाय नमः ।

He is the controller of sense organs – organs of action and organs of knowledge.

Hṛṣīka = senses. *Ēśā* = lord. I.e. he assumes the form of Kshetrajna, who controls the senses, the supreme Atman.

He delights the world by his *Keśā* (rays).

Mahabharatam (Shanti Parvam 343, 62 and 63) says – He through his rays known as *Keśā* always uphold the Universe by awaking it and causing it to sleep. By such awaking and causing to sleep, the universe is delighted.

Normally lord *Vişņu* is called *Hrişīkeśa*. But here Lord Sun is called so. This implies that there is no difference between them and both are one and the same.

In *Vişņu* sahasranamam – 47th name – *Hrişīkeśaḥ* – Lord of senses.

297. *Oṃ Padmānandāya Namaḥ* । ॐ पद्मानन्दाय नमः ।

He makes Lotus flower happy.

Padma = Lotus flower. *Ānanda* = Happiness or Bliss. Lotus flower buds blooms upon seeing the Sun. I.e. it gets happy and opens its petals.

298. *Oṃ Atinanditāya Namaḥ* । ॐ अतिनन्दिताय नमः ।

He is a very much happy person.

He is always pleasing.

He makes his devotees delighted.

299. *Oṃ Padmanābhāya Namaḥ* । ॐ पद्मनाभाय नमः ।

He is lotus navelled. Having the navel like Lotus in his hand.

He shines in the center of the Lotus like heart of the devotees.

Normally lord *Vişņu* is called *Padmanābha*. But here Lord Sun is called so. This implies that there is no difference between them and both are one and the same.

Lotus flower symbolizes the source of all the Universe which is in his navel.

In *Vişņu* sahasranamam – 48th & 196th names – *Padmanābhaḥ* – Lotus navelled.

Taitreeya Samhita (4-6-2) says "In the navel of Aja (Brahma) all this is established".

300. *Oṃ Amṛtāhārāya Namaḥ* | ॐ अमृताहाराय नमः |

One whose food is nectar (*amrut*).

He who turns the food of the devotees into nectar.

Before eating food, during *Pariśeşaŋam*, we say "*Amruta Upastharanamasi*" and drink a spoon quantity of water. It means let that water be the base foundation of the food which is *Amrut*. Similarly, after finishing the meal, we say "*Amruta Abhitanamasi*" and drink a spoon quantity of water. It means that the water should be lid of the food that is *amrut*.

That is, the food consumed between drinking two waters becomes *amrtam*.

Thus ends 100 divine names on Lord *Sūrya* from 201 to 300.

*****

301. *Oṃ Sthitimate Namaḥ* | ॐ स्थितिमते नमः ।

He is static. Any star is static. Only other celestial objects are moving.

He is stable as a mountain.

In *Viṣṇu* sahasranamam – 203rd name – *Sthiraḥ* – he is constant.

In *Śiva* sahasranamam – 1st & 524th names – *Sthiraḥ* – He is perennial.

302. *Oṃ Ketumate Namaḥ* | ॐ केतुमते नमः ।

He is endowed with brightness, which is a known fact.

He is in the form of Ketu, one of the shadow grahams among the Navagrahas.

303. *Oṃ Nabhase Namaḥ* | ॐ नभसे नमः ।

Moving in the sky or atmosphere.

In *Śiva* sahasranamam – 179th name – *Nabhaḥ* – He is unattached like the sky.

331st name below may also be referred.

304. *Oṃ Anādyantāya Namaḥ* | ॐ अनाद्यन्ताय नमः ।

He has no beginning nor end.

He does not have any birth or end. In lots of puranas and literatures we have come across the birth of Lord Ganesh, Lord Kumara, Rama, Krishna and all. In some places we have even read the end of Lord Rama, Krishna and all. But no literature mentions about the origin of Lord Sun.

In *Viṣṇu* sahasranamam – 42nd name – *Anādinidhānaḥ* – he is devoid of birth and death.

Again, in *Viṣṇu* sahasranamam – 941st name – *Anādiḥ* – He has no origin.

305. *Oṃ Acyutāya Namaḥ* I ॐ अच्युताय नमः ।

He is not shaken and will not be shaken from his own glory.

Narayana Upanishat (13) says "He is eternal, calm and unswerving".

Any *karma* is started with Ācamanam, which again starts with *Acyutāya Namaḥ*. Only after giving the first salutations to *Acyutan* any religious task, including Ganapati puja, is started.

Lord Krishna in Shrimad Bhagawad Gita says "I did not swerve from my path at any time before, hence I am called as Achyuta by that act".

In *Viṣṇu* sahasranamam – 100th & 318th names – *Acyutaḥ* – Unswerving (from his nature) being free from the six kinds of changes like birth, death, etc.

306. *Oṃ Viśvāya Namaḥ* I ॐ विश्वाय नमः ।

He is this universe or the cause of this universe.

He is the *Brahmam, Omkara Pranavam*, world or the creator of it or involver of all in him.

The very first name in *Viṣṇu* sahasranamam – *Viśwam* – the universe.

In *Śiva* sahasranamam – 947th name – *Viśwaḥ* – the universe.

307. *Oṃ Viśvāmitrāya Namaḥ* I ॐ विश्वामित्राय नमः ।

He is a friend to all. He does not have foes.

744th name below may also be referred.

308. *Oṃ Ghṛṇaye Namaḥ* I ॐ घृणये नमः ।

He has a warm feeling towards others.

In the previous name it was mentioned that he is friendly to all. Hence, he has a warm feeling to all.

745th name below may also be referred.

309. *Oṃ Virāje Namaḥ* I ॐ विराजे नमः ।

He is without any stain or sin originated by the *Rajo* character.

The prefix '*Vi*' has to be taken in the opposite sense – i.e. without the character called *Rajo*.

In *Lalitā* sahasranamam –779th name – *Virajā* – She is without any tint or sin.

746th name below may also be referred.

310. *Oṃ Āmuktakavacāya Namaḥ* I ॐ आमुक्तकवचाय नमः ।

He wears an armour as a jewel or shield.

He is liberated from Rahu.

Āmukta = liberation. He liberates all his devotees from the cycle of birth and death. He gives salvation.

311. *Oṃ Vāgmine Namaḥ* I ॐ वाग्मिने नमः ।

He is eloquent in his speech. Such a quality pertains to Brahmam.

In *Viṣṇu* sahasranamam – 267th name – *Vāgmiḥ* – He from whom speech begins.

In *Lalitā* sahasranamam – 350th name – *Vāgvādinī* – She is the speaker of the world and who has the power that prompts to speak words.

162nd name above and 500th & 626th name below may also be referred.

312. *Oṃ Kañcukine Namaḥ* I ॐ कञ्चुकिने नमः ।

He is covered with armour. This has been mentioned in 285th name above also.

In Mahabharata his son Karna was born with armour.

313. *Oṃ Viśvabhāvanāya Namaḥ* I ॐ विश्वभावनाय नमः ।

He is the existence of this Universe. He expands himself as universe or remains as pure existence.

In *Vişṇu* sahasranamam – 7th name – *Bhāvaḥ* – The absolute existence.

In *Śiva* sahasranamam – 521st name – *Bhāvaḥ* – The absolute existence.

314. *Oṃ Animittagataye Namaḥ* । ॐ अनिमित्तगतये नमः ।

He bestows unconditioned salvation to his devotees.

315. *Oṃ Śreṣṭhāya Namaḥ* । ॐ श्रेष्ठाय नमः ।

He is the greatest.

63rd above & 506th below names may also be referred.

316. *Oṃ Śaraṇyāya Namaḥ* । ॐ शरण्याय नमः ।

He is the God with whom everyone seeks refuge with.

In *Śiva* sahasranamam – 842nd name – *Śaraṇyaḥ* – he well takes care of his devotees.

27th name above & 390th name below may also be referred.

317. *Oṃ Sarvatomukhāya Namaḥ* । ॐ सर्वतोमुखाय नमः ।

He has faces in all directions.

He witnesses everything that happens in this world.

318. *Oṃ Vigāhine Namaḥ* । ॐ विगाहिने नमः ।

He plunges or penetrates into everything.

319. *Oṃ Veṇurasahāya Namaḥ* । ॐ वेणुरसहाय नमः ।

He sucks up or imbibes the juice of bamboos.

It is very difficult to make a bamboo as hollow sucking up the juice inside it. But Lord Sun only can do it.

320. *Oṃ Samāyuktāya Namaḥ* । ॐ समायुक्ताय नमः ।

He is committed and always prepared for his work.

58th name above may also be referred.

321. *Oṃ Samākratave Namaḥ* । ॐ समाक्रतवे नमः ।

He is so gigantic that there is no equivalent for him.

322. *Oṃ Dharmaketave Namaḥ* । ॐ धर्मकेतवे नमः ।

He is a strict follower of justice.

Kathopanishat (1-21) says "this Dharma is subtle or he is adored by Dharma".

In *Viṣṇu* sahasranamam – 403rd name – *Dharmaḥ* – He supports all beings.

323. *Oṃ Dharmarataye Namaḥ* । ॐ धर्मरतये नमः ।

He gets delighted by being virtue.

324. *Oṃ Saṃhartre Namaḥ* । ॐ संहर्त्रे नमः ।

He destroys well this world during great dissolution.

325. *Oṃ Saṃyamāya Namaḥ* । ॐ संयमाय नमः ।

He controls his senses, so that his mind can concentrate on his tasks.

He helps his devotees to control the senses.

326. *Oṃ Yamāya Namaḥ* । ॐ यमाय नमः ।

He is in the form of Yama, the lord of Death.

Yama is not only the lord of death, but also, a Dharmavan – strict follower of justice. Lord Sun is same as Yama.

Yama is one of the means of acquiring Yoga. He can be achieved only through Yoga and hence he is called as Yama.

In *Viṣṇu* sahasranamam – 162nd name – *Yamaḥ* – He controls the entire universe and living beings.

327. *Oṃ Praṇatārtiharāya Namaḥ* | ॐ प्रणतार्तिहराय नमः ।

He is worshipped reverentially by all.

He being the God in front of us, he is the cause for worshipping.

372nd & 612nd names below may also be referred.

328. *Oṃ Vāyave Namaḥ* | ॐ वायवे नमः ।

He is Vayu, the air God.

He is Agni – the fire God, Varuna – the Water God, Yama – the God of Death and here Vayu – the air God.

In *Viṣṇu* sahasranamam – 404th name – *Vāyuḥ* – He spreads the odour everywhere.

In Shrimad Bhagawat Gita (7-9), Lord says, I am tolerable odour in the Earth.

48th name above and 340th & 723rd names below may also be referred.

329. *Oṃ Siddhakāryāya Namaḥ* | ॐ सिद्धकार्याय नमः ।

He always accomplishes his objects (never fails).

330. *Oṃ Janeśvarāya Namaḥ* | ॐ जनेश्वराय नमः ।

He is the popular lord of entire general public (without any discrimination).

331. *Oṃ Nabhase Namaḥ* | ॐ नभसे नमः ।

Always moving in the sky or atmosphere.

303rd name above may also be referred.

332. *Oṃ Vigāhanāya Namaḥ* I ॐ विगाहनाय नमः ।

He plunges or penetrates into everything.

We all are aware that Sun rays penetrate into everything and that is what is stressed.

333. *Oṃ Satyāya Namaḥ* I ॐ सत्याय नमः ।

He is always truthful. He blesses truthful devotees.

He is so adamant in keeping up his words and promises. He has promised to protect the entire universe and he is stubborn in that.

He is the possessor of truth. Being *Paramatma*, he is the reverse of unreal.

Sat = Prāŋan, Ti = food or matter and *yam* = the Sun. He is Satyam, because his form is made of *Prāŋan* and matter.

Taitrīya Upanishat (2-1) says – Brahmam, who is with or without form is existence, knowledge and infinite

Chandokya Upanishat (8-1-5) says – *Satya Sankalpa* – Truth is his resolve.

Narāyaŋa Upanishat (79) says – Therefore, they say, Truth is Supreme. He is the truth of truth.

Brahadāraŋyaka Upanishat (4-1-20) says – The *pranas* are the truth and He is the truth of them.

In *Vişṇu* sahasranamam – 106th, 212th & 869th names – *Satyaḥ* – He is the truth.

Again, in *Vişṇu* sahasranamam –

- 289th name – *Satyadharmaparākramaḥ* – He is of true Dharma and prowess.
- 529th name – *Satyadharmā* – He is the true Dharma.

- 870th name – *Satyadharmaparāyaṇaḥ* – He is ever devoted to truthfulness and Dharma.

In *Lalitā* sahasranamam – 693rd name – *Satyasandhā* – She has unbroken promises or respects.

Again, in *Lalitā* sahasranamam – 818th name – *Satyarūpā* – Her form is full of truth unaffected at all the three times.

In *Shiva* sahasranamam – 998th name – *Satyavrataḥ* – He has taken a vow to be always truthful.

334. *Oṃ Savitre Namaḥ* I ॐ सवित्रे नमः ।

He is full of rays.

47th & 121st names above and 895th name below may also be referred.

335. *Oṃ Ātmane Namaḥ* I ॐ आत्मने नमः ।

He is the very soul in every living being.

Atma alone is the material cause of the universe and nothing else.

The word *Ātmā* has several meanings – body, mind, *Brahmam*, nature, firmness and intelligence. Since Lord Sun is in all these forms this name is very much apt for **Him**.

The word *Ātmā* here can be taken to mean *Paramātmā* (the Supreme Being).

The *Ātmā* indicates body. Hence all bodies of embodied souls are the forms of Sun only.

Chandokya Upanishat (7-24-1) says, where doth that immensity abide? In its own glory.

In *Viṣṇu* sahasranamam – 84th name – *Ātmavān* and – 985th name – *Ātmayoniḥ* – Centered in his own glory. The self-cause.

In *Lalitā* sahasranamam – 617th name – *Ātmā* – She is in the form of *Ātman* or *Jeeva* (soul).

In *Shiva* sahasranamam – 321st name – *Ātman* – he takes care of each Jeevan.

336. *Oṃ Manoharāya Namaḥ* I ॐ मनोहराय नमः ।

He is charmingly beautiful. Being the unlimited bliss, he is so charm.

117th name above may also be referred.

337. *Oṃ Hāriṇe Namaḥ* I ॐ हारिणे नमः ।

He is yellowish in colour.

In the 263rd name above & 369th name below also the same was mentioned.

338. *Oṃ Haraye Namaḥ* I ॐ हरये नमः ।

He destroys everything into ashes.

He destroys the sorrows of his devotees.

He steals the heart of his devotees.

In *Shiva* sahasranamam – 13th, 105th & 748th names – *Haraḥ* – he destroys everything during the of deluge.

339. *Oṃ Harāya Namaḥ* I ॐ हराय नमः ।

One who holds a triad as a weapon

105th name above may also be referred.

340. *Oṃ Vāyave Namaḥ* I ॐ वायवे नमः ।

He is in the form of *Vāyu*, the air god.

48th and 328th names above & 723rd names below may also be referred.

341. *Oṃ Ṛtave Namaḥ* I ॐ ऋतवे नमः ।

He creates the *Ṛtus*.

There are six Ritus (seasons) in a year. These are created by the rotation of Earth around Sun.

- *Vasanta Ritu* – Spring – from mid-April to mid-June.
- *Greeshma Ritu* – Summer – from mid-June to mid-August.
- *Varsha Ritu* – Monsoon – from mid-August to mid-October.
- *Sharad Ritu* – Autumn or fall – from mid-October to mid-December.
- *Hemanta Ritu* – Late autumn or pre-winter – from mid-December to mid-February.
- *Shishir Ritu* – Winter – from mid-February to mid-April.

533rd name below may also be referred.

342. *Oṃ Kālānaladyutaye Namaḥ* I ॐ कालानलद्युतये नमः ।

By changes in the seasons, he makes the plants to grow and bloom.

343. *Oṃ Sukhasevyāya Namaḥ* I ॐ सुखसेव्याय नमः ।

He is an easily accessible God.

344. *Oṃ Mahātejase Namaḥ* I ॐ महातेजसे नमः ।

He is of great splendid majesty.

He is full of fire.

In *Shiva* sahasranamam – 118th name – *Tejasaḥ* – he shines like a huge light.

345. *Oṃ Jagatāmekakāraṇāya Namaḥ* I ॐ जगतामेककारणाय नमः ।

He is the only cause of the universe.

He only creates, protects and destroys the universe.

346. *Oṃ Mahendrāya Namaḥ* I ॐ महेन्द्राय नमः ।

He is a great Indra.

He is lord of Devas, including Indra, the king of Devas.

He is the Lord of splendour, strength and prosperity.

In *Vişņu* sahasranamam – 268th name – *Mahendraḥ* – The great Indra.

347. *Oṃ Viṣṭutāya Namaḥ* I ॐ विष्टुताय नमः ।

He is a highly praised, extolled, Lord.

348. *Oṃ Stotrāya Namaḥ* I ॐ स्तोत्राय नमः ।

He is celebrated and praised through hymns.

We have lots of hymns praising Lord Sun, like Aditya Hrudaya Stotram, Aruna Prashnam, etc.

In the previous name, it was mentioned that he is highly praised. He is praised through hymns.

The praises are of two types – *Vaidheeka* (based on *Vedas*) and *loukeeka* (not based on *Vedas*). The characters of *loukeeka stotras* have been divided into six types by learned. They are;

1. Salutation (*namaskāra*),
2. Blessing (*Āshirvāta*),
3. Praising the attainments (talking about the *siddhāntās*),
4. Praising exploits (*parākrama*),
5. Rehearsing glory (*vibhooti*) and
6. Prayer for prosperity (*prārthanā*).

These 1,000 names in this Sahasranama, entirely fit in any one of these 6 types.

The *Vedic* praise, namely chanting the Vedic verses relating to Sun like *Aruna Prashnam*, etc. **He** is very fond of it.

In *Vişņu* sahasranamam – 679th name – *Stavyaḥ* – and – 680th name – *Stavyapriyaḥ* – **He** is praised by all, but **he** does not praise anybody and hence *Stavyaḥ*. Because of this he is interested in praising – *Stotrapriyāḥ*.

Again, In *Vişņu* sahasranamam – 683rd name – *Stotrā* – An adorer.

In *Lalitā* sahasranamam – 927th name – *Stotrapriyā* – She is fond of praises (*stotras*).

349. *Oṃ Stutihetave Namaḥ* । ॐ स्तुतिहेतवे नमः ।

He is very much fit for praising.

He is not being praised just for flatter or getting some tasks done. He is worthy of all the praises.

350. *Oṃ Prabhākarāya Namaḥ* । ॐ प्रभाकराय नमः ।

He is the light maker.

584th name below may also be referred.

351. *Oṃ Sahasrakarāya Namaḥ* । ॐ सहस्रकराय नमः ।

He has thousand hands.

When it is said as thousand, it means thousands of hands. Each of his ray is treated as a hand. No one can count the number of Sun rays. Hence it is in thousands.

In *Shiva* sahasranamam – 840th name – *Sahasrabāhuḥ* – he has thousands of hands.

352. *Oṃ Āyuṣmate Namaḥ* । ॐ आयुष्मते नमः ।

He has long life. He does not have any origin neither end. Hence his life is very long.

He blesses long life to his devotees.

Āyuṣmate is the third of the twenty-seven yogas or divisions of the ecliptic lunar mansion. He is in that form.

He possesses with vital and healthy power.

353. *Oṃ Aroṣāya Namaḥ* । ॐ अरोषाय नमः ।

He is so gentle, free from any type of anger. Not even inclined to anger.

Karma is violent, desire too is violent, so also anger is violent. He is free from all these because he has no desire to achieve.

In *Viṣṇu* sahasranamam – 906th name – *Aroudhraḥ* – He is not wrathful.

354. *Oṃ Sukhadāya Namaḥ* I ॐ सुखदाय नमः ।

He is the bestower of pleasures to his devotees.

He blesses happiness to the righteous ones and deprives the same to the wicked.

In *Viṣṇu* sahasranamam – 459th & 889th names – *Sukhadaḥ* – conferrer of happiness.

In *Lalitā* sahasranamam – 502nd name – *Samasta Bhakta Sukhadā* – She bestows happiness to all her devotees.

357th & 769th names below may also be referred.

355. *Oṃ Sukhine Namaḥ* I ॐ सुखिने नमः ।

He is always happy. Unless he is happy, he cannot bestow happiness to all as mentioned in the previous name.

768th name below may also be referred.

356. *Oṃ Vyādhighne Namaḥ* I ॐ व्याधिघ्ने नमः ।

He removes every type of disease.

In modern day allopathy also recommends to have Sun bath to get vitamin 'D' to the body, to alleviate any type of bone/ skin diseases.

Earlier also, it was mentioned that the Veda mantra "*Aruna Prashnam*" talks about cure for various diseases and also suggesting safe delivery.

357. *Oṃ Sukhadāya Namaḥ* I ॐ सुखदाय नमः ।

He is the bestower of pleasures to his devotees.

In the previous name, it was said that he cures all ailments. If there are no diseases, happiness will be obtained automatically.

354th name above & 769th name below may also be referred.

358. *Oṃ Saukhyāya Namaḥ* । ॐ सौख्याय नमः ।

He gives comfort to all.

If one person is happy and free from ailments, then happiness will automatically follow.

770th name below may be referred.

359. *Oṃ Kalyāṇāya Namaḥ* । ॐ कल्याणाय नमः ।

Giver of all auspicious things to all.

If one is happy, healthy without diseases, definitely all auspicious things will follow.

398th name below may also be referred.

360. *Oṃ Kalatāṃ Varāya Namaḥ* । ॐ कलतां वराय नमः ।

He is the decider of time (*kālam*).

361. *Oṃ Ārogyakāraṇāya Namaḥ* । ॐ आरोग्यकारणाय नमः ।

Giver of solid health.

In some names above it was mentioned as the destroyer of diseases. If there are no diseases, health is automatic.

367th name below may also be referred.

362. *Oṃ Siddhaye Namaḥ* । ॐ सिद्धये नमः ।

Always ready for any task. He does not feel lazy neither need any rest – always prepared.

363. *Oṃ Ṛddhaye Namaḥ* । ॐ ऋद्धये नमः ।

He bestows abundant prosperity to his devotees.

364. *Oṃ Vṛddhaye Namaḥ* I ॐ वृद्धये नमः ।

He is older, but feels young and beautiful.

The body may become older. But everyone should be mentally young and energetic. He is an example of this.

365. *Oṃ Bṛhaspataye Namaḥ* I ॐ बृहस्पतये नमः ।

He is *Bṛhaspati*, the Deva Guru.

281st name above may also be referred.

366. *Oṃ Hiraṇyaretase Namaḥ* I ॐ हिरण्यरेतसे नमः ।

He has golden seeds.

In 112th name above it was mentioned as *Svarṇaretase* – which has the same meaning.

187th name above may also be referred.

367. *Oṃ Ārogyāya Namaḥ* I ॐ आरोग्याय नमः ।

Giver of solid health.

361st name above may also be referred.

368. *Oṃ Viduṣe Namaḥ* I ॐ विदुषे नमः ।

He is an expert satire comedy.

369. *Oṃ Bradhnāya Namaḥ* I ॐ ब्रध्नाय नमः ।

He is Yellow in colour.

In the 263rd name above & 337th name below also the same was mentioned.

370. *Oṃ Budhāya Namaḥ* I ॐ बुधाय नमः ।

He is in the form of Mercury planet, in-charge of Wednesday.

Earlier it was mentioned that he is in the form of Jupiter (Guru) planet. It is now said that he in the form of Mercury.

Just for reference – Among Navagrahas, Mercury is Moon's son and Saturn is a son of Surya.

371. *Oṃ Mahate Namaḥ* । ॐ महते नमः ।

He is a great person fit to be worshipped.

He is the only God who can be seen by the devotees and hence it is very much apt that he is worshipped.

In *Śiva* sahasranamam – 17th name – *Mahate* – He is a very great lord. Also 115th and 821st names are – *Mahān*.

473rd, 801st, 925th & 986th names below may also be referred.

372. *Oṃ Prāṇavate Namaḥ* । ॐ प्राणवते नमः ।

He is worshipped reverentially by all.

327th name above & 612th name below may also be referred.

373. *Oṃ Dhṛtimate Namaḥ* । ॐ धृतिमते नमः ।

He consists constancy and contentment.

In *Śiva* sahasranamam – 696th name – *Dṛtimān* – He is stable minded.

374. *Oṃ Gharmāya Namaḥ* । ॐ घर्माय नमः ।

He is very hot indeed.

The very source of heat in this world is Sun.

375. *Oṃ Gharmakartre Namaḥ* । ॐ घर्मकर्त्रे नमः ।

He is the creator of heat. This name is in continuation of the previous name.

376. *Oṃ Rucipradāya Namaḥ* I ॐ रुचिप्रदाय नमः ।

He creates an appetite to all living beings.

If we roam a lot in Sunshine, we will feel hungrier.

He gives taste to all edible items. Different items taste differently. He only makes us feel the tastes.

377. *Oṃ Sarvapriyāya Namaḥ* I ॐ सर्वप्रियाय नमः ।

He is most loved by all. All are dear to him.

In Western countries, where Sunshine is not much available, people search for sea shore to take Sunbath.

378. *Oṃ Sarvasahāya Namaḥ* I ॐ सर्वसहाय नमः ।

He is most helpful to all.

He is all enduring.

379. *Oṃ Sarvaśatruvināśanāya Namaḥ* I ॐ सर्वशत्रुविनाशनाय नमः ।

He destroys all enemies of his devotees.

In the last name, it was mentioned that he is very helpful to all. Destroying enemies is the biggest help one can do.

When it is said as enemies, it need not be human outside enemies. It is internal enemies of the mind like *kama* (desire), *krodha* (anger), *lobha* (greed), *mada* (Sense of I), *moha* (attachment) and *matsarya* (partiality). Ananya Bhakti with focused mindedness can be achieved only by destroying these enemies. Lord Surya is the one who destroys those enemies and conquers the devotees.

12th, 154th and 190th names above can also be referred.

380. *Oṃ Prāṃśave Namaḥ* I ॐ प्रांशवे नमः ।

He has mother like affection to all. He does not discriminate whether poor or rich, whether a thatched hut or a villa/ bungalow.

381. *Oṃ Vidyotanāya Namaḥ* । ॐ विद्योतनाय नमः ।

He creates the lightning. Lightning is formed when clouds collide with each other.

382. *Oṃ Dyotāya Namaḥ* । ॐ द्योताय नमः ।

He makes things bright.

When things are seen in dark, the brightness would not be perceived. When Sun shines, the actual brightness is visible.

383. *Oṃ Sahasrakiraṇāya Namaḥ* । ॐ सहस्रकिरणाय नमः ।

He has thousands of rays.

The same has been mentioned in 47th, 96th, 116th, 155th, 264th, 266th and 334th names above.

384. *Oṃ Kṛtine Namaḥ* । ॐ कृतिने नमः ।

He creates the world. He does the task creation by taking the form of Lord Brahma.

As the universal soul he is considered to be as being in the bottom effort of every task.

In *Viṣṇu* sahasranamam – 83rd name – *Kṛtiḥ* – He is the effort behind every task.

385. *Oṃ Keyūriṇe Namaḥ* । ॐ केयूरिणे नमः ।

He is decorated with a bracelet on the upper arm.

It is very usual for kings and Gods to be decorated with bracelets in the upper arm. So also, Lord Sun.

In the *Sandhyāvanda Upastana* mantra also Lord Sun is addressed as "*Keyūravān Makara Kunḍalavān...*".

386. *Oṃ Bhūṣaṇodbhāsine Namaḥ* । ॐ भूषणोद्भासिने नमः ।

His radiance is more splendour on account of various jewels.

Himself is radiant and more so on account of his jewels.

387. *Oṃ Bhāsitāya Namaḥ* | ॐ भासिताय नमः ।

He reduces everything to ashes by burning them.

243rd and 338th names above also the same message was conveyed.

388. *Oṃ Bhāsanāya Namaḥ* | ॐ भासनाय नमः ।

His shine glitters like anything incomparable to anything else.

389. *Oṃ Analāya Namaḥ* | ॐ अनलाय नमः ।

He acts like fire.

His energies and powers are unlimited.

He never forgives sinning against his devotees.

An = Pranas. La = receives – *Jeevas* receive the Pranas as his Self.

Braharanyaka Upanishat (5-8-8) says "He is neither smell nor taste or who never (*na*) knows enough (*ala*).

In *Viṣṇu* sahasranamam – 293rd & 711th names – *Analaḥ* – The fire. Unlimited.

In *Śiva* sahasranamam – 498th, 586th, & 639th names – *Analaḥ* – he never gets satisfied in bestowing his blessings to his devotees. He has his limitless powers.

522nd, 639th, 816th and 898th names below may also be referred.

390. *Oṃ Śaraṇyārtiharāya Namaḥ* | ॐ शरण्यार्तिहराय नमः ।

He is the God with whom everyone seeks refuge with.

27th and 316th names above may also be referred.

391. *Oṃ Hotre Namaḥ* | ॐ होत्रे नमः ।

One who accepts all the sacrifices offered by devotees.

106th & 203rd names above and 714th name below may also be referred.

392. *Oṃ Khadyotāya Namaḥ* । ॐ खद्योताय नमः ।

He is the illuminator of the entire universe.

In North pole and South Pole, the Sun will be visible only for 6 months and next 6 months Sun will be set. Hence it will be complete dark in those six months when the Sun is set.

393. *Oṃ Khagasattamāya Namaḥ* । ॐ खगसत्तमाय नमः ।

He is like the chief of all the birds.

Like birds he is also moving in the sky and hence call as head of all birds.

394. *Oṃ Sarvadyotāya Namaḥ* । ॐ सर्वद्योताय नमः ।

He treats everyone impartially.

395. *Oṃ Bhavadyotāya Namaḥ* । ॐ भवद्योताय नमः ।

He gives equal attention to all.

In the previous name it was mentioned that he is impartial. Here it is stressed that he gives equal attention to all.

396. *Oṃ Sarvadyutikarāya Namaḥ* । ॐ सर्वद्युतिकराय नमः ।

He gives brightness to all others.

We all know that other celestial objects reflect Sun's brightness.

397. *Oṃ Matāya Namaḥ* । ॐ मताय नमः ।

He produces fire.

Still in lot many places by showing the convex lens in Sun and focusing on cotton or other objects fire is produced.

398. *Oṃ Kalyāṇāya Namaḥ* I ॐ कल्याणाय नमः ।

Giver of all auspicious things to all.

359th name above may also be referred.

399. *Oṃ Kalyāṇakarāya Namaḥ* I ॐ कल्याणकराय नमः ।

He causes prosperity or profit or good fortune.

400. *Oṃ Kalyāya Namaḥ* I ॐ कल्याय नमः ।

He is free from sickness.

In an earlier name it was mentioned that he provides healthy life to all. Unless he is healthy, he cannot provide health to others.

Thus ends 100 divine names on Lord *Sūrya* from 301 to 400.

*****

401. *Oṃ Kalyakarāya Namaḥ* | ॐ कल्यकराय नमः ।

He is well prepared for every activity, before he starts.

He is free from all sickness.

402. *Oṃ Kavaye Namaḥ* | ॐ कवये नमः ।

He is a great poet.

403. *Oṃ Kalyāṇakṛte Namaḥ* | ॐ कल्याणकृते नमः ।

He is a propitious lord, always doing good.

398th and 399th names above may also be compared.

404. *Oṃ Kalyavapave Namaḥ* | ॐ कल्यवपवे नमः ।

He prepares well in advance before starting any task.

405. *Oṃ Sarvakalyāṇabhājanāya Namaḥ* |
ॐ सर्वकल्याणभाजनाय नमः ।

He is represented in every auspicious yagnas.

In every havan, whichever purpose/ God is intented, there will definitely be one or more offerings to Lord Sun.

406. *Oṃ Śāntipriyāya Namaḥ* | ॐ शान्तिप्रियाय नमः ।

He is a peace loving God.

407. *Oṃ Prasannātmane Namaḥ* | ॐ प्रसन्नात्मने नमः ।

He is a gracious minded God. He is ever merciful.

His *Antaḥ Karaṇa* (Inner organ) is untained by the qualities of Rajas and Tamas. Hence has no desire to be satisfied.

In *Viṣṇu* sahasranamam – 237th name – *Prasannatmāḥ* – He is of delightful nature.

408. *Oṃ Praśāntāya Namaḥ* I ॐ प्रशान्ताय नमः ।

He is quiet, composed and auspicious.

Characterised by the absence of love and hatred he bestows peace to all.

Swetavastara Upanishat (6-19) says – He, who is tranquil is without any organ neither action.

In *Viṣṇu* sahasranamam – 582nd name – *Śāntaḥ* – and 587th name – *Śāntidaḥ* – He is of tranquil nature. He is the conferor of peace.

406th name above may also be referred.

409. *Oṃ Praśamapriyāya Namaḥ* I ॐ प्रशमप्रियाय नमः ।

He loves pacification.

Where there is peace, pacification is automatic.

410. *Oṃ Udārakarmaṇe Namaḥ* I ॐ उदारकर्मणे नमः ।

He is very liberal and generous in giving anything and everything to all.

In Mahabharata, his son Karna is very well known to generous in giving anything to those who asked for.

411. *Oṃ Sunayāya Namaḥ* I ॐ सुनयाय नमः ।

He has very beautiful and sharp eyes.

Earlier in multiple times, it has been mentioned that he has thousands of eyes. All are very beautiful and sharp.

He is wise and well conducted.

412. *Oṃ Suvarcase Namaḥ* I ॐ सुवर्चसे नमः ।

He is splendid, radiant and fiery.

413. *Oṃ Varcasojjvalāya Namaḥ* । ॐ वर्चसोज्ज्वलाय नमः ।

He shines with colourful luster.

414. *Oṃ Varcasvine Namaḥ* । ॐ वर्चस्विने नमः ।

He is vigorously energetic and active.

415. *Oṃ Varcasāmīśāya Namaḥ* । ॐ वर्चसामीशाय नमः ।

He is the Lord of luster.

Four names from 412th talk about the luster of Lord Sun.

416. *Oṃ Trailokyeśāya Namaḥ* । ॐ त्रैलोक्येशाय नमः ।

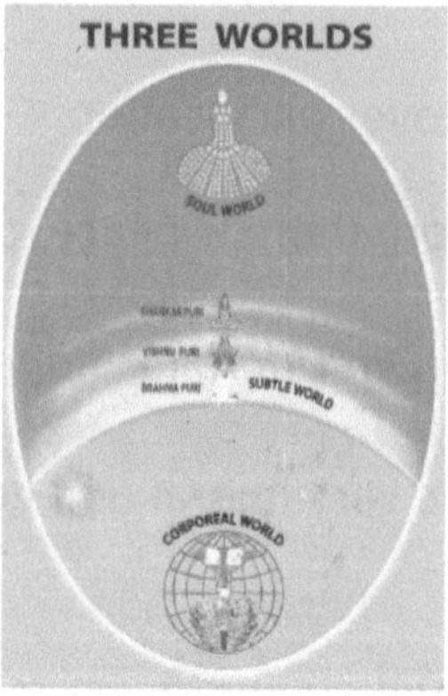

He is the lord of all the three worlds – upper, this world and the lower world.

In *Lalitā Sahasranamam* – 787th name – *Tripureśī* – She is the head of the three worlds.

417. *Oṃ Vaśānugāya Namaḥ* । ॐ वशानुगाय नमः ।

He is submissive to his devotees.

He functions on his own will.

418. *Oṃ Tejasvine Namaḥ* । ॐ तेजस्विने नमः ।

He is splendidly intellect.

425th name below may also be referred.

419. *Oṃ Suyaśase Namaḥ* । ॐ सुयशसे नमः ।

He is gloriously famous.

420. *Oṃ Varṣmiṇe Namaḥ* । ॐ वर्ष्मिणे नमः ।

He has handsome and auspicious form.

421. *Oṃ Varṇādhyakṣāya Namaḥ* I ॐ वर्णाध्यक्षाय नमः ।

He created and maintains the four social divisions and castes.

He is the planet presiding over the class/ caste.

After creating all from *Brahma* to worms, the *Vedas* were created, in order to lead the created beings into the right path. The *Vedas* are divided into two parts, the *Karma Kāṇḍa* and *Gnana Kāṇḍa* – as according to the rule, the *Devas* and lower animals have no share in the *Karma Kāṇḍa*, the (divine) Lord established righteousness (*dharma*) through *karma Kāṇḍa* after dividing human beings into four castes and four orders.

In *Lalitā Sahasranamam* – 286th name – *Varŋāśramavidhāyinī* – she established the social divisions and castes.

In *Śiva Sahasranamam* – 633rd name – *Varṇavibhāvī* – He divided the society into four. He has many coloured splendour.

422. *Oṃ Balipriyāya Namaḥ* I ॐ बलिप्रियाय नमः ।

He is fond of *bali* offerings.

He conquers his enemies like amorousness, desire, etc., can be called as *Bali*. He blesses them with affection.

During the incarnation as *Vāmanā*, *Viṣhŋu* had compassion over the emperor *Bali*. This name indicates that form.

Dheera or *Bali*, those who are able to succeed by destroying ignorance. **He** is fond of them.

During worship, for the satisfaction of deities, some articles are offered as *bali*. **He** accepts them with hilarity.

In *Lalitā Sahasranamam* – 677th name – *Balipriyā* – she is delighted with the mighty.

In *Gāyatri Sahasranamam* – 690th name – *Balipriyāyai* – she is fond of bali offerings.

In *Śiva Sahasranamam* – 235th name – *Baliḥ* – He is very strong.

423. *Oṃ Yaśasvine Namaḥ* | ॐ यशस्विने नमः ।

He is illustrious and celebrated.

He bestows fame to his devotees.

In *Śiva Sahasranamam* – 334th name – *Yaśaḥ* – He blesses his devotees with fame.

424. *Oṃ Tejonilayāya Namaḥ* | ॐ तेजोनिलयाय नमः ।

He is an abounding treasury of glory.

278th name above may also be referred.

425. *Oṃ Tejasvine Namaḥ* | ॐ तेजस्विने नमः ।

He is splendidly intellect.

418th name above may also be referred.

426. *Oṃ Prakṛtisthitāya Namaḥ* | ॐ प्रकृतिस्थिताय नमः ।

He is always in the original and natural state.

It is not known that he has taken any incarnation or any other form.

427. *Oṃ Ākāśagāya Namaḥ* | ॐ आकाशगाय नमः ।

He always moves in the sky like a bird.

129th, 158th, 239th and 393rd names above may also be referred.

428. *Oṃ Śīghragataye Namaḥ* | ॐ शीघ्रगतये नमः ।

He is swift in motion.

429. *Oṃ Āśugāya Namaḥ* | ॐ आशुगाय नमः ।

As mentioned in the previous name he moves quickly.

He is very difficult to comprehend.

430. *Oṃ Gatimate Namaḥ* | ॐ गतिमते नमः ।

He is the only source to seek refuge.

He is always in motion.

This has been mentioned multiple times in this Sahasranam.

In *Viśŋu Sahasranamam* – 566th name – *Gatisattamaḥ* – He is the refuge and the best.

In *Śiva Sahasranamam* – 859th name – *Gatiḥ* – He is the place for refugees.

431. *Oṃ Khagāya Namaḥ* | ॐ खगाय नमः ।

He is the wind god.

158th name above & 880th name below may also be referred.

432. *Oṃ Gopataye Namaḥ* | ॐ गोपतये नमः ।

He is the Lord of cows. He is the Lord of the Earth.

He is the Lord controlling the senses.

In *Viśŋu Sahasranamam* – 495th & 592nd names – *Gopatiḥ* – He is a shepherd.

In *Śiva Sahasranamam* – 702nd name – *Gopatiḥ* – He rules the Earth.

433. *Oṃ Grahadeveśāya Namaḥ* | ॐ ग्रहदेवेशाय नमः ।

He is the head of all the Navagrahas.

All the other planets in Navagrahas depend on him – go around him.

434. *Oṃ Gomate Namaḥ* | ॐ गोमते नमः ।

He is owner of entire cattle in the world.

He is in the form of *Gomati* River.

435. *Oṃ Ekāya Namaḥ* I ॐ एकाय नमः ।

He is the only God.

Chandokya Upanishat (6-2-1) says;

"Ekam Brahmam, Dvitīya Naste Neh Na Naste Kinchan".

There is only one *Brahmam* – without any attributes and without any form. Different persons attribute various forms and character to that *Brahmam* and worship. That one Brahmam is Lord Surya. That is *Advaitam*.

Since he is the concluded truth without any kind of differences that are internal or that relates to similar external objects or to dissimilar object, he is Only one.

In *Viśŋu Sahasranamam* – 725th name – *Ekaḥ* – The one.

In *Lalitā Sahasranamam* – 665th name – *Ekākinī* – She is alone.

In *Gāyatri Sahasranamam* – 104th name – *Ekāyai* – conveying the same meaning.

891st name below may also be referred.

436. *Oṃ Prabhañjanāya Namaḥ* I ॐ प्रभञ्जनाय नमः ।

He is the God of wind – in the form of *Vāyu*.

In multiple names in this Sahasranama, this has been mentioned.

437. *Oṃ Janitre Namaḥ* I ॐ जनित्रे नमः ।

He has no origin and hence no parents.

In Rudra Trishatee 161st name – *Namo̧ Agriyāya Ca̧* – he existed even before the creation of the world. That means he has no origin or birth.

In *Lalita Sahasranamam* – 183rd Name – *Nişparigraha* – She has no origin.

438. *Oṃ Prajanāya Namaḥ* I ॐ प्रजनाय नमः ।

He is the cause to living being to propagate offsprings.

439. *Oṃ Jīvāya Namaḥ* I ॐ जीवाय नमः ।

He is the living entity in all beings.

440. *Oṃ Dīpāya Namaḥ* I ॐ दीपाय नमः ।

He is like the bright light.

In multiple names in this Sahasranama, this has been mentioned.

441. *Oṃ Sarvaprakāśakāya Namaḥ* I ॐ सर्वप्रकाशकाय नमः ।

He illuminates the entire world. He reveals his form to his devotees.

231st name above may also be referred.

442. *Oṃ Sarvasākṣine Namaḥ* I ॐ सर्वसाक्षिने नमः ।

He is the witness for everything happening in this world.

He sees the entire world. **He** sees the entire world as his own form.

In *Lalitā Sahasranamam* – 384th name – *Viśvasākşiņī* – She is the witness for everything.

443. *Oṃ Yoganityāya Namaḥ* I ॐ योगनित्याय नमः ।

He is perpetualy eternal.

444. *Oṃ Nabhasvate Namaḥ* I ॐ नभस्वते नमः ।

He vaporises the water from the sea, river, etc.

He is the wind God.

445. *Oṃ Asurāntakāya Namaḥ* I ॐ असुरान्तकाय नमः ।

He destroys all the evil-people like demons.

446. *Oṃ Rakṣoghnāya Namaḥ* | ॐ रक्षोघ्नाय नमः ।

(In continuation of previous name), he is the slayer of demons by taking different forms.

447. *Oṃ Vighnaśamanāya Namaḥ* | ॐ विघ्नशमनाय नमः ।

He overcomes any obstacle. He removes any obstacles of any task of his devotees.

During Sandhyavandanam (3 times a day) 3 or 2 times argyam is being offered. The water chant with Gayatri mantra becomes arrow and removes the obstrucles on the course of Sun's movement.

Normally Lord Ganapati is worshiped to remove all the obstrucles and any task to be successfully completed. Here Lord Sun is said to remove the obstracles. That implies, Sun and Ganapati are one and the same.

448. *Oṃ Kirīṭine Namaḥ* | ॐ किरीटिने नमः ।

He is decorated with a diadem. It is very usual for any king or God wears different types of crowns. So also Lord Sun.

449. *Oṃ Sumanaḥpriyāya Namaḥ* | ॐ सुमनःप्रियाय नमः ।

He is very charmingly handsome. Hence everyone is very fond of him.

450. *Oṃ Marīcimāline Namaḥ* | ॐ मरीचिमालिने नमः ।

He shines with a garland of rays.

In multiple names in this Sahasranama, this has been mentioned.

451. *Oṃ Sumataye Namaḥ* | ॐ सुमतये नमः ।

He flies in the heaven. This has been mentioned in multiple names in this Sahasranama.

542nd & 625th names below may also be referred.

452. *Oṃ Kṛtābhikhyaviśeṣakāya Namaḥ* I
ॐ कृताभिख्यविशेषकाय नमः ।

He is an expert in performing religious ablutions.

Everyone worships him. He accepts it with love.

453. *Oṃ Śiṣṭācārāya Namaḥ* I ॐ शिष्टाचाराय नमः ।

Being a learned and virtuous Lord, he practices/ conducts every etiquette tasks.

454. *Oṃ Śubhākārāya Namaḥ* I ॐ शुभाकाराय नमः ।

He protects all the multitude of good works of his devotees.

455. *Oṃ Svacārācāratatparāya Namaḥ* I ॐ स्वचाराचारतत्पराय नमः ।

He strictly follows his own religious rules as prescribed.

456. *Oṃ Mandārāya Namaḥ* I ॐ मन्दाराय नमः ।

He has Mandara Hill as his base.

457. *Oṃ Māṭharāya Namaḥ* I ॐ माठराय नमः ।

Māṭhara is one of the Sun's attendants. He himself is in that form.

458. *Oṃ Veṇave Namaḥ* I ॐ वेणवे नमः ।

Veṇava = something made of or produced from bamboo.

Flute or Dandam stick in the hands of Sanyasis some examples. He has all these.

459. *Oṃ Kṣudhāpāya Namaḥ* I ॐ क्षुधापाय नमः ।

He creates hunger in all living beings.

460. *Oṃ Kṣmāpataye Namaḥ* I ॐ क्ष्मापतये नमः ।

He is the Lord of Earth and he protects it.

461. *Oṃ Gurave Namaḥ* I ॐ गुरवे नमः ।

He is the teacher. He is the supreme Guru to Brahma and others.

He is called *Guru* since He is the promulgator of all Vidyas.

Gu means darkness of ignorance and *Ru* removes that. Hence the word *Guru* itself means removing the darkness of ignorance.

The letter *Gu* is an existence (*Sat*) and *Ru* is knowledge (of *Brahmam*) and because one is with the knowledge of *Brahmam*, he is called *guru*.

The confirmed opinion of the *mantra sāstras* is – the teacher, the *mantra* and the deity are all one and the same and should not be distinguished.

Aruŋagirināda also sings about Lord Muruga as;
"Guruvāi Varuvāi Arulvāi Guhane".

In Viṣŋu *Sahasranamam* – 209th name – *Guruḥ* – he is the teacher of this universe.

In *Lalitā Sahasranamam* – 603rd name – *Gurumūrtiḥ* – She assumes the form of a teacher.

In *Śiva Sahasranamam* – 839th name – *Guruḥ* – conveying the same meaning.

593rd name below may also be referred.

462. *Oṃ Suviśiṣṭāya Namaḥ* I ॐ सुविशिष्टाय नमः ।

He is the most distinguished and excellent Lord.

463. *Oṃ Viśiṣṭātmane Namaḥ* I ॐ विशिष्टात्मने नमः ।

In continuation of the previous name, he is the peculiarly distinguished Lord.

464. *Oṃ Vidheyāya Namaḥ* । ॐ विधेयाय नमः ।

He is down to earth subdued Lord. He is so great and still he is submissive to his devotees.

620th name below may also be referred.

465. *Oṃ Jñānaśobhanāya Namaḥ* । ॐ ज्ञानशोभनाय नमः ।

He is very smart and very knowledgeable in all areas. He bestows knowledge to his devotees.

Knowledge is of two types. Attaining the complete form of *Brahmam*, who is not limited by anything. The second is – thinking this un-soul body and universe as soul – this is actually ignorance. He only gives both these.

He can be attained neither by *karma* (actions) nor by *karma* and *jnana*, but by *jnana* (knowledge) only.

The three – the knower, the knowledge and the object of knowledge – is called *Tripudee*. **He** is of the form hiding all these and only remaining is the knowledge/ supreme bliss.

Śreemad Bhagavad Geeta (XIII-17) says – "*Gnānam Gneyam Gnānagamyam Grudi Sarvasya Vishtitam*" – He, in the form of the knowledge, the knowable and the goal of knowledge, seated in the hearts of all.

This is called as the object and the sight. (There is a book by name *Drik Drishyam Vivekam*, the author of which is not clearly known. Someone has mentioned that this is written by *Śree Ādi Śaṇkara*).

It can also be told that **He** hides both knowledge (part of *chit*) and bliss.

In Viṣṇu *Sahasranamam* – 497th name – *Jnānagamyaḥ* – He can be obtained only through knowledge.

In *Lalitā Sahasranamam* –

#	Name	Meaning
643	*Jnānadā*	She bestows knowledge.
644	*Jnānavigrahā*	She is in the form of knowledge.
979	*Jnānamudrā*	She is in the form of (symbol of knowledge).
980	*Jnānagamyā*	She can be reached through knowledge
981	*Jnānajneyasvaroopiṇee*	She is in the form of knowledge and the object of knowledge.

466. *Oṃ Mahāśvetāya Namaḥ* । ॐ महाश्वेताय नमः ।

He is of a dazzling white colour.

467. *Oṃ Priyāya Namaḥ* । ॐ प्रियाय नमः ।

He loves all and is loved by all.

40th name above may also be referred.

468. *Oṃ Jñeyāya Namaḥ* । ॐ ज्ञेयाय नमः ।

He has to be learnt or understood or ascertained or investigated or perceived or inquired about through knowledge.

469. *Oṃ Sāmagāya Namaḥ* । ॐ सामगाय नमः ।

He is an expert in *Sāma Veda* (Gānam).

He can be pleased by chanting *Sāma Veda*.

Hearing *Sāma Veda* will be so sweet to the ears like music. It is also said that the music originates only from *Sāma Veda*. *Parameshwara* is also very much interested in *Sāma Veda* songs.

In *Śreemad Rāmāyana, Uttara Kāṇḍa* (16-33) – *Rāvanā* sang *Sāmaveda* and pleased *Parameshwara*.

It can also be said that those who follow *Sāma Veda* are so dear to **Him**, as **His** own life.

Śreemad Bhagavad Geeta (X-22) Lord Krishna says – Among Vedas, I am the Sama Veda.

In Vişŋu *Sahasranamam* – 576th name – *Sāma* – He is the *Sāma Veda.*

Again, in Vişŋu *Sahasranamam* – 575th name – *Sāmagaḥ* – He is the chanter of *Sāma Veda.*

In *Lalitā Sahasranamam* – 909th name – *Sāma Gāna Priyā* – She is fond of *Sāmaveda* songs.

In *Gāyatri Sahasranamam* – 970th name – *Sāma Gāna Priyāyai* – conveying the same meaning.

470. *Oṃ Mokṣadāyakāya Namaḥ* I ॐ मोक्षदायकाय नमः ।

He is the bestower of liberation (*moksha*) to his devotees.

In *Śiva Sahasranamam* – 928th name – *Mokṣadvāraḥ* – He is the gateway to salvation.

557th, 655th & 939th names below may also be referred.

471. *Oṃ Sarvavedapragītātmane Namaḥ* I ॐ सर्ववेदप्रगीतात्मने नमः ।

He is an expert in all Vedas.

Earlier itself, it was mentioned that he taught all the Vedas to Lord Anjaneya.

Taitrīya Brāhmaŋam (3-55) says – the one who does not know the *Vedas* knows not the omnipresent one.

Śreemad Bhagavad Geeta (X-11) Lord Krishna says – Out of mere compassion for them, I, abiding in their Self, destroy the darkness born of ignorance, by the luminous lamp of wisdom called *Vedas.*

Again, *Śreemad Bhagavat Geeta* (XV – 15) Lord *Krişhŋa says* – I am verily that which has to be known by all the *Vedas.*

In Vişŋu *Sahasranamam* –

#	Name	Meaning
127	*Vedaḥ*	He is in the form of scriptures
128 & 131	*Vedavit*	He is the knower of all Vedas
130	*Vedāngaḥ*	He has Vedas as his own organs
163	*Vedyaḥ*	He spreads the knowledge of *Vedas*
547	*Vedhāḥ*	He is in the form of Brahma.

In *Lalitā Sahasranamam* –

335	*Vedavedyā*	She can be known through the *Vedas*
338	*Vedajananī*	She only created the *Vedas*
652	*Vedyavarjitā*	She has nothing more to know.

In *Gāyatri Sahasranamam* – 1,005th name – *Vedagarbhāyai* – She is the mother of all Vedas.

472nd, 475th, 680th & 711th names below may also be referred.

472. *Oṃ Sarvavedalayāya Namaḥ* I ॐ सर्ववेदलयाय नमः ।

He is an expert in all Vedas.

471st name above 475th, 680th & 711th names below may be referred.

473. *Oṃ Mahate Namaḥ* I ॐ महते नमः ।

371st name above and 801st, 925th & 986th names below may also be referred.

474. *Oṃ Vedamūrtaye Namaḥ* I ॐ वेदमूर्तये नमः ।

He is in the form of all Vedas.

475. *Oṃ Caturvedāya Namaḥ* I ॐ चतुर्वेदाय नमः ।

He is an expert in all Vedas.

471st & 472nd names above and 680th & 711th names below may be referred.

476. *Oṃ Vedabhṛte Namaḥ* I ॐ वेदभृते नमः ।

He is full of Vedas. He is Veda personified.

477. *Oṃ Vedapāragāya Namaḥ* I ॐ वेदपारगाय नमः ।

He thoroughly knows all the Vedas.

478. *Oṃ Kriyāvate Namaḥ* I ॐ क्रियावते नमः ।

He is the cause of every activity/ task/ ritual.

238th name above may also be referred.

479. *Oṃ Asitāya Namaḥ* I ॐ असिताय नमः ।

He is in dark red in colour.

480. *Oṃ Jiṣṇave Namaḥ* I ॐ जिष्णवे नमः ।

He is always triumphant. He bestows victory to his devotees.

481. *Oṃ Varīyāṃśave Namaḥ* I ॐ वरीयांशवे नमः ।

He is easily accessible by devotees and farther away for others.

482. *Oṃ Varapradāya Namaḥ* I ॐ वरप्रदाय नमः ।

He is the bestower of boons.

Granter of objects desired. He gives the boons desired by the devotees in their minds.

He becomes the doer of sacrificial fire and gives the boons.

In *Viṣṇu Sahasranamam* – 330th name – *Varadaḥ* – the granter of boons.

In *Lalitā Sahasranamam* – 331st name – *Varadā* – she bestows boons to all.

In *Śiva Sahasranamam* – 880th name – *Varadaḥ* – conveying the same meaning.

483. *Oṃ Vratacāriṇe Namaḥ* I ॐ व्रतचारिणे नमः ।

He is always engaged in religious vow observance.

484. *Oṃ Vratadharāya Namaḥ* I ॐ व्रतधराय नमः ।

He entirely fulfills the wishes of his devotees who observe any vow.

485. *Oṃ Lokabandhave Namaḥ* I ॐ लोकबन्धवे नमः ।

He is friend/ relative of the whole world.

486. *Oṃ Alaṅkṛtāya Namaḥ* I ॐ अलङ्कृताय नमः ।

He is always decorated/ adorned with ornaments.

Lord Shiva is a lover of bathing with various items and *Vishnu* is a lover of decoration, the saying goes.

487. *Oṃ Alaṅkārākṣarāya Namaḥ* I ॐ अलङ्काराक्षराय नमः ।

He protects the decoration of his devotees.

488. *Oṃ Vedyāya Namaḥ* I ॐ वेद्याय नमः ।

He is a physician. Earlier it was mentioned that he gives healthy life and hence he is called as physician here.

He is knowable by those who desire supreme good.

In *Viṣṇu Sahasranamam* – 163th name – *Vedyaḥ* – the knowable.

489. *Oṃ Vidyāvate Namaḥ* I ॐ विद्यावते नमः ।

He is highly learned.

645th & 734th names below may also be referred.

490. *Oṃ Viditāśayāya Namaḥ* I ॐ विदिताशयाय नमः ।

He creates thirst and hunger.

583rd name below may also be referred.

491. *Oṃ Ākārāya Namaḥ* | ॐ आकाराय नमः ।

Devotees can ask anything (legal) to him – he will also definitely oblige. Definitely not illegal things. When it is said as legal, it does not only mean national laws but also Dharmic laws.

492. *Oṃ Bhūṣaṇāya Namaḥ* | ॐ भूषणाय नमः ।

He is decorated with ornaments and embellishments.

493. *Oṃ Bhūṣyāya Namaḥ* | ॐ भूष्याय नमः ।

This has the same meaning as 492nd name above.

494. *Oṃ Bhūṣṇave Namaḥ* | ॐ भूष्णवे नमः ।

He adorns the entire world.

In *Viṣṇu Sahasranamam* – 629th name – *Bhūṣaṇaḥ* – by his various incarnations he adorns the world.

495. *Oṃ Bhuvanapūjitāya Namaḥ* | ॐ भुवनपूजिताय नमः ।

He is worshipped by the entire world.

496. *Oṃ Cakrapāṇaye Namaḥ* | ॐ चक्रपाणये नमः ।

He has a discuss in his hand.

Usually Lord *Viṣṇu* is called as *Cakrapāṇi*, since a discuss is his main weapon. This name confirms that Vishnu and Surya are one and the same.

497. *Oṃ Dhvajadharāya Namaḥ* | ॐ ध्वजधराय नमः ।

He bears a flag.

Any king or God, will have a unique flag on the top of his chariot. So also Sun God. Even from a distance, by looking at the flag, the king or God can be identified.

498. *Oṃ Sureśāya Namaḥ* | ॐ सुरेशाय नमः ।

He is the lord of all lords.

213th name above may also be referred.

499. *Oṃ Lokavatsalāya Namaḥ* | ॐ लोकवत्सलाय नमः ।

He is affectionate to the entire world.

The whole world is affectionate to him.

500. *Oṃ Vāgmipataye Namaḥ* | ॐ वाग्मिपतये नमः ।

He is very eloquent in speech.

Lord Hanuman, his disciple, is well known for his loquacious speech.

162nd & 311th names above & 626th name below may also be referred.

Thus ends 100 divine names on Lord *Sūrya* from 401 to 500.

*****

501. *Oṃ Mahābāhave Namaḥ* I ॐ महाबाहवे नमः ।

He has great/ broad shoulders.

Any warrior will have broad shoulders. So also, Sun God.

In Valmiki Ramayana, Sita addresses Rama as '*Mahābāhu*'.

In Bhagawad Gita, Krishna addresses Arjuna in many a place as '*Mahābāhu*'.

502. *Oṃ Prakṛtaye Namaḥ* I ॐ प्रकृतये नमः ।

He is the nature. He is this world.

He has various forms.

In *Śiva Sahasranamam* – 828th name – *Vikṛtaḥ* – conveying the same meaning.

503. *Oṃ Vikṛtaye Namaḥ* I ॐ विकृतये नमः ।

He is unnatural. This gives just an opposite meaning of the previous name.

In other words, this can also be interpreted as multi-faceted.

Ashtotra arcana on Goddess Lakshmi starts with *Prakrutyai*, *Viktutyai*, etc.

All these natural, unnatural and all are illusions of ignorant people like us. He is Brahmam – *niroopa, Nirguna*.

504. *Oṃ Guṇāya Namaḥ* I ॐ गुणाय नमः ।

He becomes or appears as merit with attributes.

In this name *Nirguṇa Brahmam* is addressed as *Guṇāya*. What an irony!

505. *Oṃ Andhakārāpahāya Namaḥ* I ॐ अन्धकारापहाय नमः ।

He throws off the darkness.

Here darkness can mean both without light and ignorance as well.

506. *Oṃ Śreṣṭhāya Namaḥ* । ॐ श्रेष्ठाय नमः ।

He is the greatest.

63rd & 315th names above may also be referred.

507. *Oṃ Yugāvartāya Namaḥ* । ॐ युगावर्ताय नमः ।

He lives throughout the ages (*Yug*).

He manages the cycle of four *Yugas*.

In *Vişŋu Sahasranamam* – 301st name – *Yugāvartaḥ* – He only brings the cycle of *Yugas*.

508. *Oṃ Yugādikṛte Namaḥ* । ॐ युगादिकृते नमः ।

He only does all the initial tasks of the beginning of a *Yug*.

In the beginning of a *Yug* there would be many a task such as, drying the floods, creation of each and every living beings, etc. He only does all these tasks.

509. *Oṃ Aprameyāya Namaḥ* । ॐ अप्रमेयाय नमः ।

He is immeasurable/ indefinable.

The *jeevas* with him are infinite and immeasurable.

He is devoid of sense-objects and hence he cannot be reached by any of the senses, nor through inference, nor through analogy. He is without parts and hence no comparison can be made. It is impossible to attain anything without him, because he is the very existence himself.

In *Vişŋu Sahasranamam* – 46th name – *Aprameyaḥ* – again 248th name – *Aprameyātmā* – Immeasurable self.

510. *Oṃ Sadāyogine Namaḥ* । ॐ सदायोगिने नमः ।

He always practices yogas.

511. *Oṃ Nirahaṅkārāya Namaḥ* I ॐ निरहङ्काराय नमः ।

One who is without any ego.

Ego is of three kinds – *Vaikhareeka, Taijasa* and *Bhutādi* – according to *satva, rajas* and *tamas* characters, respectively.

He is without *Nirguṇā* – **he** is beyond the three characters viz. *satva, rajas* and *tamas*. Accordingly, **he** does not have the ego relating to those characters also. Hence *Nirahankāra*.

In *Lalitā Sahasranamam* – 161st name – *Nirahankārā* – she is without any self-image.

512. *Oṃ Īśvarāya Namaḥ* I ॐ ईश्वराय नमः ।

Worshiped by all spiritual masters – *Īśvar* for all *yogeswaras*.

Saguna-Brahmam himself is called *Īśvara* in Advaita texts.

Unification of separate things is called Yoga. What is different from us is the nature of God. The unifying tool is yoga. Yogis are those who have acquired this God quality through this.

In *Viṣṇu Sahasranamam* – 36th name – *Īśvaraḥ* – The great.

In *Lalitā* Sahasranamam – 274th name – *Pancha Krutya Parāyaṇā* — One who is devoted to the five functions viz., creation, protection, destruction, Tirodhāna (bondage) and Anugraha (release). She has much interest and involvement in all these five tasks.

Brahadaranyaka Upanishat (6-4-22) says – He is the Lord of all.

It can also be interpreted that all the five functions depend on Her. The five functions viz. creation, protection, destruction, annihilation and causing the reappearance of the universe are that of Brahma, Viṣṇu, Rudra, Ēśvara and Paramaśiva. These five are different forms or Śaktis of that of Śrī Devī only.

513. *Oṃ Śubhapradāya Namaḥ* I ॐ शुभप्रदाय नमः ।

He bestows all auspicious things to all.

517th name below may also be referred.

514. *Oṃ Śubhāya Namaḥ* । ॐ शुभाय नमः ।

He himself is auspicious. Then only he can bestow auspicious to all, as mentioned in the previous name.

515. *Oṃ Śāstre Namaḥ* । ॐ शास्त्रे नमः ।

An unfailing follower of the *Shastras*.

516. *Oṃ Śubhakarmaṇe Namaḥ* । ॐ शुभकर्मणे नमः ।

He always does noble/ virtuous acts.

517. *Oṃ Śubhapradāya Namaḥ* । ॐ शुभप्रदाय नमः ।

He bestows all auspicious things to all.

513th name above may also be referred.

518. *Oṃ Satyavate Namaḥ* । ॐ सत्यवते नमः ।

He is always veracious/ truthful in all his words and acts.

519. *Oṃ Śrutimate Namaḥ* । ॐ श्रुतिमते नमः ।

He has the Veda as source or authority for his words and acts.

All his words and acts are based on or conformable to sacred tradition or the Vedas.

520. *Oṃ Uccairnakārāya Namaḥ* । ॐ उच्चैर्नकाराय नमः ।

His voice is majestic like that of a tiger.

521. *Oṃ Vṛddhidāya Namaḥ* । ॐ वृद्धिदाय नमः ।

His blessings always cause advancement or prosperity.

522. *Oṃ Analāya Namaḥ* । ॐ अनलाय नमः ।

He is like a fire or act as a fire.

389th name above and 639th, 816th & 898th names below may also be referred.

389th name above can also be referred.

523. *Oṃ Balabhṛte Namaḥ* I ॐ बलभृते नमः ।

He is powerfully strong.

524. *Oṃ Baladāya Namaḥ* I ॐ बलदाय नमः ।

He confers or imparts strength/ power.

525. *Oṃ Bandhave Namaḥ* I ॐ बन्धवे नमः ।

He is a relative/ kinsman to all.

526. *Oṃ Matimate Namaḥ* I ॐ मतिमते नमः ।

He is the most wise and intelligent.

527. *Oṃ Balināṃ Varāya Namaḥ* I ॐ बलिनां वराय नमः ।

He bestowed boon to the emperor Bali.

As lord Vishnu in the incarnation of Vamana, gave boon to Bali to rule the lower world and come to this world once in a year (on Onam day).

528. *Oṃ Anaṅgāya Namaḥ* I ॐ अनङ्गाय नमः ।

He is without any body organ.

It has been mentioned in multiple places, that Brahmam is Niroopam (without any form). Hence Sun is without body, i.e. without any body parts.

529. *Oṃ Nāgarājendrāya Namaḥ* I ॐ नागराजेन्द्राय नमः ।

He is the supreme sovereign of snakes.

In Puranas, lot many snakes like Adi Sheshan, Vasuki, Dakshagan and so on, have been mentioned as king of snakes. He is in all these forms.

530. *Oṃ Padmayonaye Namaḥ* I ॐ पद्मयोनये नमः ।

He is lotus born. He has lotus in his naval.

Lotus symbolizes the source of the Universe which is his navel.

He has a lotuslike navel. He shines in the center of the lotus like hearts of the devotees.

He is seated in the pericarp of the lotus.

Taitreeya Samhitai (4-6-2) says – in the navel of *Aja* (Brahma) all this is established.

In *Viṣṇu Sahasranamam* – 48th, 196th & 346th names – *Padmanābhaḥ* – Lotus navelled.

537th name below may also be referred.

531. *Oṃ Gaṇeśvarāya Namaḥ* I ॐ गणेश्वराय नमः ।

One of the primary meanings of the word *Gaṇa* in Samskrutam is group. In Modern Algebra section of Mathematics also we have something called 'Set', which is a collection of objects. This is called as *Gaṇam* in most of the languages like Tamil, Hindi, Samskrutam, etc. Hence, *Gaṇeśvar* is leader or head of that group.

11th Anuvakam of Sri Rudra Namakam says there are thousands of Rudra *Gaṇas*. For all those *Gaṇas Gaṇeśvar* is the head.

But, in practice the word *Gaṇapati* has started to mean by default, Lord *Vinayaka*. Because he is the leader of Deva *Gaṇas* – all the groups of Devas. Lord *Gaṇapati* and Lord Sun are one and the same.

532. *Oṃ Saṃvatsarāya Namaḥ* I ॐ संवत्सराय नमः ।

He creates the year.

He, being the controller of time, he creates the year. Earth takes one year to go around the Sun. Hence this name.

533. *Oṃ Ṛtave Namaḥ* | ॐ ऋतवे नमः ।

He creates the *Ṛtus*.

341st name above may also be referred.

534. *Oṃ Netre Namaḥ* | ॐ नेत्रे नमः ।

He is the eyes (of the world).

He is the witness for every happening in this world. Hence it is symbolically mentioned as he is the eyes of this world.

535. *Oṃ Kālacakrapravartakāya Namaḥ* | ॐ कालचक्रप्रवर्तकाय नमः ।

He sets in motion the time cycle.

536. *Oṃ Padmekṣaṇāya Namaḥ* | ॐ पद्मेक्षणाय नमः ।

He sleeps on a Lotus.

In reality he never sleeps. For our sake, he is seemingly sleeping.

537. *Oṃ Padmayonaye Namaḥ* | ॐ पद्मयोनये नमः ।

He is lotus born. He has lotus in his naval.

530th name above may also be referred.

538. *Oṃ Prabhāvate Namaḥ* | ॐ प्रभावते नमः ।

He has conciliation beauty.

He is of superior origin. Actually, he does not have any origin. That is what is indirectly mentioned here.

In *Viṣṇu* sahasranamam – 34th name – *Prabhavaḥ* – His birth place (no one knows).

539. *Oṃ Amarāya Namaḥ* | ॐ अमराय नमः ।

There is no end for him. All the Devas are called *Amaras*, since they have drunk amrutam, there is no death for them. Sun is one among the Devas. Hence, he is *Amarā*.

540. *Oṃ Prabhave Namaḥ* | ॐ प्रभवे नमः ।

He in the one from whom all things were born. I bow Him.

18th name above may also be referred.

541. *Oṃ Sumūrtaye Namaḥ* | ॐ सुमूर्तये नमः।

He has a good/ beautiful form.

542. *Oṃ Sumataye Namaḥ* | ॐ सुमतये नमः।

He flies in the heaven. This has been mentioned in multiple names in this Sahasranama.

451st name above & 625th name below may also be referred.

543. *Oṃ Somāya Namaḥ* | ॐ सोमाय नमः ।

He lives alongwith the consort *Uma*.

Usually, Lord Shiva is called *Somaḥ*, since he lives with his consort *Uma*. Here Lord Sun is called as *Somaḥ*, since Lord Shiva and Lord Sun are one and the same. As another evidence for this concept, *Śiva* sahasranamam 60th name is *Sūryaḥ*.

In *Śiva* sahasranamam 57th name – *Somaḥ* – he lives with *Uma*.

544. *Oṃ Govindāya Namaḥ* | ॐ गोविन्दाय नमः ।

He is the Lord of Earth/ cows. *Go* = earth/ cow. *Vinda* = lord. Hence, he is lord of both earth and cows.

Vid is the root word, which means to know. Hence, *Vinda* means knower.

The text called *Vishnu Tilaka* says – you to be known only through Vedas and hence you are called *Govinda*.

Go + *Vid* has following 10 meanings;

1. *Svarga* (heaven) – he transcends the heaven.
2. Arrows – He has all the divine arrows.
3. Cattle – he is the lord of all ignorant ones (cattle like people).
4. Speech – he is the lord of speech.
5. Thunder – he creates the thunder.
6. Quarter – he is known in all quarter.
7. Eyes – he is the person residing in eyes. Devi Puranas say that Sun, Moon and Agni are the three eyes of Sri Devi.
8. Sun – himself.
9. Earth – he is the lord of Earth.
10. Water – he creates the cycle of rain.

Normally Lord Vishnu is called as Govinda. Here Lord Sun is addressed so. Hence Lord Vishnu and Lord Sun are one and the same.

In *Vişŋu* Sahasranamam – 187th and 539th names – *Govindaḥ* – he is known only by Vedas or maxims of Vedanta.

In *Lalitā* Sahasranamam – 267th name – *Govindarūpiŋī* – she is in the form of *Govinda*. There is no difference between Sri Devi and Lord Vishnu.

In *Gāyatri* Sahasranamam – 209th name – *Govindacaraṇākrāntā* – she is the who can easily approach Govinda. Other than her, nobody else can easily approach Sri Govinda. *Gāyatri* is one of the consorts of Lord Sun. Hence, she can approach him easily.

545. *Oṃ Jagadādijāya Namaḥ* I ॐ जगदादिजाय नमः ।

He was the first born in this world. Actually, he has no origin. He only crated the entire world. But it is symbolically mentioned as first born.

He manifests himself as Hiranyagarbha in the beginning of the Universe.

Thiruvalluvar also mentions as *Ādi Bhagavan* at the very beginning of Thirukkural.

In *Vişŋu* Sahasranamam – 145th name – *Jagadādijaḥ* – he was the first born in this Universe.

546. *Oṃ Pītavāsase Namaḥ* । ॐ पीतवाससे नमः ।

He is dressed in Yellow colour.

It was already been mentioned in many places that he himself is yellow in colour.

547. *Oṃ Kṛṣṇavāsase Namaḥ* । ॐ कृष्णवाससे नमः ।

He is dressed in Black colour.

548. *Oṃ Digvāsase Namaḥ* । ॐ दिग्वाससे नमः ।

He lives in all directions. From every nook and corner of this world he is visible. Hence, he is in all directions.

He is a kind of mendicant without any dress.

Earlier it was mentioned as he is dressed in yellow/ black colours. Actually, He is *Nirguna, Niroopa Brahmam*. To the uninitiated ignorant people like us, he seems to be dressed in yellow or black colours.

549. *Oṃ Indriyātigāya Namaḥ* । ॐ इन्द्रियातिगाय नमः ।

He overpowers his senses/ organs. He has control over his senses.

He also helps his devotees to control their senses.

550. *Oṃ Atīndriyāya Namaḥ* । ॐ अतीन्द्रियाय नमः ।

He is beyond all senses. He transcends all senses.

Katopanishat (3-15) says – he is soundless and untouched.

In *Vişŋu* Sahasranamam – 169th name – *Atīndriyaḥ* – transcending all senses.

551. *Oṃ Anekarūpāya Namaḥ* । ॐ अनेकरूपाय नमः ।

He has many forms. In reality he, in the form of Supreme Being, is *niroopa* (without any form) *Brahmam*. Ironically, it is mentioned as he has multiple images. Though he is without any form as an actor **he** takes up different characters and shows different forms.

He has four forms viz., *Virāt* (imperishable), *Sūtram* (formulae), *Avyākrutam* (unmanifested) and *Turīyam* (fourth). He has four different colours in each of these forms as white, red, yellow and black.

Shruti says *Rudra* has billions of forms. *Śree Rudram – Asankhyātāḥ Sahasrāni Ye Rudra Atibhūmyām*. He in the form of such a billion forms of *Shiva* and hence **he** also has many forms.

Many texts like *Varāha Purāŋam, Narasimha Upapurāŋam* and *Tripura Siddhāntam* clearly says that he has many a form.

Vişhŋu Sahasranāma – 721st name – *Anekamūrtiḥ*, 723rd name – *Śatamūrtiḥ* and 765th name – *Chaturmūrtiḥ* – he takes many forms in the self-imposed incarnations to help the human beings and Devas. On account of various alternatives, different forms are created from a single knowledge matter and hence *Śatamūrtiḥ*.

In *Lalitā* Sahasranamam – 824th name – *Bahurūpā* – she has many forms.

552. *Oṃ Skandāya Namaḥ* I ॐ स्कन्दाय नमः ।

He dries everything – *Skand* = to dry.

He dries up the miseries of his devotees.

He is so sweet to his devotees. Usually Lord Kumara is called as Skanda. But here Lord Sun is called as Skanda. This implies that both are one and the same.

Vişhŋu Sahasranāma – 327th name – *Skandaḥ* – He is as sweet as nectar.

590th name below may also be referred.

553. *Oṃ Parapurañjayāya Namaḥ* I ॐ परपुरञ्जयाय नमः ।

He conquers the city of enemies.

554. *Oṃ Śaktimate Namaḥ* | ॐ शक्तिमते नमः ।

He is possessed of or united with his *shakti* (energy).

874th name below may also be referred.

555. *Oṃ Jaladhṛge Namaḥ* | ॐ जलधृगे नमः ।

He makes the tears to come out of the corner of the eyes.

If anyone roams in hot Sun, tears will come out of the eyes and the same is mentioned here.

556. *Oṃ Bhāsvate Namaḥ* | ॐ भास्वते नमः ।

He is splendidly luminous.

No need to exclusively mention about the brightness of Sun. Neverthless, it has been stressed in many places.

557. *Oṃ Mokṣahetave Namaḥ* | ॐ मोक्षहेतवे नमः ।

He is the bestower of liberation (*moksha*) to his devotees.

470th name above and 655th & 939th names below may also be referred.

558. *Oṃ Ayonijāya Namaḥ* | ॐ अयोनिजाय नमः ।

He is self-born and not being born from a womb.

559. *Oṃ Sarvadarśine Namaḥ* | ॐ सर्वदर्शिने नमः ।

He is visible to all freely.

He alone is *Pratyaksha* God. Visible to the naked eye for everyone .

560. *Oṃ Jitādarśāya Namaḥ* | ॐ जितादर्शाय नमः ।

He cannot be overcome or enslaved by anyone.

585th name below may also be referred.

561. *Oṃ Duḥsvapnā Śubhanāśanāya Namaḥ* I
ॐ दुःस्वप्नाशुभनाशनाय नमः ।

He is the destroyer of bad dreams. He shows good dreams to his devotees and removes the bad dreams.

Vişhŋu Sahasranāma – 922th name – *Duḥsvapnanāśanaḥ* – the dispeller of evil dreams that forebode the forthcoming evils.

Śiva Sahasranāma – 422nd name – *Susvapnaḥ* – controller of dreams.

562. *Oṃ Māṅgalyakartre Namaḥ* I ॐ माङ्गल्यकर्त्रे नमः ।

He is in-charge of the sacred thread (fortuitous string) worn by sumangali ladies from her wedding onwards.

As per horoscope Lord Sun's position decides the wedding of a lady. Hence he is *Māṅgalyakartre*.

601st, 602nd, 603rd, 604th & 605th names below may also be referred.

563. *Oṃ Taraṇaye Namaḥ* I ॐ तरणये नमः ।

He makes his devotees to swim across the ocean of samsara.

115th name above may also be referred.

564. *Oṃ Vegavate Namaḥ* I ॐ वेगवते नमः ।

He is a swift traveller.

565. *Oṃ Kaśmalāpahāya Namaḥ* I ॐ कश्मलापहाय नमः ।

He is blemishless.

566. *Oṃ Spaṣṭākṣarāya Namaḥ* I ॐ स्पष्टाक्षराय नमः ।

He is a distinctly pronouncing person during speech.

It has been mentioned that he is an expert in Vedas. For chanting of Vedas, one of the important qualities is distinctly pronouncing. In that way he is an expert. Further, he makes his devotees to distinctly pronounce Vedas and other speeches.

567. *Oṃ Mahāmantrāya Namaḥ* । ॐ महामन्त्राय नमः ।

In-charge of the great *mantra*, called *Gāyatri mantra*.

According to some puranas, Gayatri (Savitru) Devi is one of the consorts of Lord Sun. Gayatri mantra is the greatest among all the *mantras*. Hence he is *Mahāmantrāya*.

It is mentioned in Vedas as "*Gāyatrīm Chandasām Mātaḥ*" – *chandas* here means *Vedas* – *Gāyatri mantra* is the mother of all *Vedas*.

In *Shrimad Bhagavad Gita* (10.34), Lord *Krishna* says – Among the *mantras*, I am in the form of *Gāyatri mantra*.

Only after chanting *Gāyatri mantra*, any karta becomes eligible to do any other puja or to chant any other mantra.

Chanting of *Gāyatri mantra* only will eradicate any type of sins committed.

568. *Oṃ Viśākhāya Namaḥ* । ॐ विशाखाय नमः ।

Śākhā = branch. *Viśākhā* = without branches. There is only one Sun in the whole universe.

Viśākhā, also means equal branches. Lord Sun is in the middle of the Universe.

569. *Oṃ Yajanapriyāya Namaḥ* । ॐ यजनप्रियाय नमः ।

He is fond of performance of sacrifices and acceptance of gifts. Even if it is for others.

570. *Oṃ Viśvakarmaṇe Namaḥ* । ॐ विश्वकर्मणे नमः ।

Viśvakarmā is the architect for Devas. He is in that form.

Just for reference Mayan is the architect for Asuras.

571. *Oṃ Mahāśaktaye Namaḥ* । ॐ महाशक्तये नमः ।

He is very powerful and mighty.

572. *Oṃ Dyutaye Namaḥ* । ॐ द्युतये नमः ।

As mentioned in many a name, he is shining brightly.

731st name below may also be referred.

573. *Oṃ Īśāya Namaḥ* । ॐ ईशाय नमः ।

He is always fresh, active and powerful.

926th name below may also be referred.

574. *Oṃ Vihaṅgamāya Namaḥ* । ॐ विहङ्गमाय नमः ।

He moves (flies) in the sky like a bird.

575. *Oṃ Vicakṣaṇāya Namaḥ* । ॐ विचक्षणाय नमः ।

He is distinctly clear sighted.

576. *Oṃ Dakṣāya Namaḥ* । ॐ दक्षाय नमः ।

He is in the form of *Dakṣan*, one of the *Prajapatis*. He is the father of *Dākṣāyaṇi*, one of the incarnations of Parvati Devi. He was so fortunate to be father-in-law of Lord Shiva.

577. *Oṃ Indrāya Namaḥ* । ॐ इन्द्राय नमः ।

He is in the form of *Indran*, the king of Devas.

578. *Oṃ Pratyūṣāya Namaḥ* । ॐ प्रत्यूषाय नमः ।

He is the day breaker or dawn.

579. *Oṃ Priyadarśanāya Namaḥ* । ॐ प्रियदर्शनाय नमः ।

He is pleasant and grateful to the sight for everyone.

580. *Oṃ Akhinnāya Namaḥ* I ॐ अखिन्नाय नमः ।

He is always unwearied.

581. *Oṃ Vedanilayāya Namaḥ* I ॐ वेदनिलयाय नमः ।

He is the abode of all Vedas.

582. *Oṃ Vedavide Namaḥ* I ॐ वेदविदे नमः ।

He is very conversant with all Vedas.

Earlier also it was mentioned that he taught all Vedas to Hanuman.

Taitreeya Brahmanam (3-55) says – the one who does not know the Vedas knows not the omnipresent one.

He understands by the Vedas hundreds of Dharmas, which are to be learned.

It has been mentioned in many a place in *Vedas* that they originated from *Brahmam – Yasya Nisvasitam Vedāḥ, Asya Mahato Bhootasya Nisvashitametadrugvedo Yajurveda, Ruchaḥ Sāmāni Jagjire*, etc.

Shrimad Bhagawad Gita (10-11), Lord Krishna says – out of mere compassion for them, I, abiding in their self, destroy the darkness born of ignorance, by the luminour lamp of wisdom.

Again, Shrimad Bhagawad Gita (15-15), Lord Krishna says – *Vedaiccha Sarvairahameva Vedhyaḥ* – I am the author of the Vedanta, as well as the knower of the Vedas.

Viṣhŋu Sahasranāma –

127	*Vedaḥ*	He is in the form of all scriptures.
128 & 131	*Vedavit*	Knower of all Vedas
130	*Vedāngaḥ*	He has Vedas as his parts.
163	*Vedyaḥ*	The knowable by those desire supreme good.
547	*Vedhāḥ*	He is in the form of Brahma.

Mahabharata says – All the Vedas, all the Vidyas, all the shastras, all the yajnas and all offerings, are Krishna.

Lalitā Sahasranāma – 335th name – *Vedavedyā* & 338th name – *Vedajananī* – she can be realised only through the *Vedas*. She is the mother of all the *Vedas*.

583. *Oṃ Viditāśayāya Namaḥ* I ॐ विदिताशयाय नमः ।

He creates thirst and hunger.

490th name above may also be referred.

584. *Oṃ Prabhākarāya Namaḥ* I ॐ प्रभाकराय नमः ।

He is the light maker.

350th name above may also be referred.

585. *Oṃ Jitaripave Namaḥ* I ॐ जितरिपवे नमः ।

He cannot be overcome or enslaved by anyone.

560th name above may also be referred.

586. *Oṃ Sujanāya Namaḥ* I ॐ सुजनाय नमः ।

He is a good or virtuous or kind or benevolent person.

587. *Oṃ Aruṇasārathaye Namaḥ* I ॐ अरुणसारथये नमः ।

He has *Aruṇan* as the driver of his chariot.

Aruṇan is the elder brother of Garuda, the vehicle of Narayana. He does not have both the legs. He is the father Sambati and Jatayu, brother eagles, in Ramayana.

In the very early morning when the Sun rises in the East, *Aruṇan* only is visible first before even Sun, because he is sitting in front in the chariot. Hence it is called as rising of *Aruṇan*. At that time the sky will be in pink red colour.

In the dhyana verse of Lalita Sahasranama, Sri Lalita is said to be in *Aruṇa* colour i.e. in pink reddish colour.

588. *Oṃ Kunāśine Namaḥ* | ॐ कुनाशिने नमः ।

He destroys all the evil elements.

589. *Oṃ Suratāya Namaḥ* | ॐ सुरताय नमः ।

He has yoked to an excellent chariot.

93rd name above & 653rd names below may also be referred.

590. *Oṃ Skandāya Namaḥ* | ॐ स्कन्दाय नमः ।

He dries everything – *Skand* = to dry.

552nd name above may also be referred.

591. *Oṃ Mahitāya Namaḥ* | ॐ महिताय नमः ।

He is a great person worshipped by all.

592. *Oṃ Abhimatāya Namaḥ* | ॐ अभिमताय नमः ।

Everyone is longing for him.

593. *Oṃ Gurave Namaḥ* | ॐ गुरवे नमः ।

He is the teacher. He is the supreme Guru to Brahma and others.

461st name above may also be referred.

594. *Oṃ Graharājāya Namaḥ* | ॐ ग्रहराजाय नमः ।

Planet Jupiter and Moon are called *Graharāja* – king among the Navagragas. He is in those forms.

595. *Oṃ Grahapataye Namaḥ* | ॐ ग्रहपतये नमः ।

Moon is called *Grahapati* – leader among the Navagragas. He is in that form.

596. *Oṃ Graha Nakṣatra Maṇḍalāya Namaḥ* I
ॐ ग्रहनक्षत्रमण्डलाय नमः ।

He resides in the realm of planets and groups of stars.

597. *Oṃ Bhāskarāya Namaḥ* I ॐ भास्कराय नमः ।

No one is so bright as Lord Sun.

270th name above may also be referred.

598. *Oṃ Satatānandāya Namaḥ* I ॐ सततानन्दाय नमः ।

He is in aperpetually happy state.

599. *Oṃ Nandanāya Namaḥ* I ॐ नन्दनाय नमः ।

He is the source of happiness for all beings.

29th name above may also be referred.

600. *Oṃ Naravāhanāya Namaḥ* I ॐ नरवाहनाय नमः ।

He has a man as his vehicle.

Thus ends 100 divine names on Lord *Sūrya* from 501 to 600.

*****

601. *Oṃ Maṅgalāya Namaḥ* I ॐ मङ्गलाय नमः ।

He is in-charge of the sacred thread (fortuitous string) worn by sumangali ladies from her wedding onwards.

562nd name above and 602nd, 603rd, 604th & 605th names below may also be referred.

602. *Oṃ Maṅgalavate Namaḥ* I ॐ मङ्गलवते नमः ।

He is in-charge of the sacred thread (fortuitous string) worn by sumangali ladies from her wedding onwards.

562nd & 601st names above and 603rd, 604th & 605th names below may also be referred.

603. *Oṃ Māṅgalyāya Namaḥ* I ॐ माङ्गल्याय नमः ।

He is in-charge of the sacred thread (fortuitous string) worn by sumangali ladies from her wedding onwards.

562nd, 601st & 602nd names above and 604th & 605th names below may also be referred.

604. *Oṃ Maṅgalāvahāya Namaḥ* I ॐ मङ्गलावहाय नमः ।

He is in-charge of the sacred thread (fortuitous string) worn by sumangali ladies from her wedding onwards.

562nd, 601st, 602nd & 603rd names above and 605th name below may also be referred.

605. *Oṃ Maṅgalyacārucaritāya Namaḥ* I ॐ मङ्गल्यचारुचरिताय नमः ।

He is in-charge of the sacred thread (fortuitous string) worn by sumangali ladies from her wedding onwards.

562nd, 601st, 602nd, 603rd and 604th names above may also be referred.

606. *Oṃ Śīrṇāya Namaḥ* I ॐ शीर्णाय नमः ।

He makes the leaves shrunken on account of dryness.

607. *Oṃ Sarvavratāya Namaḥ* । ॐ सर्वव्रताय नमः ।

He strictly follows all vows.

He makes all his devotees to follow all the vows. Only by following the vows devotees can realise the Lord Sun.

608. *Oṃ Vratine Namaḥ* । ॐ व्रतिने नमः ।

He is always engaged in a religious observance/ vow.

He makes his devotees to engage in a religious observance/ vow.

609. *Oṃ Caturmukhāya Namaḥ* । ॐ चतुर्मुखाय नमः ।

He has four faces/ heads.

It is usual to address Lord Brahma as *Caturmukhan* (having four faces). Here Lord Sun is addressed so. This implies Lord Brahma and Sun are one and the same.

610. *Oṃ Padmamāline Namaḥ* । ॐ पद्ममालिने नमः ।

He wears a garland of Lotus flowers.

611. *Oṃ Pūtātmane Namaḥ* । ॐ पूतात्मने नमः ।

He is the pure Atma. Any thought that he is attached to Sattva and other gunas is by his own wish or the devotees' wish.

38th name above may also be referred.

612. *Oṃ Praṇatārtighne Namaḥ* । ॐ प्रणतार्तिघ्ने नमः ।

He is worshipped reverentially by all.

327th and 372nd names above may also be referred.

613. *Oṃ Akiñcanāya Namaḥ* । ॐ अकिञ्चनाय नमः ।

He is voluntarily poor. He has no interest in wealth and any other things. Hence, it is mentioned as poor.

614. *Oṃ Satāmīśāya Namaḥ* | ॐ सतामीशाय नमः ।

He is an excellent lord. He is a gorgeous lord.

615. *Oṃ Nirguṇāya Namaḥ* | ॐ निर्गुणाय नमः ।

He is without any attributes/ characters.

He is *Nirguna* and *Niroopa Brahmam*. On account of our ignorance, we add forms and attributes to him. As being, in truth, he is devoid of attributes.

Shvetashvatara Upanishat (6-15) says – *Sākshee Chetā Kevalo Nirguŋasca* – he is pure and devoid of qualities. Witness, the philosopher, one who is uncontaminated and who is free from characters.

This has been explained in *Matsya* and *Padma puranās* also. The traits of *Devas* are their identities; characters are related to bodies. Since *Sun* is in the form of *Chit*, **he** has no characters neither identity.

Viṣŋu Sahasranamam – 840th name – *Nirguṇaḥ* – He that transcends all attributes.

Lalitā Sahasranamam – 139th name – *Nirguṇā* – One who is beyond the three characters – *Guŋas*.

Gāyatri Sahasranamam – 378th & 505th names – *Nirguṇāyai* – conveying the same meaning.

616. *Oṃ Guṇavate Namaḥ* | ॐ गुणवते नमः ।

He is endowed with good qualities, virtues, merits and excellences.

In the previous name it was mentioned as without attributes. Contrary to the same here it is being mentioned as with good attributes. Because of he being the universal soul and the lord of creation, protection and destruction, by means of Satva, Rajas and Tamo qualities.

The *Sānkhya* doctrine says that though the qualities are specifically three viz. *sattva*, *rajas* and *tamas*, they have endless modifications. **He** is the treasure house of all such qualities.

Guṇa means aggregate (*Vyoohas*). Like nine *nidhies*, these *vyoohas* also are nine in number. *Sun* is of the form of these nine aggregates of qualities. The nine *vyoohas* are;

1. *Kālavyooha* (time)
2. *Kulavyooha* (family race)
3. *Nāmavyooha* (name)
4. *Gnānavyooha* (knowledge)
5. *Chittavyooha* (mind)
6. *Nadavyooha* (*Nātha*)
7. *Binduvyooha* (*Bindu*)
8. *Kalpavyooha* (*Kalpa*) and
9. *Jeevavyooha* (soul).

The word *Guṇa* also means rope. The rope called *Vairikā*, which tied the ship during the *pralaya*. This great rope called as *Vatrikā* is nine *Yojanas* long and three cubits broad. The following story occurs in the *Matsya* and *Kālika Purāṇas* thus; at the time of dissolution all seeds and sages entered the boat at the command of *Manu*, who was directed by the Lord *Viṣṇu* and the boat was tied to the horn of the fish-incarnation. That rope became firm when *Sun* held it. *Sun* who is the protector of the universe, the great *Māyā*, the father of the world, the world itself, will make that rope firm so that it will not give away.

Viṣṇu Sahasranamam – 839th name – *Guṇabhṛt* – He is possessed with attributes. This name is contrary to the next name.

Lalitā Sahasranamam – 604th name – *Guṇanidhiḥ* – she is the treasure house of qualities.

617. *Oṃ Śucaye Namaḥ* । ॐ शुचये नमः ।

He is brightly shining.

618. *Oṃ Sampūrṇāya Namaḥ* । ॐ सम्पूर्णाय नमः ।

He is the complete absolute entirely filled.

The below verse is worth noting here;

Oṃ Pūrṇamadaḥ Pūrṇamidaṃ Pūrṇātpūrṇamudacyate |
Pūrṇasya Pūrṇamādāya Pūrṇamevāvaśiṣyate ||

Out of the Infinite Being the finite has come, yet being infinite, only infinite remains. Peace in my heart, peace with each other, peace in the cosmos. Thou art every One and ever whole.

678th & 750th names below may also be referred.

619. *Oṃ Puṇḍarīkākṣāya Namaḥ* | ॐ पुण्डरीकाक्षाय नमः ।

He is a lotus like eyed lord. Pervading the lotus in the heart.

Narayana Upanishat (10) says – there is a lotus in the center of the city (body).

Viṣṇu Sahasranamam – 111th name – *Puṇdarīkākṣaḥ* – He has lotuslike eyes.

620. *Oṃ Vidheyāya Namaḥ* | ॐ विधेयाय नमः ।

He is down to earth subdued Lord. He is so great and still he is submissive to his devotees.

Vaishnavites always call themselves as *Videhan*.

464th name above may also be referred.

621. *Oṃ Yogatatparāya Namaḥ* | ॐ योगतत्पराय नमः ।

He has Yoga as his main principle.

The realization of oneness of the individual and the Supreme spirit, by keeping the senses of knowledge together with the mind under control is called Yoga. He can be reached only through such Yogas.

Yoga means union, *Jnana* and *Samadhi*. He who controls his self with his self is Yogi. He can be reached only by Yogis.

Yoga has four parts – *mantra, Laya, hata* and *rāja*. *Rājayoga* has three parts – *Sānkya, Tāraka* and *Amanska*. These details are to be learnt from *Yoga shāstras*.

Yogis are obstructed (in their progress) by Yogic impediments and (consequently) fall off from their own position. These obstructions have to be overcome to reach him.

Vişŋu Sahasranamam – 18th name – *Yogaḥ* – 849th name – *Yogiḥ* – 850th name – *Yogīśaḥ* – He is the *Yoga*, He can be reached only by *Yogis*, He is the lord of *Yogis*.

Lalitā Sahasranamam – 653rd name – *Yoginī* – 654th name – *Yogadā* – 655th name – *Yogyā* – she has a *Yoga* form, she bestows yoga to her devotees, she can be reached only by Yoga.

Śiva Sahasranamam – 79th & 782nd names – *Yogiḥ* – 79th name – *Yojyaya* – he is a great yogi. He can be reached only through Yogas. He is in the form of Yoga.

622. *Oṃ Sahasrāṃśave Namaḥ* I ॐ सहस्रांशवे नमः ।

He is with thousand rays.

264th name above & 780th name below may also be referred.

623. *Oṃ Kratumataye Namaḥ* I ॐ क्रतुमतये नमः ।

He is endowed with intelligence. He endows intelligence to his devotees.

624. *Oṃ Sarvajñāya Namaḥ* I ॐ सर्वज्ञाय नमः ।

He is omniscient. He knows everything.

272nd name above may also be referred.

625. *Oṃ Sumataye Namaḥ* I ॐ सुमतये नमः ।

He flies in the heaven. This has been mentioned in multiple names in this Sahasranama.

451st & 542nd names above may also be referred.

626. *Oṃ Suvāce Namaḥ* I ॐ सुवाचे नमः ।

He is very eloquent in his speech.

162nd, 311th & 500th names above may also be referred.

627. *Oṃ Suvāhanāya Namaḥ* I ॐ सुवाहनाय नमः ।

He has a very good vehicle. He travels non-stop (24 x 7). Hence his vehicle needs to be very good – no break-downs.

628. *Oṃ Mālyadāmne Namaḥ* I ॐ माल्यदाम्ने नमः ।

He wears garlands, normally of flowers.

629. *Oṃ Kṛtāhārāya Namaḥ* I ॐ कृताहाराय नमः ।

He is the one who has accomplished his past and present duties. And he will also accomplish his future duties and be contented.

251st name above may also be referred.

630. *Oṃ Haripriyāya Namaḥ* I ॐ हरिप्रियाय नमः ।

He is very fond of *Hari* (Lord *Vishnu*). Lord *Hari* is very fond of him.

631. *Oṃ Brahmaṇe Namaḥ* I ॐ ब्रह्मणे नमः ।

He is in the form of Lord Brahma, the creator. He is in the form of Brahmam, the universal soul.

Viṣṇu Sahasranamam – 663rd name – *Brahmā* – 664th name – *Brahma* – He is the Brahmam and Lord *Brahmā*.

Lalitā Sahasranamam – 265th name – *Brahmārūpiṇī* – she is in the form of Brahma.

632. *Oṃ Pracetase Namaḥ* I ॐ प्रचेतसे नमः ।

He is very wise. He is always delighted.

633. *Oṃ Prathitāya Namaḥ* | ॐ प्रथिताय नमः ।

He is a widely renowned Lord.

634. *Oṃ Prayatātmane Namaḥ* | ॐ प्रयतात्मने नमः ।

He is so pure and hence holy.

189th name above may also be referred.

635. *Oṃ Sthirātmakāya Namaḥ* | ॐ स्थिरात्मकाय नमः ।

He is steadfast/ firm-minded.

636. *Oṃ Śatavindave Namaḥ* | ॐ शतविन्दवे नमः ।

He is at peak at a particular hour of the day (at noon).

He gains heat when the time passes in a day.

637. *Oṃ Śatamukhāya Namaḥ* | ॐ शतमुखाय नमः ।

He has hundred faces (heads).

When it is said as hundred, it means hundreds of faces.

We all are aware that when Lord Krishna took Virat form, he had countless (hundreds of) heads. Lord Sun and Krishna are one and the same.

Viṣṇu Sahasranamam – 723rd name – *Śatamūrtiḥ* – 724th name – *Śatānanaḥ* – He has hundreds of forms. He has hundreds of faces.

Śiva Sahasranamam – 835th name – *Śatajihvāḥ* – he has hundreds of tongues. When the tongues are in hundreds, naturally the mouths and hence the heads also need to be in hundreds.

638. *Oṃ Garīyase Namaḥ* | ॐ गरीयसे नमः ।

His devotees are very dearer to him than anything else.

He is very dearer to his devotees than anything else.

639. *Oṃ Analaprabhāya Namaḥ* | ॐ अनलप्रभाय नमः ।

He acts like fire. His energies and powers are unlimited.

389th & 522nd names above and 816th and 898th names below may also be referred.

640. *Oṃ Dhīrāya Namaḥ* | ॐ धीराय नमः ।

He encourages and makes his devotees at a comfort level.

641. *Oṃ Mahattarāya Namaḥ* | ॐ महत्तराय नमः ।

He is so large and greater than anybody else. He is the eldest person and most respectable.

He is very strong and mighty.

642. *Oṃ Viprāya Namaḥ* | ॐ विप्राय नमः ।

He is a brahmin, who very well knows *Vedas*.

Shrimad Bhagavatam defines the word *Vipra* as Veda knowing brahmin.

He travels like a flight.

643. *Oṃ Purāṇapuruṣottamāya Namaḥ* | ॐ पुराणपुरुषोत्तमाय नमः ।

As per Puranas, he is the best of men.

In Shrimad Bhagavad Gita (15-18) Sri Krishna says – since I excel the destructible and am more excellent also than the indestructible in the world and in the Vedas, I am proclaimed as *'Purushottama'*.

Viṣṇu Sahasranamam – 24th name – *Puruṣottamaḥ* – best among men.

644. *Oṃ Vidyārājādhirājāya Namaḥ* | ॐ विद्याराजाधिराजाय नमः ।

He is an emperor of knowledge.

645. *Oṃ Vidyāvate Namaḥ* I ॐ विद्यावते नमः ।

He is highly learned.

489th name above & 734th name below may also be referred.

646. *Oṃ Bhūtidāya Namaḥ* I ॐ भूतिदाय नमः ।

He is part of a group of deceased ancestors. There are various groups of pitrus called Vishwedevas. He is a part of one of such groups.

647. *Oṃ Sthitāya Namaḥ* I ॐ स्थिताय नमः ।

He is stable and permanent.

225th name above & 932nd name below may also be referred.

648. *Oṃ Anirdeśyavapave Namaḥ* I ॐ अनिर्देश्यवपवे नमः ।

He has an indefinable and incomparable form.

As he transcends with all attributes, his form cannot be defined by anyone.

Viṣṇu Sahasranamam – 177th & 656th names – *Anirdeśyavapuḥ* – he has an indefinable/ indescribable form.

649. *Oṃ Śrīmate Namaḥ* I ॐ श्रीमते नमः ।

He is so splendorous.

163rd & 170th names above may also be referred.

650. *Oṃ Vipāpmane Namaḥ* I ॐ विपाप्मने नमः ।

He is free from any type of sufferings.

651. *Oṃ Bahumaṅgalāya Namaḥ* I ॐ बहुमङ्गलाय नमः ।

He walks in the path of prosperity and happiness.

He shows the way to prosperity and happiness to his devotees.

652. *Oṃ Svaḥsthitāya Namaḥ* | ॐ स्वःस्थिताय नमः ।

He is very independent, not dependent on anybody. He is in a state of welfare.

653. *Oṃ Surathāya Namaḥ* | ॐ सुरथाय नमः ।

He has yoked to an excellent chariot.

93rd & 589th names above may also be referred.

654. *Oṃ Svarṇāya Namaḥ* | ॐ स्वर्णाय नमः ।

He is in gold colour. He shines like a gold.

655. *Oṃ Mokṣadāya Namaḥ* | ॐ मोक्षदाय नमः ।

He is the bestower of liberation (*moksha*) to his devotees.

470th & 557th names above and 939th name below may also be referred.

656. *Oṃ Baliketanāya Namaḥ* | ॐ बलिकेतनाय नमः ।

He acts as a councilor or adviser to the victims, so that they turn to the correct path.

657. *Oṃ Nirdvandvāya Namaḥ* | ॐ निर्द्वन्द्वाय नमः ।

He is a pure follower of Advaita principle. He does not advocate dvaita principle.

He is indifferent to the alternatives or opposite pairs.

658. *Oṃ Dvandvaghne Namaḥ* | ॐ द्वन्द्वघ्ने नमः ।

He pairs the opposite sides to make peace. This name is seeming opposite to the previous name.

659. *Oṃ Sargāya Namaḥ* | ॐ सर्गाय नमः ।

He is very natural himself. He is the primary creation.

660. *Oṃ Sarvagāya Namaḥ* I ॐ सर्वगाय नमः ।

He consists wholly of the Gayatri (mantra).

Sun God and Gayatri mantra are inseparable twins. To have more understanding about Gayatri mantra and also to stress the significance, a separate chapter has been included in this book.

In some other place, it has been mentioned that Gayatri mantra pertains to Brahmam. Lord Sun is the Brahmam and hence Gayatri pertains to Sun God.

794th and 945th names below may also be referred.

661. *Oṃ Saṃprakāśakāya Namaḥ* I ॐ संप्रकाशकाय नमः ।

He manifests various forms as different Gods.

662. *Oṃ Dayālave Namaḥ* I ॐ दयालवे नमः ।

He is disinclined to pity to evil persons.

663. *Oṃ Sūkṣmadhiye Namaḥ* I ॐ सूक्ष्मधिये नमः ।

He is subtly intelligent.

664. *Oṃ Kṣāntaye Namaḥ* I ॐ क्षान्तये नमः ।

He has much patience and forgives the sinners.

665. *Oṃ Kṣemā Kṣema Sthiti Priyāya Namaḥ* I
ॐ क्षेमाक्षेमस्थितिप्रियाय नमः ।

Whether happy or otherwise he is firm or stable.

He bestows firmness or stability on his devotees whether they are with great joy when they are well and great sorrow when they are not.

666. *Oṃ Bhūdharāya Namaḥ* I ॐ भूधराय नमः ।

Bhūdhara = number 7. Lord Sun's connection with number 7 has been mentioned in lots of places in this Sahasranama. For details 75th name above can be referred.

667. *Oṃ Bhūpataye Namaḥ* | ॐ भूपतये नमः ।

He is the head of this world.

668. *Oṃ Vaktre Namaḥ* | ॐ वक्त्रे नमः ।

He has a very good organ of speech and hence he is an expert in speech.

In Ramayana, his disciple Anjaneya has been described as an expert in speech.

669. *Oṃ Pavitrātmane Namaḥ* | ॐ पवित्रात्मने नमः ।

He is a holy/ sacred/ saintly soul.

670. *Oṃ Trilocanāya Namaḥ* | ॐ त्रिलोचनाय नमः ।

He has three eyes. Lord Shiva, Goddess Lalita and various other Gods are also said to three eyes.

In Lalita Sahasranamam – 477th name – *Trilochanā* – she has three eyes.

671. *Oṃ Mahāvarāhāya Namaḥ* | ॐ महावराहाय नमः ।

He is a great king.

He is a great bore. Lord Vishnu took the incarnation like a bore. Lord Sun is in that form.

672. *Oṃ Priyakṛte Namaḥ* | ॐ प्रियकृते नमः ।

He is a friend/ benefactor/ well wishes to his devotees. He does all activities very willingly. He does all actions which please most.

673. *Oṃ Dātre Namaḥ* | ॐ दात्रे नमः ।

He holds a sort of sickle or crooked knife.

674. *Oṃ Bhoktre Namaḥ* । ॐ भोक्त्रे नमः ।

He is an enjoyer. He enjoys everything. He enjoys the Supreme Bliss.

The enjoyer of insentient Prakruti or matter.

Vişŋu sahasranamam – 143rd, 500th & 888th names – *Bhoktāḥ* – the enjoyer.

675. *Oṃ Abhayapradāya Namaḥ* । ॐ अभयप्रदाय नमः ।

He bestows safety and protection to his devotees.

He drives away all the fears from the cycle of birth and deaths.

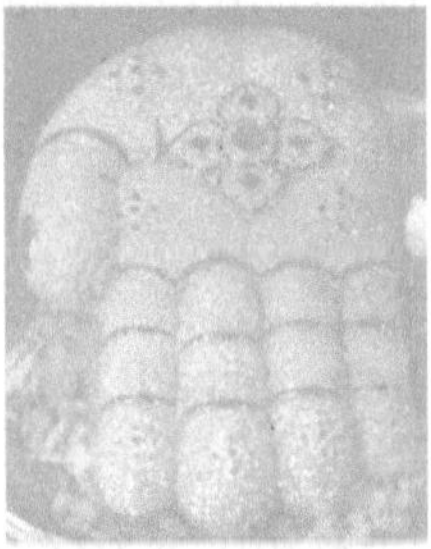

Veda says – *Ānandam Brahmaŋo Vidwan Na Bhibheti Kutaschana* – One who has reached eternal bliss knows no fear.

Normally all Gods/ Goddesses show the hand symbols of boon and *abhayam* (no fear).

Vişŋu sahasranamam – 834th name – *Bhayanāshanaḥ* – He destroys the fear for those who do follow the convention of caste and *ashramas*.

Again, Vişŋu sahasranamam – 935th name – Bhayāpahaḥ – he relieves his devotees from the fear of cycle of birth and death.

Lalita Sahasranamam – 121st name – *Bhayāpahā* – she dispels all fears.

676. *Oṃ Cakravartine Namaḥ* । ॐ चक्रवर्तिने नमः ।

He is an emperor – king of all kings.

In Lalita Sahasranama, Sri Devi is depicted as emperess ruling from Sripuram.

677. *Oṃ Dhṛtikarāya Namaḥ* । ॐ धृतिकराय नमः ।

He is a self-commanding person. There is nobody else above him to command.

678. *Oṃ Sampūrṇāya Namaḥ* I ॐ सम्पूर्णाय नमः ।

He is the complete absolute entirely filled.

618th name above and 750th name below may also be referred.

679. *Oṃ Maheśvarāya Namaḥ* I ॐ महेश्वराय नमः ।

He is the supreme sovereign.

65th name above may also be referred.

680. *Oṃ Caturvedadharāya Namaḥ* I ॐ चतुर्वेदधराय नमः ।

He is an expert in all Vedas.

471st, 472nd & 475th names above and 711th name below may also be referred.

681. *Oṃ Acintyāya Namaḥ* I ॐ अचिन्त्याय नमः ।

He has an incomprehensible/ inconceivable form.

682. *Oṃ Vinindyāya Namaḥ* I ॐ विनिन्द्याय नमः ।

He never reproaches anybody. Noone can abuse him.

683. *Oṃ Vividhāśanāya Namaḥ* I ॐ विविधाशनाय नमः ।

He has different sorts of seats. Various types of food are offered to him.

684. *Oṃ Vicitrarathāya Namaḥ* I ॐ विचित्ररथाय नमः ।

He has wonderful/ diversified chariot. His chariot has only one wheel. Nobody else has such a chariot.

685. *Oṃ Ekākine Namaḥ* I ॐ एकाकिने नमः ।

He is all alone. There is nobody who can be equal or superior to him. This name best indicates Advaita (no two) philosophy.

Chandogya Upanishat (6-2-1) says – there is only one without a second.

Viṣṇu sahasranamam – 725th name – *Ekaḥ* – The one.

686. *Oṃ Saptasaptaye Namaḥ* | ॐ सप्तसप्तये नमः ।

Number seven is highly connected with Lord Sun in many ways.

75th & 188th names above and 747th, 748th, 749th, 757th, 758th & 854th names below may also be referred.

687. *Oṃ Parātparāya Namaḥ* | ॐ परात्पराय नमः ।

He is superior to the best.

He is beyond the very great *Trimoortis - Brahma, Viṣhṇu* and *Rudra*.

According to *Kāli Purāṇa* – one day (one day and night) of *Brahma* is called as *Para*. His day and night are of equal duration and they are called *Parārdham* (it can be reminded that during any *Sankalpa* [declaring the desire to do *pooja*, etc.] this is being used). But, for the person, who is subtler than the subtle and minute than the minutest there is no bindings like day, night, year, etc., because he only creates the time and he is not controlled by time

Lalita Trishatee – 236th name – *Samānādhikavarjitā* – there is no one equal to or above **Her**.

Lalita Sahasranamam – 809th name – *Parātparā* – she is the most supreme of the supreme.

688. *Oṃ Sarvodadhisthitikarāya Namaḥ* |
ॐ सर्वोदधिस्थितिकराय नमः ।

He only maintains/ controls all water forms like ocean, river, pond, etc.

689. *Oṃ Sthitistheyāya Namaḥ* | ॐ स्थितिस्थेयाय नमः ।

He is always still and to be stationed or fixed or settled. He is always the same.

Viṣṇu sahasranamam – 203rd name – *Sthitaraḥ* – He is constant.

690. *Oṃ Sthitipriyāya Namaḥ* | ॐ स्थितिप्रियाय नमः ।

He is very fond of firmness or stability.

691. *Oṃ Niṣkalāya Namaḥ* | ॐ निष्कलाय नमः ।

He is not connected with any stain (the result of sin). Sin cannot near him and hence this name.

Íshāvāsya Upanishad (8th verse) reads as – *Śuddamapāpavitram* – pure and untouched by sins.

Lalita Sahasranamam – 153rd name – *Niṣkalankā* – she is blemishless.

692. *Oṃ Puṣkalāya Namaḥ* | ॐ पुष्कलाय नमः ।

He is magnificently powerful.

693. *Oṃ Vibhave Namaḥ* | ॐ विभवे नमः ।

He is the bestower of all wealth.

19th name above may also be referred.

694. *Oṃ Vasumate Namaḥ* | ॐ वसुमते नमः ।

He is the owner of entire wealth.

He is of great mind. His mind is not polluted with the afflictions of desires, aversion and pride.

Viṣṇu sahasranamam – 105th name – *Vasumanāḥ* – He is of great mind.

695. *Oṃ Vāsavapriyāya Namaḥ* | ॐ वासवप्रियाय नमः ।

He is fond of Indra, the king of Devas.

Indra, the king of Devas is very obedient to Lord Sun.

696. *Oṃ Paśumate Namaḥ* I ॐ पशुमते नमः ।

He is a blemishless and error free God.

206th name above may also be referred.

697. *Oṃ Vāsavasvāmine Namaḥ* I ॐ वासवस्वामिने नमः ।

He is the Lord of Indra, the king of Devas.

698. *Oṃ Vasudhāmne Namaḥ* I ॐ वसुधाम्ने नमः ।

He grants liberal wealth and treasures to his devotees.

699. *Oṃ Vasupradāya Namaḥ* I ॐ वसुप्रदाय नमः ।

He is the conferrer of salvation.

172nd name above may also be referred.

700. *Oṃ Balavate Namaḥ* I ॐ बलवते नमः ।

He possesses strong power.

Thus ends 100 divine names on Lord *Sūrya* from 601 to 700.

*****

701. *Oṃ Jñānavate Namaḥ* । ॐ ज्ञानवते नमः ।

He is knowledge personified.

The three – the knower, the knowledge and the object of knowledge – are called *'Tripudee'*. **He** is of the form hiding all these and only remaining is the knowledge/ supreme bliss.

With the blessings of Lord Sun, the knowledge expands further and knowledge only will remain at the end. Our little knowledge expands and become the supreme one.

Lalita Sahasranamam – 644th name – *Jnānavigrahā* – her form is knowledge.

702. *Oṃ Tattvāya Namaḥ* । ॐ तत्त्वाय नमः ।

He is the reality. He is the knower of truth.

The words *'Tattva'*, *'Amruta'*, *'Satya'*, etc., are all synonyms and mean the same Brahmam, which is the real truth.

Those that last till great dissolution and be enablers of the souls to enjoy are called *Tattvas*. The objects like body, pot, etc., do not qualify to be called as *tattva*.

The combination of the *Sat* (eternal), *Chit* (energy) and *Ānanda* (bliss) *tattvas* is the supreme bliss. It indicates *Satchitānanda*. Hence He is called as *Tattvāya*.

The literal meaning of *tattva*, in Samskrutam, is philosophy. According to different principles the number of *tattvas* vary as 25, 36, 51 and 94.

Viṣṇu sahasranamam – 963rd name – *Tattvam* and 964th name – *Tattvavit* – He is the real and knower of the real truth.

Lalita Sahasranamam – 907th name – *Tattvamayī* – she is in the form of all *Tattvas*.

703. *Oṃ Oṃṅkārāya Namaḥ* । ॐ ओङ्काराय नमः ।

He is in the form of *Oṅkārā*, the *Pranava mantra*.

The *praṇava* has three parts[5]. They are (A) *akāra*, **(U)** *ukāra* and (M) *makāra*. To bring out any sound there are three actions in the mouth – opening, lips joining and closing of lips. During these three actions the sound coming out are *akāra*, *ukāra* and *makāra* respectively. This is irrespective of any language. Looking at another perspective, the *praṇava mantra* has five parts viz. *akāra*, *ukāra*, *makāra*, *bindhu* and *nādam*. Consequently, this is also one of the glorious *Panchākşara mantra*. That is the reason this glorious *mantra* is being attached with all the *mantras* irrespective of Gods.

The *Mandukya* Upanishat, belonging to Atharva Veda and contains twelve verses, is an exposition of the principle of *Oṃ* as consisting of three elements A, U, M, which refer to the three states of waking, dream and deep sleep. The supreme self is manifested in the universe in its gross, subtle and causal aspects. Answering to the four states of consciousness namely wakefulness, dream, deep sleep and transcendental consciousness, the last aspect of godhead being all inclusive and ultimately real.

Oṃ Ityetadakşaraṃ Idaṃ Sarvaṃ, Tasyo'pavyākhyānaṃ, Bhūtaṃ Bhavad Bhaviśyad Iti Sarvaṃ Oṃkāra Eva, Yac Cānyat Trikālātītaṃ Tadapyoṃkārameva.

Oṃ, this syllable is all this. All that is past, the present and the future, all these are only the syllable *Oṃ*. And whatever else there is beyond the threefold time, that too is only the syllable *Oṃ*.

Taittarīya Upanişat (I.vli .1);

Oṃ Iti Brahma, Oṃ Itīdaṃ Sarvaṃ, Oṃ Ityetad Anukṛtiḥ Ha Sma Vā Apyośrāvayetyāśrāvayanti, Oṃ Iti Sāmāni Gāyanti, Oṃ Śomiti Śastrāṇi Śamśaṃthi, Oṃ Iti Adhvaryuḥ, Pratigāraṃ Pratigṛṇāti, Oṃ Iti Brahma Prasauti, Oṃ Ityagnihotraṃ Anujānāti, Oṃ Iti Brāhmaṇaḥ Pravakşyann Āha, Brahmopāpnavānīti, Brahmaivovāpnoti.

Oṃ is Brahma. *Oṃ* is these all. *Oṃ*, this, verily, is compliance. On uttering `recite', they recite. With *Oṃ*, they sing the chants of Sama

---

[5] The author of this book has written a separate book titled "Vedas – an Analytical Approach". In this book he has written a separate chapter detailing various aspects of Pranava Mantra.

Veda. With *Oṃ*, they resite the prayers. With *Oṃ* the advaryu priest utters the response. With *Oṃ* does the priest utter the introductory eulogy. With *Oṃ*, one assents to the offering to fire. The symbol *Oṃ* is used to indicate the indescribable Brahman, whose true nature, like the riot of colours in the summer sky, can be felt, but the experience remains supremely personal.

704. *Oṃ Triṣu Saṃsthitāya Namaḥ* I ॐ त्रिषु संस्थिताय नमः ।

He is well settled in all the three worlds.

705. *Oṃ Saṅkalpayonaye Namaḥ* I ॐ सङ्कल्पयोनये नमः ।

He has source or origin in will/ desire.

706. *Oṃ Dinakṛte Namaḥ* I ॐ दिनकृते नमः ।

He is the maker of day, i.e. day and night.

100th name above may also be referred.

707. *Oṃ Bhagavate Namaḥ* I ॐ भगवते नमः ।

He is with complete wealth, charity, fame, liberation, etc.

he knows everything about the living beings like birth, death, destruction, movement, knowledge, ignorance, etc., hence *Bhagavate*.

The word *Bhaga* has various meanings – beauty, desire, detachment, discrimination, dispassion, effort, excellence, fame, glory, liberation, lordliness, magnanimity, power, prosperity, omniscience, righteousness, supremacy, trying, wisdom, womb, worldly concerns, etc. He is possessor of all these qualities and hence *Bhagavate*.

Viṣhṇu Sahasranāma – 558th name – *Bhagavān* – He has complete wealth, charity, fame, liberation, etc.

Lalitā Sahasranāma – 279th name – *Bhagavat* – She is with prosperity.

886th, 944th & 1,006th names below may also be referred.

708. *Oṃ Kāraṇāpahāya Namaḥ* । ॐ कारणापहाय नमः ।

He is beyond any type of reasoning. He can be realised only through knowledge.

709. *Oṃ Nīlakaṇṭhāya Namaḥ* । ॐ नीलकण्ठाय नमः ।

He has a blue neck. Only Lord Shiva is said to have blue neck. Here Lord Sun is said so. Hence both Lord Shiva and Sun are one and the same.

Lord Shiva's neck turned black due to the ingestion of poison. He drank the poison to save the Devas (the world) regardless of the permanent disfigurement that might occur to his neck. His mercy is incomparable. We all know this story.

Sri Rudra Namakam (1.8) – Lord Parameshwara who has a black neck due to the poisoning, is going into the visible solar system in red colour. Our salutations to him.

Asau Yo'vasarpati Nīlagrīvo Vilohitaḥ ।

Sri Rudra Namakam (1.9) – Our salutations to Lord Parameshvara, who has thousands of eyes, gives everything sought for to the devotees and has a blue neck.

Namo Astu Nīlagrīvāya Sahasrākṣāya Mīḍhuṣe ।

Related area in Rudra Namakam 11th Anuvakam;

Nīlagrīvāḥ Śitikaṇṭhāḥ Śarvā Adhaḥ Kṣamācarāḥ ॥ 11.3
Nīlagrīvāḥ Śitikaṇṭhā Divarudrā Upaśritāḥ ॥ 11.4
Ye Vṛkṣeṣu Saspiṃjarā Nīlagrīvā Vilohitāḥ ॥ 11.5

We request thee Oh Black necked Rudra! To order your soldiers who are in thousands, to keep their thousands of weapons, which are of thousand kinds and thousand miles away from us.

And those soldiers, who do exist, whose half side of neck is blue and the other half is white, and live under the earth in Patala. And those soldiers, who do exist, whose neck is blue (on account of drinking poison) and was white (before drinking poison). The meaning of this is that if the weapons are sent far away, they cannot be aimed at us.

Devas are immortal only when they drink *Amruta*. But Lord Shiva drinks poison and still he is immortal. That is why he is *Mahadevan*, head of all devas.

Lalita Sahasranamam – 392nd name – *Śrīkanṭhārdha Śarīriṇī* – **She** has *Paramashiva as* **Her** half body or **She** has in-differentiable half body with *Paramashiva.*

710. *Oṃ Dhanādhyakṣāya Namaḥ* I ॐ धनाध्यक्षाय नमः ।

He is a treasurer or overseer of a treasury.

In general, *Kuberā* is said to be the presiding deity of wealth. He is one of the famous worshippers of Sun. The scriptures say that there is no distinction between the worshipper and the worshipped deity. In that fashion Sun is the *Kubera*. Hence **He** is the head of wealth.

Lalita Sahasranamam – 885th name – *Dhanādhyakshā* – **She** is the head of wealth.

711. *Oṃ Caturvedapriyaṃvadāya Namaḥ* I ॐ चतुर्वेदप्रियंवदाय नमः ।

He is an expert in all Vedas. He is very compassionate towards the reciters of the Vedas.

471st, 472nd, 475th and 680th names above may also be referred.

712. *Oṃ Vaṣaṭkārāya Namaḥ* I ॐ वषट्काराय नमः ।

He on whose account *Vaṣaṭkāraḥ* is offered. *Vaṣaṭkāraḥ* is a technical word through which oblations are offered in fire to various Gods.

He pleases all Gods by himself being the soul of *Vaṣaṭkāra* and other mantras.

Taitreeya Samhita (1-7-4) says – sacrifice indeed is God.

The Veda says – the Lord Prajapati and *Vaṣaṭkāraḥ*.

Viṣhṇu Sahasranāma – 3rd name – *Vaṣaṭkāraḥ* – He is in the form of sacrifice.

713. *Oṃ Udgātre Namaḥ* I ॐ उद्गात्रे नमः ।

He is the chief priest who chants hymns from Sama Veda. The main acharya who performs homam.

714. *Oṃ Hotre Namaḥ* I ॐ होत्रे नमः ।

One who accepts all the sacrifices offered by devotees.

106th, 203rd and 391st names above may also be referred.

715. *Oṃ Svāhākārāya Namaḥ* I ॐ स्वाहाकाराय नमः ।

He is in the form of *Svaha* mantra.

Svaha and *Svadha* are two consorts of Lord *Agni*. *Svaha* or *Svadha* is uttered when something is offered in holy fire. Both *Svaha* and *Svadha* carry the offerings to the concerned to whom the offering was aimed at. *Svaha* is uttered when the offereing is for Devas/ Gods. *Svadha* is uttered when the offering is for *pitrus* (ancestors).

Lalita Sahasranamam – 535th name – *Svāhā* – and – 536th name – *Svadā* – She is in the forms of *Svāhā* and *Svadā*, the sacred exclamations with which oblations are made in sacrificial fire for Devas/ Gods/ Pitrus.

716. *Oṃ Hutāhutaye Namaḥ* I ॐ हुताहुतये नमः ।

He arranges to deliver the oblations just offered immediately to the concerned person to whom it was intended.

717. *Oṃ Janārdanāya Namaḥ* I ॐ जनार्दनाय नमः ।

He is the promulgator of Vedas.

He is an excited or agitated person. He is wicked, since he sends the sinners to hell.

He whom men (*Jana*) pray (*Ardanā*) for all kinds of prosperity and eternal happiness.

Usually, Lord Krishna or Vishnu is only addressed as *Janārdanān*. Here Lord Sun is addressed so. Hence Lord Vishnu and Sun are one and the same.

Vişhŋu Sahasranāma – 126th name – *Janārdanaḥ* – oppresser of men.

718. *Oṃ Janānandāya Namaḥ* I ॐ जनानन्दाय नमः ।

He is the head of human beings. He bestows supreme bliss to people.

719. *Oṃ Narāya Namaḥ* I ॐ नराय नमः ।

He is in the form of *Nara*.

This name goes together with the below 720th name.

720. *Oṃ Nārāyaṇāya Namaḥ* I ॐ नारायणाय नमः ।

He is in the form *Nārāyaṇa*.

Nara-Narayana is a duo of sage-brothers, generally regarded to be the partial-incarnation (*aṃśa-avatara*) of Vishnu, on earth. Nara means 'male being', and Narayana refers to Vishnu.

Monier-Williams dictionary says Nara is "the primeval Man or eternal Spirit pervading the universe always associated with Narayana, "son of the primeval man".

The scripture Mahabharata identifies the prince Arjuna with Nara, and the deity Krishna with Narayana. Here Lord Sun is in both the forms. The legend of Nara-Narayana is also mentioned in the scripture Bhagavata Purana. It is believed that the pair still dwells in a cave at Badrinath, where their most important temple is situated.

719th name above may also be referred.

721. *Oṃ Ambudāya Namaḥ* I ॐ अम्बुदाय नमः ।

He provides water to the Earth in the form of cloud.

722. *Oṃ Sandehanāśanāya Namaḥ* | ॐ सन्देहनाशनाय नमः ।

He frees his devotees from doubt.

No matter what, some people do, unnecessarily suspicious about everything and everybody. They do not trust anyone or anything. He clears such doubts.

723. *Oṃ Vāyave Namaḥ* | ॐ वायवे नमः ।

He is in the form Vāyu, the air god.

48th, 328th and 340th names above below may also be referred.

724. *Oṃ Dhanvine Namaḥ* | ॐ धन्विने नमः ।

He is armed with a bow (of course with arrows).

725. *Oṃ Suranamaskṛtāya Namaḥ* | ॐ सुरनमस्कृताय नमः ।

He is worshiped by the Devas. It is not unusual for humans to worship him. All Devas also always bow down him.

726. *Oṃ Vigrahine Namaḥ* | ॐ विग्रहिने नमः ।

He is the minister for war for Devas, i.e. commander-in-chief for Devas.

727. *Oṃ Vimalāya Namaḥ* | ॐ विमलाय नमः ।

He is stainlessly pure. *Mala* (impurity) belongs to *avidyā* (ignorance). Sun is the full form of knowledge. **He** is without ignorance and impurity.

Lalita Sahasranamam – 135th name – *Nirmalā* – and – 347th name – *Vimalā* – She is unsullied.

728. *Oṃ Vindave Namaḥ* | ॐ विन्दवे नमः ।

It is very difficult to realise/ reach him. He can be reached only by focused and dedicated devotion.

729. *Oṃ Viśokāya Namaḥ* | ॐ विशोकाय नमः ।

He has no sign of any grief. He removes all the sorrows of his devotees.

730. *Oṃ Vimaladyutaye Namaḥ* | ॐ विमलद्युतये नमः ।

He shines without any imperfection. When we see a full Moon there would be a stain-like mark. There is no such mark in Sun. mark

731. *Oṃ Dyutimate Namaḥ* | ॐ द्युतिमते नमः ।

As mentioned in many a name, he is shining brightly.

572nd name above may also be referred.

732. *Oṃ Dyotanāya Namaḥ* | ॐ द्योतनाय नमः ।

He only illuminates the whole world and hence enables us to see other things.

733. *Oṃ Vidyute Namaḥ* | ॐ विद्युते नमः ।

He has radiant eyes as bright as a lightning.

734. *Oṃ Vidyāvate Namaḥ* | ॐ विद्यावते नमः ।

He is highly learned.

489th & 645th names above may also be referred.

735. *Oṃ Viditāya Namaḥ* | ॐ विदिताय नमः ।

His perceiverance and understanding capacity is very high.

736. *Oṃ Baline Namaḥ* | ॐ बलिने नमः ।

He is mighty and robust. There is no one stronger than him.

737. *Oṃ Gharmadāya Namaḥ* । ॐ घर्मदाय नमः ।

He causes heat and he only creates heat.

Gāyatri Sahasranamam – 234th name – *Gharmadāyai* – She creates heat and makes the water of ocean as vapour and hence causes the rain.

738. *Oṃ Himadāya Namaḥ* । ॐ हिमदाय नमः ।

He is dispeller of dews. Early in the morning when the Sun started to rise, the dew drops on the flowers, leaves and tips of grasses start to get dispelled.

739. *Oṃ Hāsāya Namaḥ* । ॐ हासाय नमः ।

He is always smiling. He causes his devotees to laugh.

In the dhyana verse of Lalita Sahasranamam, she is addressed as *Smita Mukhīm* – one who has a smiling face.

740. *Oṃ Kṛṣṇavartmane Namaḥ* । ॐ कृष्णवर्त्मने नमः ।

His path is black. As soon as he passes the darkness creeps in, so that it becomes black.

741. *Oṃ Sutājitāya Namaḥ* । ॐ सुताजिताय नमः ।

He conquers/ attracts the children. This may not be much understood in tropical countries like India. But in cold countries this is very much true.

742. *Oṃ Sāvitrībhāvitāya Namaḥ* । ॐ सावित्रीभाविताय नमः ।

Souls of devotees are purified by meditating on the universal soul or whose thoughts are fixed on the Supreme Spirit through the Verses or prayers addressed to Sun.

743. *Oṃ Rājñe Namaḥ* । ॐ राज्ञे नमः ।

He is an emperor – king of kings.

676th name above may also be referred.

744. *Oṃ Viśvāmitrāya Namaḥ* | ॐ विश्वामित्राय नमः ।

He is a friend to all. He does not have foes.

307th name above may also be referred.

745. *Oṃ Ghṛṇaye Namaḥ* | ॐ घृणये नमः ।

He has a warm feeling towards others.

308th name above may also be referred.

746. *Oṃ Virāje Namaḥ* | ॐ विराजे नमः ।

He is without any stain or sin originated by the *Rajo* character.

309th name above may also be referred.

747. *Oṃ Saptārciṣe Namaḥ* | ॐ सप्तार्चिषे नमः ।

He rides in a chariot with seven horses.

75th, 188th & 686th names above and 748th, 749th, 757th, 758th & 854th names below may also be referred.

748. *Oṃ Saptaturagāya Namaḥ* | ॐ सप्ततुरगाय नमः ।

He rides in a chariot with seven horses.

Above 75th, 188th, 686th, 747th names and 749th, 757th, 758th & 854th names below may also be referred.

749. *Oṃ Saptalokanamaskṛtāya Namaḥ* | ॐ सप्तलोकनमस्कृताय नमः ।

He is worshipped by all the seven worlds.

Above 75th, 188th, 686th, 747th, 748th names and 757th, 758th & 854th names below may also be referred.

750. *Oṃ Sampūrṇāya Namaḥ* | ॐ सम्पूर्णाय नमः ।

He is the complete absolute entirely filled.

618th and 678th names above may also be referred.

751. *Oṃ Jagannāthāya Namaḥ* | ॐ जगन्नाथाय नमः ।

The lord of this whole world.

250th name above may also be referred.

752. *Oṃ Sumanase Namaḥ* | ॐ सुमनसे नमः ।

He is very good-minded. His mind never gets corrupted.

753. *Oṃ Śobhanapriyāya Namaḥ* | ॐ शोभनप्रियाय नमः ।

He is very fond of beauty/ welfare/ virtues.

754. *Oṃ Sarvātmane Namaḥ* | ॐ सर्वात्मने नमः ।

He is the soul of every being.

Śiva Sahasranamam – 8th name – *Sarvātmaḥ* – conveying the same meaning.

755. *Oṃ Sarvakṛte Namaḥ* | ॐ सर्वकृते नमः ।

He is the producer of anything and everything. We all are aware that no life or crop or plant can grow without Sunlight.

756. *Oṃ Sṛṣṭaye Namaḥ* | ॐ सृष्टये नमः ।

He is filled with every type of ornament.

757. *Oṃ Saptimate Namaḥ* | ॐ सप्तिमते नमः ।

He rides in a chariot with seven horses.

75th, 188th, 686th, 747th, 748th & 749th names above and 758th & 854th name below may also be referred.

758. *Oṃ Saptamīpriyāya Namaḥ* | ॐ सप्तमीप्रियाय नमः ।

He is fond of Saptami tithi (7th day of lunar cycle).

We all are aware that Bheeshma attained Moksha after waiting on Ratha Saptami day. It is customary for everyone to do Tarpanam to Surya on that day.

75th, 188th, 686th, 747th, 748th, 749th & 757th names above and 854th name below may also be referred.

759. *Oṃ Sumedhase Namaḥ* । ॐ सुमेधसे नमः ।

He is very nourishing. He bestows nourishment to his devotees.

Sumedhas is the name of the Manu, in-charge of fifth manvantaram. He is in that form.

Sumedhas is a particular class of ancestors. He is the head of that class.

Viṣṇu Sahasranamam – 752nd name – *Sumedhā* – he is of bright intelligence.

760. *Oṃ Medhikāya Namaḥ* । ॐ मेधिकाय नमः ।

He is unequivocally intelligent.

761. *Oṃ Medhyāya Namaḥ* । ॐ मेध्याय नमः ।

He consistently display his intelligence.

762. *Oṃ Medhāvine Namaḥ* । ॐ मेधाविने नमः ।

He is a very learned teacher.

984th name below may also be referred.

763. *Oṃ Madhusūdanāya Namaḥ* । ॐ मधुसूदनाय नमः ।

The slayer of the demon called Madhu.

Usually, Lord Vishnu is called as *Madhusūdanan*. Here Lord Sun is address so, since there is no difference between Lord Vishnu and Sun.

It is mentioned in Mahabharata – The Virat Purusha slew the great Asura Madhu born to Karnamishra, in compliance with the request of Brahma. Hence the sages, Devas and others started to call him as *Madhusūdanan.*

Sri Devi Mahatmyam, first chapter is about slaying the twin demons Madhu and Kaidabha by Lord Vishnu, with the background support from Sri Devi.

Viṣŋu Sahasranamam – 73rd name – *Madhusūdanaḥ* – slayer of Madhu.

764. *Oṃ Aṅgiraḥpataye Namaḥ* । ॐ अङ्गिरःपतये नमः ।

Aṅgiraḥ = hymns of Atharva Veda. They are mostly about Lord Sun. Hence, he is the Lord of *Aṅgiraḥ*.

765. *Oṃ Kālajñāya Namaḥ* । ॐ कालज्ञाय नमः ।

He knows the fixed times or seasons. He is a great astrologer.

766. *Oṃ Dhūmaketave Namaḥ* । ॐ धूमकेतवे नमः ।

Dhūmaketu means meteor, fire, comet and smoke marked. He is in all these forms.

767. *Oṃ Suketanāya Namaḥ* । ॐ सुकेतनाय नमः ।

He always has good intentions and bestow benevolents to his devotees.

768. *Oṃ Sukhine Namaḥ* । ॐ सुखिने नमः ।

He is always happy.

355th name above may also be referred.

769. *Oṃ Sukhapradāya Namaḥ* । ॐ सुखप्रदाय नमः ।

He is the bestower of pleasures to his devotees.

354th & 357th names above may also be referred.

770. *Oṃ Saukhyāya Namaḥ* । ॐ सौख्याय नमः ।

He gives comfort to all.

358th name above may also be referred.

771. *Oṃ Kāmine Namaḥ* । ॐ कामिने नमः ।

He loves all and he is loved by all.

Since he possess all good qualities, he is desired by all.

He destroys all the desires.

772. *Oṃ Kāntaye Namaḥ* । ॐ कान्तये नमः ।

Since He is effulgent, he looks like the Ultimate beauty. The luster is the beauty and brightness of the body.

66th name above may also be referred.

773. *Oṃ Kāntipriyāya Namaḥ* । ॐ कान्तिप्रियाय नमः ।

He is fond of beauty enhanced by love.

774. *Oṃ Munaye Namaḥ* । ॐ मुनये नमः ।

He is in-charge of Ursa Major. Ursa Major, also known as the Great Bear, is a constellation in the northern sky that includes the Big Dipper asterism. It is the third largest constellation in the sky and the largest in the Northern Hemisphere.

775. *Oṃ Santāpanāya Namaḥ* । ॐ सन्तापनाय नमः ।

He does the act of afflicting burning.

776th name below may also be referred.

776. *Oṃ Santapanāya Namaḥ* । ॐ सन्तपनाय नमः ।

He is in a tormenting warm status.

775th name above may also be referred.

777. *Oṃ Ātapāya Namaḥ* | ॐ आतपाय नमः ।

He is hot like anything.

778. *Oṃ Tapasāṃ Pataye Namaḥ* | ॐ तपसां पतये नमः ।

He is head of ascetincs/ sages.

779. *Oṃ Umāpataye Namaḥ* | ॐ उमापतये नमः ।

He is the Lord of Uma.

543rd name above may also be referred.

780. *Oṃ Sahasrāṃśave Namaḥ* | ॐ सहस्रांशवे नमः ।

He is with thousand rays.

264th & 622nd names above may also be referred.

781. *Oṃ Priyakāriṇe Namaḥ* | ॐ प्रियकारिणे नमः ।

He shows the act of kindness to all, including the sinners.

782. *Oṃ Priyaṅkarāya Namaḥ* | ॐ प्रियङ्कराय नमः ।

He is excitingly or attractingly pleasing to look at.

783. *Oṃ Prītaye Namaḥ* | ॐ प्रीतये नमः ।

He is always in a pleased or delighted or satisfied mind.

784. *Oṃ Vimanyave Namaḥ* | ॐ विमन्यवे नमः ।

He is distinguishly honoured person.

785. *Oṃ Ambhotthāya Namaḥ* | ॐ अम्भोत्थाय नमः ।

He creates water-born clouds.

786. *Oṃ Khañjanāya Namaḥ* I ॐ खञ्जनाय नमः ।

He is in the form of God of Love, Cupid (*Manmata*).

787. *Oṃ Jagatāṃ Pataye Namaḥ* I ॐ जगतां पतये नमः ।

He is the head of this universe.

Śiva Sahasranamam – 1,008th name – *Jagataḥ* – He is this world.

788. *Oṃ Jagatpitre Namaḥ* I ॐ जगत्पित्रे नमः ।

He is the father of this whole world.

Normally Lord Shiva is said to be the father of this world (*Jagatpita*) and Sri Devi as mother of this world (*Jaganmatha*).

In the Raghuvamsam (1-10) Kalidasa refers to Parvati and Parameshvara as "*Jagataḥ Pitharou*". *'Pitharou'* means parents. The suffix *'Rou'* means dual number.

Vāgarthāviva Sampruktou Vāgarthapratipattaye I
Jagataḥ Pitarou Vande Pārvatiparameśvarou II

789. *Oṃ Prītamanase Namaḥ* I ॐ प्रीतमनसे नमः ।

He is in a pleased or gratified status of mind.

790. *Oṃ Sarvāya Namaḥ* I ॐ सर्वाय नमः ।

He is entirely everything in the universe.

791. *Oṃ Kharvāya Namaḥ* I ॐ खर्वाय नमः ।

His devotees are large in number.

792. *Oṃ Guhāya Namaḥ* I ॐ गुहाय नमः ।

He is concealed, in the cave called the heart of the devotees.

205th name above may also be referred.

793. *Oṃ Acalāya Namaḥ* I ॐ अचलाय नमः ।

He is constantly static/ immobile.

794. *Oṃ Sarvagāya Namaḥ* I ॐ सर्वगाय नमः ।

He consists wholly of the Gayatri (mantra).

660th name above and 945th name below may also be referred.

795. *Oṃ Jagadānandāya Namaḥ* I ॐ जगदानन्दाय नमः ।

He rejoices the whole world.

796. *Oṃ Jagannetre Namaḥ* I ॐ जगन्नेत्रे नमः ।

He is the eyes of this world. Nothing can be missed out of his sight.

534th name above can also be referred.

797. *Oṃ Surārighne Namaḥ* I ॐ सुरारिघ्ने नमः ।

He destroys the enemies of the Devas. On and off there used to be battles between Devas and Demons. Always the demons are destoyed.

798. *Oṃ Śreyase Namaḥ* I ॐ श्रेयसे नमः ।

He bestows welfare and ultimately bliss to his devotees.

799. *Oṃ Śreyaskarāya Namaḥ* I ॐ श्रेयस्कराय नमः ।

He is conducive to happiness or prosperity.

800. *Oṃ Jyāyase Namaḥ* I ॐ ज्यायसे नमः ।

He is the greatest among all. There is no one equal or above him.

Thus ends 100 divine names on Lord *Sūrya* from 701 to 800.

*****

801. *Oṃ Mahate Namaḥ* | ॐ महते नमः |

He is a great person fit to be worshipped.

371st & 473rd names above and 925th & 986th names below may also be referred.

802. *Oṃ Uttamāya Namaḥ* | ॐ उत्तमाय नमः |

He is an excellent person. No one can be better than him.

804th name below may also be referred.

803. *Oṃ Udbhavāya Namaḥ* | ॐ उद्भवाय नमः |

The universe originated from him. Samsara came to existence through him, but he is free from Samsara.

Viṣṇu Sahasranamam – 373rd name – *Udbhavaḥ* – He is responsible for the origin of everything.

804. *Oṃ Uttamāya Namaḥ* | ॐ उत्तमाय नमः |

He is an excellent person.

802nd name above may also be referred.

805. *Oṃ Merumeyāya Namaḥ* | ॐ मेरुमेयाय नमः |

He is the backbone of every activity of the world.

According to the saying – *Meruḥ Sumeruḥ Hemādriḥ* – *Meru* is a golden mountain.

The gem called *Meru* in the garland of chanting or when counted in fingers, the base line of the middle finger of the palm is called *Meru*. He has this place as his dwelling.

Lalitā Sahasranāmam – 775th name – *Merunilayā* – She dwells in the *Meru*. It is customary to worship Mahameru and/ or Sri Chakram as Sri Devi herself.

806. *Oṃ Athāya Namaḥ* | ॐ अथाय नमः ।

Noone is comparable to him or above him.

807. *Oṃ Dharaṇāya Namaḥ* | ॐ धरणाय नमः ।

He sends beam of light rays in a row or line to the Earth.

808. *Oṃ Dharaṇīdharāya Namaḥ* | ॐ धरणीधराय नमः ।

He sustains the earth.

Viṣṇu Sahasranamam – 235th name – *Dharaṇīdharaḥ* – He is the sustainer of this earth in the form of Adhisesha or Boar.

809. *Oṃ Dharādhyakṣāya Namaḥ* ॐ धराध्यक्षाय नमः ।

He supports the Earth. He supports the mountains.

Viṣṇu Sahasranamam – 756th name – *Dharādharaḥ* – He supports the mountains. In his Krishna incarnation he lifted the Govardhana Mountain.

810. *Oṃ Dharmarājāya Namaḥ* | ॐ धर्मराजाय नमः ।

He is a just or a righteous king. Rules/ laws conceived as a king.

Generally, *Yama*, the king of death, is called as *Dharmarāja*. In Mahabharata, his son Yudhishthira was also called as *Dharmaraja*. Here Lord Sun is called so, since he is in that form.

811. *Oṃ Dharmā Dharma Pravartakāya Namaḥ* |
ॐ धर्माधर्मप्रवर्तकाय नमः ।

He only promotes or sets in motion/ action both Dharma and Adharma.

860th and 978th names below may also be referred.

812. *Oṃ Rathādhyakṣāya Namaḥ* ॐ रथाध्यक्षाय नमः ।

He is the leader of all chariots.

813. *Oṃ Rathagataye Namaḥ* । ॐ रथगतये नमः ।

He only decides the path of the chariot(s). He always moves in a chariot.

814. *Oṃ Taruṇāya Namaḥ* । ॐ तरुणाय नमः ।

He is always young and fresh.

815. *Oṃ Tanitāya Namaḥ* । ॐ तनिताय नमः ।

He is very slender. He is the youngest of all.

Earlier in one name, he was mentioned as the eldest of all. Here it is said that he is the youngest. In Sri Rudra Namakam, Lord Shiva is addressed as *Jyeşţāya* and *Kanişţāya* – he is both eldest and youngest.

816. *Oṃ Analāya Namaḥ* । ॐ अनलाय नमः ।

He acts like fire. His energies and powers are unlimited.

389th, 522nd & 639th names above and 898th name below may also be referred.

817. *Oṃ Uttarāya Namaḥ* । ॐ उत्तराय नमः ।

He moves towards North. This name has to be read in coherence with the next name.

818. *Oṃ Anuttarastāpine Namaḥ* । ॐ अनुत्तरस्तापिने नमः ।

He moves towards South. In a year, he travels towards south for six months (Dakshinayanam) and travels towards North (Uttarayanam) for another six months.

Anuttara is a class of Gods among Jains. He is in that form. It was earlier itself mentioned that Jains also worship Sun God.

819. *Oṃ Avākpataye Namaḥ* । ॐ अवाक्पतये नमः ।

He is the Lord of Southern hemisphere.

820. *Oṃ Apāṃ Pataye Namaḥ* | ॐ अपां पतये नमः ।

In continuation of the previous name, he is the Lord of Norther hemisphere also.

Why this has to be mentioned in a split way? During Dakshinayanam he rules over southern hemisphere and during uttarayanam he rules over northern hemisphere.

821. *Oṃ Puṇyasaṅkīrtanāya Namaḥ* | ॐ पुण्यसङ्कीर्तनाय नमः ।

He praises, glorifies and celebrates virtues.

822. *Oṃ Puṇyāya Namaḥ* | ॐ पुण्याय नमः ।

He is virtue personified. He nullifies the sins of his devotees by his very thought.

Vişŋu Sahasranamam – 687th & 925th names – *Puṇyaḥ* – He is very holy.

823. *Oṃ Hetave Namaḥ* | ॐ हेतवे नमः ।

He is the material and instrumental cause of everything.

Vişŋu Sahasranamam – 366th name – *Hetuḥ* – He is the means of the desired things.

824. *Oṃ Lokatrayāśrayāya Namaḥ* | ॐ लोकत्रयाश्रयाय नमः ।

He protects all the three worlds.

825. *Oṃ Svarbhānave Namaḥ* | ॐ स्वर्भानवे नमः ।

He shines like a gem.

826. *Oṃ Vigatānandāya Namaḥ* | ॐ विगतानन्दाय नमः ।

He does not have a specific dwelling house.

We always connect Lord Vishnu to Vaikuntam, Lord Shiva to Kailash, Sri Devi to Sripuram, etc. In the similar fashion we are not able to connect any specific place to Lord Sun.

827. *Oṃ Viśiṣṭotkṛṣṭakarmakṛte Namaḥ* । ॐ विशिष्टोत्कृष्टकर्मकृते नमः ।

He is peculiarly outstanding and prominent skillful in work.

828. *Oṃ Vyādhipraṇāśanāya Namaḥ* । ॐ व्याधिप्रणाशनाय नमः ।

He causes to disappear the diseases of his devotees.

829. *Oṃ Kṣemāya Namaḥ* । ॐ क्षेमाय नमः ।

He ensures his devotees to rest safely. He blesses final emancipation to his devotees.

830. *Oṃ Śūrāya Namaḥ* । ॐ शूराय नमः ।

He is a great warrior for good.

831. *Oṃ Sarvajitāṃ Varāya Naṃaḥ* । ॐ सर्वजितां वराय नमः ।

He bestows the boon of success in all endeavours of his devotees.

832. *Oṃ Ekarathāya Namaḥ* । ॐ एकरथाय नमः ।

He is an eminent warrior.

833. *Oṃ Rathādhīśāya Namaḥ* । ॐ रथाधीशाय नमः ।

He is a lord or master of chariots.

834. *Oṃ Śanaiścarasyanamaḥ* । ॐ शनैश्चरस्यनमः ।

He moves slowly.

Lord Saturn is called as *Śanaiścaran*, since he moves slowly – he takes 30 years to complete one cycle of all the 12 rashis. Lord Sun is in that form.

835. *Oṃ Pitre Namaḥ* I ॐ पित्रे नमः ।

He is the father of all – *Jagatpita*.

836. *Oṃ Vaivasvata Gurave Namaḥ* I ॐ वैवस्वत गुरवे नमः ।

Vaivasvata indicates Saturn, Yama or one of the Manus. He is the Guru (teacher) of all those.

837. *Oṃ Mṛtyave Namaḥ* I ॐ मृत्यवे नमः ।

He is the Lord of death.

838. *Oṃ Dharmanityāya Namaḥ* I ॐ धर्मनित्याय नमः ।

He is eternally hooked to *Dharma*. He never deviates from *Dharma* for any reason, whatsoever.

839. *Oṃ Mahāvratāya Namaḥ* I ॐ महाव्रताय नमः ।

He has undertaken solemn religious duties or vows.

840. *Oṃ Pralambahārasañcāriṇe Namaḥ* I ॐ प्रलम्बहारसञ्चारिणे नमः ।

He wanders after slaying Pralambasura. Pralambasura is a demon in Hindu mythology who was killed by Lord Sun in the form of Balarama. Pralambasura represents lusty desires that disguise themselves as friends and promise pleasure.

Pralambasura is mentioned in the Vishnu Purana and the Mahabharata. Pralambasura disguised himself as a cowherd and tried to join Krishna and Balarama in a game. Pralambasura lost the game and was forced to carry Balarama on his back. Pralambasura then transformed into a larger form and tried to run away with Balarama, but Krishna stopped him. Balarama then attacked Pralambasura and killed him.

841. *Oṃ Pradyotāya Namaḥ* I ॐ प्रद्योताय नमः ।

He irradicates darkness and illuminates this world.

Darkness should be construed as ignorance of human being and illumination is eradicating the ignorance and showing the path to understand the Brahmam.

842. *Oṃ Dyotitānalāya Namaḥ* । ॐ द्योतितानलाय नमः ।

He is Illustrated as abodeless.

843. *Oṃ Santāpahṛte Namaḥ* । ॐ सन्तापहृते नमः ।

He removes heat and cools everything.

In reality, what we all consider, is Sun creates heat. But ironically, it is mentioned as he removes heat.

844. *Oṃ Parasmai Namaḥ* । ॐ परस्मै नमः ।

He is the Supreme. There is no one above or equal to him.

845. *Oṃ Mantrāya Namaḥ* । ॐ मन्त्राय नमः ।

He is enchanted/ mesmerised with spells or charms.

888th name below may also be referred.

846. *Oṃ Mantramūrtaye Namaḥ* । ॐ मन्त्रमूर्तये नमः ।

He is mantras personified.

Mantras, both in Hinduism and Buddhism, a sacred utterance (syllable, word, or verse) that is considered to possess mystical or spiritual efficacy. Mantras need to be chant without moving the lips, i.e., merely sounded internally in one's thoughts and they are repeated continuously for some time. Thus, repetition of or meditation on a particular mantra can induce a trancelike state in the participant and can lead him to a higher level of spiritual awareness.

It is said that there are seven crores (70 million) of *mantras*. He is in the form of all these *mantras*. Or His form itself is these *mantras*.

Mantras are also classified as *āgneya* (fiery) and *saumya* (pleasing).

They should be repeated at the beginning and end of the asterisms and the halves. The *āgneya* mantra is generally laid down as having the asterism at the end and the fire and the ether (in greater proportions). The rest are said to be *saumya*.

The concerned Gods are in the form of relevant mantras. The sages have categorically stressed that the respective deities exist in the form of the relevant mantra itself. Mantras have different number of letters. A mantra shastra text called *Mahodati* names different mantras based on the number of letters it has. A mantra with one syllable is called ***pindam***. The two-syllable mantra is called ***Karttree***. Mantras with three to nine syllables are called ***beejam***, mantras of ten to twenty syllables are called ***mantras***, mantras of more than twenty syllables are called ***mala-mantras***. For example;

- Single lettered mantra called a *bījamantra* or *bījākṣara – Oṃ*
- Two lettered mantra – *Rāma*
- Five lettered mantra – *Pancākṣara*
- Eight lettered mantra – *Oṃ Namo Nārāyaŋāya*
- Twelve lettered mantra – *Oṃ Namo Bhagavate Vāsudevāya*
- 15 lettered mantra – Sri Vidya – *Pancadashī*
- 16 lettered mantra – *Śoḍashī*
- 24 lettered mantra – *Gāyatri* mantra.
- And so on. There are mantras with 90+ letters also.

He is in the form of *mantras* in the method of worshipping called *Mantratva*, one of the six *tattvas*

Lalitā Sahasranāma – 204th name – *Sarvamantrasvarūpiŋī* – She is in the form (very essence) of all *mantras*.

847. *Oṃ Mahābalāya Namaḥ* | ॐ महाबलाय नमः |

Balā means strong. *Mahābalā* means very powerful.

17th name above may also be referred.

848. *Oṃ Śreṣṭhātmane Namaḥ* | ॐ श्रेष्ठात्मने नमः |

He is the most excellence and superior *Atma*.

The second of the five-Brahma aspects of Lord Shiva is *Vāmadevā*. The corresponding mantra in Sri Rudra Namakam says – he is the *Jyeṣṭha* and *Śreṣṭha*.

Vāmadevāya Namo Jyeṣṭhāya Namaḥ
Śreṣṭhāya Namo Rudrāya Namaḥ Kālāya Namaḥ |

I bow down to Vamadeva; I pay homage to the great and I bow down to the most excellent.

849. *Oṃ Supriyāya Namaḥ* | ॐ सुप्रियाय नमः ।

He is sweet hearted, very dear and pleasant.

850. *Oṃ Śambhave Namaḥ* | ॐ शम्भवे नमः ।

He is so much helpful to his devotees.

The word *Śambhu* normally denotes Lord Shiva. Lord Sun is in that form and hence he Is also addressed in the same manner.

Śambhu is one of the sons of Lord Vishnu. He is in that form.

851. *Oṃ Marutāmīśvareśvarāya Namaḥ* | ॐ मरुतामीश्वरेश्वराय नमः ।

Marut is the God of various types of winds and fragrances. He is in the lord of all those.

852. *Oṃ Saṃsāragativicchettre Namaḥ* | ॐ संसारगतिविच्छेत्त्रे नमः ।

He is the protector of his devotees from *Saṃsāra* – The circuit of mundane existence.

236th name above & 853rd name below may also be referred.

853. *Oṃ Saṃsārārṇavatārakāya Namaḥ* | ॐ संसारार्णवतारकाय नमः ।

He is the protector of his devotees from *Saṃsāra* – The circuit of mundane existence.

236th & 852nd names above may also be referred.

854. *Oṃ Saptajihvāya Namaḥ* । ॐ सप्तजिह्वाय नमः ।

He has seven tongues. Usually Agni, the fire god is said to be with seven tongues. Here Lord Sun is said so. That means Agni and Sun are one and the same.

75th, 188th 686th, 747th, 748th, 749th, 757th & 758th names above may also be referred.

855. *Oṃ Sahasrārciṣe Namaḥ* । ॐ सहस्रार्चिषे नमः ।

Thousand rayed Lord. It has been mentioned in this Sahasranamam in multiple places about thousands of rays of Lord Sun.

856. *Oṃ Ratnagarbhāya Namaḥ* । ॐ रत्नगर्भाय नमः ।

He is filled (pregnant) with precious stones/ jewels. He bestows his devotees with precious jewels.

Viṣŋu Sahasranamam – 473rd name – *Ratnagarbhaḥ* – jewel wombed.

857. *Oṃ Aparājitāya Namaḥ* । ॐ अपराजिताय नमः ।

He is undefeated/ unconquered. Nobody can win over him.

858. *Oṃ Dharmaketave Namaḥ* । ॐ धर्मकेतवे नमः ।

He has justice as his exceptional character.

859. *Oṃ Ameyātmane Namaḥ* । ॐ अमेयात्मने नमः ।

He is of indefinable nature possessing immense powers.

Viṣŋu Sahasranamam – 102nd & 179th names – *Ameyātmā* – he is of remarkable intelligence that cannot be measured.

860. *Oṃ Dharmā Dharmavara Pradāya Namaḥ* ।
ॐ धर्माधर्मवरप्रदाय नमः ।

He only promotes or sets in motion/ action both Dharma and Adharma.

811th name above and 978th name below may also be referred.

861. *Oṃ Lokasākṣiṇe Namaḥ* । ॐ लोकसाक्षिणे नमः ।

He is the witness for the entire world. No activity in this world can miss his sight.

862. *Oṃ Lokagurave Namaḥ* । ॐ लोकगुरवे नमः ।

He is the teacher (*guru*) for the entire world.

He is the promulgator of all *Vidyas*. He is the supreme guru to all from Brahma onwards.

The confirmed opinion of the *mantra sāstras* is – the teacher, the *mantra* and the deity are all one and the same and should not be distinguished.

Aruŋagirināda also sings about Lord Muruga as
"Guruvāi Varuvāi Arulvāi Guhane".

Gu means darkness of ignorance and *Ru* removes that. Hence the word *Guru* itself means removing of the darkness of ignorance.

The letter *Gu* is an existence (*Sat* letter) and *Ru* is knowledge (of *Brahmam*) and because one is with the knowledge of *Brahmam*, he is called *guru*.

Vişŋu Sahasranamam – 209th name – *Guruḥ* – he is the teacher.

Lalitā Sahasranamam – 603rd name – *Gurumūrtiḥ* – She assumes the form of a teacher.

863. *Oṃ Lokeśāya Namaḥ* । ॐ लोकेशाय नमः ।

He is the lord of the world.

864. *Oṃ Caṇḍavāhanāya Namaḥ* । ॐ चण्डवाहनाय नमः ।

He has impetuous heat as his vehicle. He only creates the heat and he lives with it.

865. *Oṃ Dharmayūpāya Namaḥ* | ॐ धर्मयूपाय नमः ।

He has *Dharma* as his way (means) of living. He does not deviate from *Dharma* at any point of time.

866. *Oṃ Yūpavṛkṣāya Namaḥ* | ॐ यूपवृक्षाय नमः ।

He is in the form of holy/ sacrificial tree. When the Milky Ocean was churned for getting *Amruta,* holy Karpaga tree occurred from it. He is in that form.

867. *Oṃ Dhanuṣpāṇaye Namaḥ* | ॐ धनुष्पाणये नमः ।

He is armed with a bow. It is very usual for every God to hold one or other weapon. In that fashion, he holds a bow and arrows.

868. *Oṃ Dhanurdharāya Namaḥ* | ॐ धनुर्धराय नमः ।

He is a great archer. In the previous name it was mentioned that he holds a bow. One has to be an archer to hold a bow.

Viṣṇu Sahasranamam – 857th name – *Dhanurdharaḥ* – the wielder of the bow. In his incarnation as Rama, he wielded the bow.

869. *Oṃ Pinākadhṛte Namaḥ* | ॐ पिनाकधृते नमः ।

Pinākam is name of the bow in the hands of Lord Shiva and hence he is called as *Pinākapāṇi*. Lord Sun in the form of Lord Shiva holds it.

Sri Rudra Namakam (10.10) – *Ācara Pinākaṃ Vibhradāgahi* || –you have your bow called *Pinākaṃ* only for decoration. The idea is that there will not be any need to use it.

870. *Oṃ Mahotsāhāya Namaḥ* | ॐ महोत्साहाय नमः ।

He has great power or strength or energy. He is always in happy mood.

871. *Oṃ Mahāmāyāya Namaḥ* । ॐ महामायाय नमः ।

Māyā is illusion. *Mahāmāyā* is great illusion. He is in that form.

174th name above may also be referred.

872. *Oṃ Mahāśanāya Namaḥ* । ॐ महाशनाय नमः ।

He is a voracious eater. Sun's heat eats everything in this world and hence this name.

In *Mahabharata*, *Bheema*, second of the Pandavas, is called as *Mahāśanān*, since he is also a voracious eater.

873. *Oṃ Vīrāya Namaḥ* । ॐ वीराय नमः ।

He is a great warrior. No one can win over him.

874. *Oṃ Śaktimatāṃ Śreṣṭhāya Namaḥ* । ॐ शक्तिमतां श्रेष्ठाय नमः ।

He is the greatest among all those who are special with energy.

554th name above may also be referred.

875. *Oṃ Sarvaśastrabhṛtāṃ Varāya Namaḥ* ।
ॐ सर्वशस्त्रभृतां वराय नमः ।

He carries all types of *Shastrams*. He bestows all shastras as boon to his worshippers.

In archery when a bow is aimed with some mantras it is called *Astram*. When an enemy sends an *Astram*, a counter missile is being sent – for instance *Varuṇāstram* against *Agniastram*, *Garudāstram* against *Nāgāstram* and so on. The original missile is called *Astram* and that counter missile is called *Śastram*.

876. *Oṃ Jñānagamyāya Namaḥ* । ॐ ज्ञानगम्याय नमः ।

He is attainable only by well understanding him.

He is difficult to worship by the incompetent and for those who cannot control their senses and sensory organs. Impossible to be worshipped by the fickle-minded.

877. *Oṃ Durārādhyāya Namaḥ* | ॐ दुराराध्याय नमः ।

It is very difficult to propitiate or win or overcome him.

Soundaryalaharee 95th verse says – *Taralakaraṇānā-Masulabhā* – To control the senses and to have focus in the mind lot of effort is required and it is very difficult.

Lalitā Sahasranamam – 771st name – *Durārādhyā* – She is difficult to understand.

878. *Oṃ Lohitāṅgāya Namaḥ* | ॐ लोहिताङ्गाय नमः ।

He is red in colour. He is in the form of Mars, who is red in colour.

879. *Oṃ Vivardhanāya Namaḥ* | ॐ विवर्धनाय नमः ।

He blesses prosperity and growth to his devotees.

936th name below may also be referred.

880. *Oṃ Khagāya Namaḥ* | ॐ खगाय नमः ।

He is the wind god.

158th & 431st names above may also be referred.

881. *Oṃ Andhāya Namaḥ* | ॐ अन्धाय नमः ।

He makes others blind. Anyone seeing him with naked eye, especially during eclipse will become blind.

882. *Oṃ Dharmadāya Namaḥ* | ॐ धर्मदाय नमः ।

He gives or grants virtues to all.

883. *Oṃ Nityāya Namaḥ* | ॐ नित्याय नमः ।

He is eternal. The soul is eternal.

183rd & 210th names above may also be referred.

884. *Oṃ Dharmakṛte Namaḥ* | ॐ धर्मकृते नमः ।

He is virtuous and ensure maintenance of order.

885. *Oṃ Citravikramāya Namaḥ* | ॐ चित्रविक्रमाय नमः ।

He has stable strength.

886. *Oṃ Bhagavate Namaḥ* | ॐ भगवते नमः ।

He is with complete wealth, charity, fame, liberation, etc.

707th name above and 944th & 1,006th name below may also be referred.

887. *Oṃ Ātmavate Namaḥ* | ॐ आत्मवते नमः ।

He is a self-possessed soul.

888. *Oṃ Mantrāya Namaḥ* | ॐ मन्त्राय नमः ।

He is enchanted/ mesmirised with spells or charms.

845th name above may also be referred.

889. *Oṃ Tryakṣarāya Namaḥ* | ॐ त्र्यक्षराय नमः ।

His name consists of three syllables (*Āditya*). He is in the form of all three syllable mantras.

893rd name below may also be referred.

890. *Oṃ Nīlalohitāya Namaḥ* | ॐ नीललोहिताय नमः ।

He is in dark-blue and red mixed or purple colour.

Lord Shiva is usually addressed as *Nīlalohitaḥ* in Sri Rudra Namakam (10.1). This means that his body is half black and half red. i.e. Lord Shiva's part is red and Uma Devi's part is black.

Among the 11 Rudras invoked in 11 kalasas, 5th Rudran is Nīlalohitaḥ.

891. *Oṃ Ekāya Namaḥ* I ॐ एकाय नमः ।

He is the only God.

435th name above may also be referred.

892. *Oṃ Anekāya Namaḥ* I ॐ अनेकाय नमः ।

In contradiction to the previous name a single form, this name denotes he is in multiple form.

He takes various forms at his own wish, during different incarnations to protect the world.

Viṣŋu Sahasranamam – 721st name – *Anekamūrtiḥ* – He is many-formed.

893. *Oṃ Trayine Namaḥ* I ॐ त्रयिने नमः ।

He is in the form of all triples – for instance;

- Three *Guṇas – Sathwa, Rajas, Tamas*
- Three *Mūrties – Brahma, Viṣŋu, Śiva*
- Three *Rāmas – Balarāma, Śrirāma, Paraśurāma*
- Three *Agnis – Āhavanīyāgni, Gārhapatyāgni, Dākṣināgni*
- Three *Vyāhritis – Bhūḥ, Bhuvaḥ, Suvaḥ*

He is the embodiment of three *Vedas – Rig, Yajus* and *Sāma* – it has become a practice to address these three *Vedas* as triple revelation. It can be noted that the *Atharva* Veda is later addition.

This name indicates the three *kāndās* (sections) of each of the four *Vedas – karma* (action), *upāsanā* (devotional practice) and *gnāna* (knowledge).

The verses of *Rig, Yajus* and *Sāma Vedas* (*Agnimeele, Ishetvā, Agna Āyāhi*) begins with the syllables *A, E* and *A*. According to Samskruta grammar, if these letters are merged, we get the letter I. According to *tantras* it is called as *Trayee*.

Lalita Sahasranamam – 872nd name – *Trayī* – She is the embodiment of three *Vedas* – *Rig, Yajus* and *Sāma*.

889th name above may also be referred.

894. *Oṃ Kālāya Namaḥ* I ॐ कालाय नमः ।

He is in the form of time. He causes the calculation of time.

146th name above may also be referred.

895. *Oṃ Savitre Namaḥ* I ॐ सवित्रे नमः ।

One who is full of rays.

47th, 121st & 334th names above may also be referred.

896. *Oṃ Samitiñjayāya Namaḥ* I ॐ समितिञ्जयाय नमः ।

He is always victorious in all battles. He is eminent in an assembly.

He is the destroyer of all pains of all the *jeevas*.

Viṣṇu Sahasranamam – 362nd name – *Samitinjayaḥ* – He is always victorious.

897. *Oṃ Śārṅgadhanvane Namaḥ* ॐ शार्ङ्गधन्वने नमः ।

He is armed with a bow called *Śārṅgam*. The bow of Lord Vishnu is called *Śārṅgam*. He is in the form of Lord *Vishnu* and hence he is called as *Śārṅgadhanvane*.

898. *Oṃ Analāya Namaḥ* I ॐ अनलाय नमः ।

He acts like fire. His energies and powers are unlimited.

389th, 522nd, 639th and 816th names above may also be referred.

899. *Oṃ Bhīmāya Namaḥ* I ॐ भीमाय नमः ।

He is awesome, tremendous and terrific.

He is, who everyone fears. Or else, if the '*A*' is prefixed it becomes *Abhīmā* – causing no fear to those who follow righteous path.

Katopanishat (6-2) – it is a great fear like an uplifted thunder-bolt.

Vişŋu Sahasranamam – 357th & 948th names – *Bhīmaḥ* – He is awe-inspiring. He is the terror.

900. *Oṃ Sarvapraharaṇāyudhāya Namaḥ* I ॐ सर्वप्रहरणायुधाय नमः ।

He is armed with all types of weapons.

He wields all kinds of destructive weapons.

Vişŋu Sahasranamam – 1000th name – *Sarvapraharaṇāyudhaḥ* – He is armed with all kinds of destructive weapons.

Thus ends 100 divine names on Lord *Sūrya* from 801 to 900.

*****

901. *Oṃ Sukarmaṇe Namaḥ* । ॐ सुकर्मणे नमः ।

He always performs virtuous activities.

He is a good architect – *Vishwakarma* is the architect for Devas and *Mayan* is the architect for demons. Together these two architects created the city of Sripura for Sri Devi and Indraprastha for the Pandavas. He is in both their forms.

902. *Oṃ Parameṣṭhine Namaḥ* । ॐ परमेष्ठिने नमः ।

Parameṣṭhina is the superior or chief god of Jains. He is in that form.

903. *Oṃ Nākapāline Namaḥ* । ॐ नाकपालिने नमः ।

He is the guardian of skies.

904. *Oṃ Divisthitāya Namaḥ* । ॐ दिविस्थिताय नमः ।

He always stays in sky – not in any of the worlds.

905. *Oṃ Vadānyāya Namaḥ* । ॐ वदान्याय नमः ।

He always speaks kindly, agreeably, fair enough and convincingly.

906. *Oṃ Vāsukaye Namaḥ* । ॐ वासुकये नमः ।

He is very divine.

He is in the form of *Vāsuki*, the snake used as a rope while churning the milky ocean for nectar.

907. *Oṃ Vaidyāya Namaḥ* । ॐ वैद्याय नमः ।

He is a very great physician. He is a master all *Vidyas*.

Viṣṇu Sahasranamam – 164th name – *Vaidhyaḥ* – He is a physician.

908. *Oṃ Ātreyāya Namaḥ* । ॐ आत्रेयाय नमः ।

He is a descendant of sage *Atreya*. Sage Atreya was a renowned scholar of Ayurveda and a school of early Ayurveda was founded based on his teachings.

909. *Oṃ Parākramāya Namaḥ* | ॐ पराक्रमाय नमः ।

He is a person of valour, strength and energy.

910. *Oṃ Dvāparāya Namaḥ* | ॐ द्वापराय नमः ।

He is uncertain when he will shine in some places. He is still shining right from *Dvapara Yug*

911. *Oṃ Paramodārāya Namaḥ* | ॐ परमोदाराय नमः ।

He is supremely generous, readily responding to the prayers of his devotees.

Udārā also means very big. He is very big both in space and time. Since he is very big, he is called as *Paramodāra*.

This name can be split as – *Para* = supreme, *moda* = bliss, *Ārā* = complete. That is, he bestows complete and supreme happiness to his devotees.

The name can also be split as – *Parama* + *Uda* + *Āra*. In that case, very great water i.e. ocean; ocean here meaning the ocean of worldly existence; *Ārā* = weapons. He is the destroyer of the worldly existence of his devotees.

By prefixing '*A*' to the name we get *Aparamodārā*; if this is split as *Aparama* + *Udāra*. *Apa* = gone, *Rama* = wealth or joy. i.e. for the poor and miserable people, he is, *Udāra*.

Para = great, *Āmoda* + sweet smell, i.e. fame. *Para* = great, *Ā* = spreads on all sides, *moda* = happiness. He embodies the ultimate bliss of realisation.

Lalitā Sahasranamam – 939th name – *Paramodārā* & 940th name – *Paramodā* – She is extremely generous. She is supremely reputed.

912. *Oṃ Paramāya Namaḥ* | ॐ परमाय नमः ।

He is the greatest in all things and in all ways.

He limits and shows us the immeasurable *Brahmam*.

The word *Parama* means "at a distance". i.e. he is at a distance for those who do not have devotion.

According to *Vișhŋu Purāŋa*, the supreme being has four forms viz., Male, Twice Born, Time and *Param*. He is in the fourth form *Param*.

This name also means he is the *Paramātma*.

Lalitā Sahasranamam – 618th name – *Paramā* – She is the greatest in all ways.

913. *Oṃ Brahmacaryavate Namaḥ* । ॐ ब्रह्मचर्यवते नमः ।

He practices chastity. He leads the life of a Brahmachari – a religious student.

914. *Oṃ Udīcyaveṣāya Namaḥ* । ॐ उदीच्यवेषाय नमः ।

He enters North direction, during *Uttarayana*.

915. *Oṃ Mukuṭine Namaḥ* । ॐ मुकुटिने नमः ।

He wears a (beautiful) diadem.

916. *Oṃ Padmahastāya Namaḥ* । ॐ पद्महस्ताय नमः ।

He has a lotus flower in his hand. Almost all the Gods and Goddesses are depicted with lotus flower in hands or sitting on a lotus flower.

917. *Oṃ Himāṃśubhṛte Namaḥ* । ॐ हिमांशुभृते नमः ।

He lends his light to cool Moon.

918. *Oṃ Sitāya Namaḥ* । ॐ सिताय नमः ।

He offers sacrifice to Furrows to keep cool.

919. *Oṃ Prasannavadanāya Namaḥ* । ॐ प्रसन्नवदनाय नमः ।

He has a bright face.

It is worth noting here, in every puja and all we start with;

Śuklāmbaradaram Viṣṇum Śaśivarnam Chaturbhujam
Prasanna Vadanam Dhyāyeth

Niroopa (formless) Brahmam is meditated upon with a bright face.

920. *Oṃ Padmodaranibhānanāya Namaḥ* I ॐ पद्मोदरनिभाननाय नमः ।

He has a lotuslike stomach.

Lord Vishnu is used to be called as *Padmanabhaḥ* – having lotuslike navel. In the same way it is mentioned here that Lord Sun has a lotuslike stomach.

921. *Oṃ Sāyaṃ Divā Divyavapuṣe Namaḥ* I
ॐ सायं दिवा दिव्यवपुषे नमः ।

He is splendorous wonderful during day-time especially in the evening.

922. *Oṃ Anirdeśyāya Namaḥ* I ॐ अनिर्देश्याय नमः ।

He has of indefinable form. As he transcends all attributes, his form cannot be defined in one way or other.

Viṣṇu Sahasranamam – 177th & 656th names – *Anirdeśyavapuḥ* – His form is indefinable.

923. *Oṃ Mahālayāya Namaḥ* I ॐ महालयाय नमः ।

Mahalayam means great merger. He enables the merger of *Jeevatma* with *Paramathma*.

Mahalayam also means gathering together. 15 days from the Full Moon Day of Purattasi month (September – October) is called *Mahalaya Paksham*. It is believed that at that time, *Pitrus* (ancestors) will come to earth in groups. *Sradham, Tarpanam,* etc. are performed during that period.

924. *Oṃ Mahārathāya Namaḥ* । ॐ महारथाय नमः ।

He possesses a great chariot.

He riding on a chariot, possessing a chariot, description of his chariot, etc., have occurred in multiple places in this Sahasranamam.

925. *Oṃ Mahate Namaḥ* । ॐ महते नमः ।

He is a great person fit to be worshipped.

371st, 473rd & 801st names above and 986th name below may also be referred.

926. *Oṃ Īśāya Namaḥ* । ॐ ईशाय नमः ।

He is always fresh, active and powerful.

573rd name above may also be referred.

927. *Oṃ Śeṣāya Namaḥ* । ॐ शेषाय नमः ।

He causes or allows other solar system object to remain in the concerned places.

928. *Oṃ Sattvarajastamase Namaḥ* । ॐ सत्त्वरजस्तमसे नमः ।

He is possessed of sattva, rajas and tamo qualities. Basically, he is *Nirguna* – without any qualities. He assumes sattva, rajas and tamo qualities whenever and wherever required.

929. *Oṃ Dhṛtātapatrapratimāya Namaḥ* । ॐ धृतातपत्रप्रतिमाय नमः ।

As a counter charm he holds an umbrella. It may be a joke that Sun himself holds an umbrella. But it is for the devotees' sake, to satisfy them.

930. *Oṃ Vimarṣine Namaḥ* । ॐ विमर्षिने नमः ।

He always well considers, reflects on, tries, examines and considers before start of any task.

931. *Oṃ Nirṇayāya Namaḥ* I ॐ निर्णयाय नमः ।

He decides/ judges anything in an unbiased manner.

932. *Oṃ Sthitāya Namaḥ* I ॐ स्थिताय नमः ।

He is stable and permanent.

225th & 647th names above may also be referred.

933. *Oṃ Ahiṃsakāya Namaḥ* I ॐ अहिंसकाय नमः ।

He is innocuous and harmless.

934. *Oṃ Śuddhamataye Namaḥ* I ॐ शुद्धमतये नमः ।

He absolutely follows the religion and enables his devotees also to follow.

935. *Oṃ Advitīyāya Namaḥ* I ॐ अद्वितीयाय नमः ।

He is unique and matchless. There is no one equal to him.

This name clearly stressed that the God is only one – *Advaita*.

Brahma Tanmangalam Viduḥ – *Brahmam* is the only one that is auspicious, says *Vişhŋu Purāŋa*.

936. *Oṃ Vivardhanāya Namaḥ* I ॐ विवर्धनाय नमः ।

He blesses prosperity and growth to his devotees.

879th name above may also be referred.

937. *Oṃ Sarvadāya Namaḥ* I ॐ सर्वदाय नमः ।

He is eternal and lives forever at all times.

938. *Oṃ Dhanadāya Namaḥ* I ॐ धनदाय नमः ।

He gives booty or treasures to the needy.

196th name above may also be referred.

939. *Oṃ Mokṣāya Namaḥ* I ॐ मोक्षाय नमः ।

He is the bestower of liberation (*moksha*) to his devotees.

470th, 557th & 655th names above may also be referred.

940. *Oṃ Vihāriṇe Namaḥ* I ॐ विहारिणे नमः ।

He always wanders with pleasure for a joy. He is never static.

941. *Oṃ Bahudāyakāya Namaḥ* I ॐ बहुदायकाय नमः ।

He can be seen in many ways or forms in all directions.

942. *Oṃ Cārurātriharāya Namaḥ* I ॐ चारुरात्रिहराय नमः ।

He elegantly wins over the night. He enables to overcome the darkness of ignorance to please his devotees and bestows *Gnana* (knowledge).

943. *Oṃ Nāthāya Namaḥ* I ॐ नाथाय नमः ।

He is the protector of this world. He in the form of *Vishnu* protects this world.

944. *Oṃ Bhagavate Namaḥ* I ॐ भगवते नमः ।

He is with complete wealth, charity, fame, liberation, etc.

707th & 886th name above and 1,006th name below may also be referred.

945. *Oṃ Sarvagāya Namaḥ* I ॐ सर्वगाय नमः ।

He consists wholly of the Gayatri (mantra).

660th and 794th name above may also be referred.

946. *Oṃ Avyayāya Namaḥ* I ॐ अव्ययाय नमः ।

He is indestructible.

When the *Brahmam* feels to create, the form taken by it on account of *māyā* (illusion) is called *Avyaktam*. According to the Samkhya School, it is expressed by the words, *Prakruti* (matter), *pradhāna* (foundation) and *avyakta*.

It is said in the text called *Samkhyasaptami* that *avyakta* is subtle, without characteristics, inanimate, without beginning or end, capable of production, without parts, one and universal.

Viroopaksha Panchasikhā also says, *Pradhāna*, say the wise, is the *avyakta*, which is without beginning or middle, beyond *Mahat* and permanent. It is the collective form of the three qualities.

The *Samkhya Sūtra* (VI-39) says, *Satva* and the rest are not qualities of that *Brahmam*, because they are the qualities of that *avyakta*.

By the word *Avyakta* the *Brahmam* is indicated. In *Brahma Sūtra* (III-2-23) it is said, that *Brahmam* is *avyakta* for the scriptures say so;

Tadavyaktamāha Hi.

Muņḍako Upanishad (III-1-8) says - He is not to be felt by the eyes, nor by the speech, nor by the other senses, nor by penance, nor by actions;

Nachakshushā Gruhyate Nāpi Vāchā Nanyaidevais
Tapasā Karmanā Va".

Further this has been evidenced through *Brahāraņyaka Upanishat* (III-9-26), *Muņḍaka Upanishat* (II-1-6) and *Taitrīya Upansihat* (II-7-1).

Śrīmad Bhagavad Gīta (II-25) also says – this *ātman* is said to be unmanifested, unthinkable and immutable. Therefore, knowing it as such you should not grieve.

The *Linga Purāņa* says that *avyakta* means *Vişhņu*. The names of *Vişhņu*, who is ever capable of creation, are *Pradhāna*, *Avyaya*, *Yoni* [origin), *Avyakta*, *Prakruti* and *Tamas*. This name stresses that *Sun* is in the form of *Vişhņu*.

Brahadaranyaka Upanishat (6-4-25) says – he is undecaying and immortal.

Viṣṇu Sahasranamam – 13th name – *Avyayaḥ* & 30th name – *Avyaya Nidhiḥ* – He is unchanging. He is resting place during pralaya.

Again, *Viṣṇu* Sahasranamam – 305th name – *Vyaktarūpaḥ* – his gross form as universe can be clearly perceived. It need not be mentioned that this is opposite to the meaning of *Avyakta*.

Lalitā Sahasranamam – 398th name – *Avyaktā* – She is not visibly seen – is in an un-manifested state.

947. *Oṃ Manoharavapave Namaḥ* । ॐ मनोहरवपवे नमः ।

He is appealingly clean shaved.

948. *Oṃ Śubhrāya Namaḥ* । ॐ शुभ्राय नमः ।

He travels in a radiant chariot.

949. *Oṃ Śobhanāya Namaḥ* । ॐ शोभनाय नमः ।

He is smart, beautiful and splendorous.

950. *Oṃ Suprabhāvanāya Namaḥ* । ॐ सुप्रभावनाय नमः ।

He is omnipotent almighty.

951. *Oṃ Suprabhāvāya Namaḥ* । ॐ सुप्रभावाय नमः ।

He is a great might – almighty.

952. *Oṃ Supratāpāya Namaḥ* । ॐ सुप्रतापाय नमः ।

He creates a fine dawn. Every living being gets a fresh beautiful dawn.

953. *Oṃ Sunetrāya Namaḥ* । ॐ सुनेत्राय नमः ।

He is fair eyed or having a good eye sight.

Sunetra is one of the 9 kinds of acquiescences. *Sunetra* is also the name of a Maraputra, son of the Tempter. He is in both these forms.

954. *Oṃ Digvidikpataye Namaḥ* I ॐ दिग्विदिक्पतये नमः ।

He is the master of cardinal and intermediate directions. Right form nursery classes, all the directions are defined only by making us facing Sun.

955. *Oṃ Rājñīpriyāya Namaḥ* I ॐ राज्ञीप्रियाय नमः ।

He is very fond of his queens. Chaya, Usha and Swarcalamba are the queens of Lord Sun. He is very fond of all of them.

956. *Oṃ Śabdakarāya Namaḥ* I ॐ शब्दकराय नमः ।

He is the cause of noise or sound creation.

957. *Oṃ Graheśāya Namaḥ* I ॐ ग्रहेशाय नमः ।

Sun is the head or leader of all the nine-planets (*Navagrahas*).

958. *Oṃ Timirāpahāya Namaḥ* I ॐ तिमिरापहाय नमः ।

He only dispels darkness (ignorance).

505th name above can also be referred.

959. *Oṃ Saiṃhikeyaripave Namaḥ* I ॐ सैंहिकेयरिपवे नमः ।

Lord of Simhika. Simhika is a demoness. When Hanuman crossed the ocean, she pulled his shadow and disturbed him.

According to some sources, Simhika is one the wives of the Sun and the mother of Svarbhānu, who is later known as Rahu and Ketu.

According to Vishnu Purana, Simhika was the daughter of Kashyapa Prajapati and Tithi and the sister of the asuras Hiranyakashipu and Hiranyaksha. Also known as Holika, according to one version, she is said to have plotted to take the life of Prahlada, the son of Hiranyakashipu, by setting him on fire.

960. *Oṃ Devāya Namaḥ* I ॐ देवाय नमः ।

Since, he sports with tasks of creation, etc., he is a *Devan*. He protects all beings including Devas.

101st name above may also be referred.

961. *Oṃ Varadāya Namaḥ* । ॐ वरदाय नमः ।

He bestows all the boons to his devotees.

32nd & 134th names above may also be referred.

962. *Oṃ Varanāyakāya Namaḥ* । ॐ वरनायकाय नमः ।

He bestows all the boons sought for by the devotees immediately.

963. *Oṃ Caturbhujāya Namaḥ* । ॐ चतुर्भुजाय नमः।

He has four shoulders. It has become a convention to depict all the Gods as having four hands.

Viṣṇu Sahasranamam – 766th name – *Caturbāhuḥ* – Having four arms.

Again, referring to the verse used in every puja while starting;

Śuklāmbaradaram Viṣṇum Śaśivarnam Chaturbhujam
Prasanna Vadanam Dhyāyeth

Niroopa (formless) Brahmam is meditated upon with four hands.

964. *Oṃ Mahāyogine Namaḥ* । ॐ महायोगिने नमः ।

He is a great Yogi. I bow him.

14th, 33rd and 64th names above may also be referred.

965. *Oṃ Yogīśvarapataye Namaḥ* ॐ योगीश्वरपतये नमः ।

In the previous name it was mentioned that he is a great Yogi. Here is described that he is head of all Yogis and all Yogis worship him.

966. *Oṃ Anādirūpāya Namaḥ* । ॐ अनादिरूपाय नमः ।

His form is without origin or birth.

967. *Oṃ Aditijāya Namaḥ* । ॐ अदितिजाय नमः ।

He is a son of Aditi, wife of sage Kashyapar.

He is very divine.

968. *Oṃ Ratnakāntaye Namaḥ* । ॐ रत्नकान्तये नमः ।

He is a mine of precious stones.

969. *Oṃ Prabhāmayāya Namaḥ* । ॐ प्रभामयाय नमः ।

He shines brightly and provides light to all.

970. *Oṃ Jagatpradīpāya Namaḥ* । ॐ जगत्प्रदीपाय नमः ।

He shines like a great lamp to the world.

971. *Oṃ Vistīrṇāya Namaḥ* । ॐ विस्तीर्णाय नमः ।

He gives light to a broad area. Nobody can measure the area covered by Sun Light.

972. *Oṃ Mahāvistīrṇamaṇḍalāya Namaḥ* ।
ॐ महाविस्तीर्णमण्डलाय नमः ।

He provides light to a very extensive zone.

973. *Oṃ Ekacakrarathāya Namaḥ* । ॐ एकचक्ररथाय नमः ।

He rides in a chariot with a single wheel.

91st name above may also be referred.

974. *Oṃ Svarṇarathāya Namaḥ* । ॐ स्वर्णरथाय नमः ।

He has a golden chariot. Multiple times, in this Sahasranama, his chariot has been described by various methods.

975. *Oṃ Svarṇaśarīradhṛṣe Namaḥ* । ॐ स्वर्णशरीरधृषे नमः ।

We can keep on staring at his amazing golden body.

976. *Oṃ Nirālambāya Namaḥ* I ॐ निरालम्बाय नमः ।

He is a self-supported independent God.

977. *Oṃ Gaganagāya Namaḥ* I ॐ गगनगाय नमः ।

He is a planet moving in the air/ sky.

978. *Oṃ Dharma Karma Prabhāvakṛte Namaḥ* I
ॐ धर्मकर्मप्रभावकृते नमः ।

He only promotes or sets in motion/ action both Dharma and Adharma.

811th and 860th names above may also be referred.

979. *Oṃ Dharmātmane Namaḥ* I ॐ धर्मात्मने नमः ।

He is virtuous and religious minded.

Viṣṇu Sahasranamam – 477th name – *Dharmī* – supporter of Dharma.

980. *Oṃ Karmaṇāṃ Sākṣiṇe Namaḥ* I ॐ कर्मणां साक्षिणे नमः ।

He is the witness for all activities.

The same message was conveyed in various names like 153, 272, 317, 442, 861 and so on in this Sahasranama.

981. *Oṃ Pratyakṣāya Namaḥ* I ॐ प्रत्यक्षाय नमः ।

He is a visible deity. He is the only deity practically seen by all.

The *Upastana* mantra chant during Madhyanikam, on a daily basis – this is chant by seeing the Sun with the naked eyes;

Paśyema Śaradaśśatam Jīvema Śaradaśśatam
Nandāma Śaradaśśatam Modāma Śaradaśśatam
Bhavāma Śaradaśśatam Ṣruṇuvāma Śaradaśśatam
Prabravāma Śaradaśśatam Ajītāsyāma Śaradaśśatam ||

May we be blessed with seeing him for a hundred autumns (years). May we live and carry on our active life for a hundred autumns. May we be happy and rejoice for a hundred autumns. May we live in our chosen places for a hundred autumns. May we hear the Vedas and have upadesham (from appropriate Gurus) for a hundred autumns. May we impart what we learnt to deserving disciples for a hundred autumns. May we defeat our enemies and let us be able to see Hi, the effulgent Sun, for a hundred autumns.

982. *Oṃ Parameśvarāya Namaḥ* I ॐ परमेश्वराय नमः ।

He is the supreme being. Usually, Lord Shiva only is addressed as *Parameśvarā*. But here Lord Sun is addressed so. This stresses that Lord Shiva and Sun are one and the same.

983. *Oṃ Merusevine Namaḥ* I ॐ मेरुसेविने नमः ।

He dwells in the Meru hill. The middle bead in a garland of beads is called Meru bead. The lower and middle lines of the right-hand middle finger is also called Meru area. When any Japa is chant it is always around the Meru.

984. *Oṃ Sumedhāvine Namaḥ* I ॐ सुमेधाविने नमः ।

He is a very learned and good teacher. He is very nourishing and intelligent.

762nd name above may also be referred.

985. *Oṃ Merurakṣākarāya Namaḥ* I ॐ मेरुरक्षाकराय नमः ।

He is the protector of Meru hill.

983rd name above may also be referred.

986. *Oṃ Mahate Namaḥ* I ॐ महते नमः ।

He is a great person fit to be worshipped.

371st, 473rd, 801st & 925th names above may also be referred.

987. *Oṃ Ādhārabhūtāya Namaḥ* I ॐ आधारभूताय नमः ।

He is the *Ādhāra Śakti*. He only supports others; he does not need any support.

He is the cardinal who provides basic needs to all living beings. He dwells in the *Mūlādhāra* of the body. *Mūlādhāra* is the lower abdomen in the body, just beneath the backbone. He resides in the Lotus in that place. 514th name of *Sri Lalita Sahasranamam* – *Mūlādhārāmbujārūḍhā* can also be referred.

Gāyatri Sahasranamam – 15th & 52nd names – *Adharāyai* and 51st name – *Adharanilayāyai* – She dons the whole world. She dwells in the *Mūlādhāra* of the body.

988. *Oṃ Ratimate Namaḥ* I ॐ रतिमते नमः ।

He has enjoyment and pleasure in all his tasks. If everyone does their tasks passionately that will be a great success. He himself is shown to be the greatest example with this name.

In the form of Cupid, he is accompanied by Rati Devi.

989. *Oṃ Dhanadhānyakṛte Namaḥ* I ॐ धनधान्यकृते नमः ।

He only creates wealth and grains.

No grain can grow without Sun Shine. From grains wealth is created.

Lalitā Sahasranama – 886th name – *Dhanadhānya Vivardhinī* – She is increasing the wealth and grain.

990. *Oṃ Pāpasantāpahartre Namaḥ* I ॐ पापसन्तापहर्त्रे नमः ।

He removes all sins of his devotees and make them comfort.

Viṣṇu Sahasranama – 992nd name – *Pāpanāśanaḥ* – Destroyer of all sins.

991. *Oṃ Manovāñchitadāyakāya Namaḥ* I
ॐ मनोवाञ्छितदायकाय नमः ।

He readily satisfies all the wishes sought for by the devotees.

The devotees need not openly ask for. Even when they think in the mind immediately it is bestowed. Sages go one step further – the devotees need not ask for or think of any wish. God knows what is needed for the devotees.

992. *Oṃ Rogahartre Namaḥ* | ॐ रोगहर्त्रे नमः ।

He cures all the diseases of his devotees.

In this connection many names like 287th, 356th, 828th and so on in this Sahasranama can be referred.

993. *Oṃ Rājyadāyine Namaḥ* | ॐ राज्यदायिने नमः ।

He bestows the kingdom to his devotees. He supports kings. In Ramayana, King Dasaratha and Rama are said to be born in Sun Dynasty.

994. *Oṃ Ramaṇīyaguṇāya Namaḥ* | ॐ रमणीयगुणाय नमः ।

He has charmful and virtuous character. In reality he is characterless (*Nirguna*). Ironically his character is described as virtuous.

995. *Oṃ Anṛṇine Namaḥ* | ॐ अनृणिने नमः ।

He releases the debts of his devotees. He himself is debt free.

He is not indebted to his devotees. He bestows more than what is expected by them.

Lalitā Sahasranama – 754th name – *Aparŋā* – She is without any debt.

996. *Oṃ Kālatrayānantarūpāya Namaḥ* | ॐ कालत्रयानन्तरूपाय नमः ।

He is in the form of all the three times – past, present and future.

997. *Oṃ Munivṛndanamaskṛtāya Namaḥ* | ॐ मुनिवृन्दनमस्कृताय नमः ।

He is worshipped/ bowed by all the groups of Munis/ sages.

998. *Oṃ Sandhyārāgakarāya Namaḥ* I ॐ सन्ध्यारागकराय नमः ।

He creates the beautiful red twilight during Sandhya time (meeting of day and night).

999. *Oṃ Siddhāya Namaḥ* I ॐ सिद्धाय नमः ।

He is always readily available for any task.

He is in the form of Siddas. In general, a siddha is a perfected being who has achieved a high level of intellect and liberation or enlightenment. They are Liberated souls, Great masters and Mystics of ancient India. It is said that there are eighteen main Siddhas. He is in all these forms.

1000. *Oṃ Sandhyā Vandana Vanditāya Namaḥ* I
ॐ सन्ध्यावन्दनवन्दिताय नमः ।

He is worshipped by all during *Sandhya Vandanam* – thrice a day on a daily basis.

All those who are eligible for a *Yagnopaveetam* have to perform Sandhya Vandanam thrice a day. During this Sandhyavandam, argyam (water chant with Gayatri Mantra – *Gāyatriyā Abhimantritena Āpaḥ*) is mainly intended to remove the obstacles in the path of Sun's movement. P*racana mantra*, *upastana mantra* and almost the complete Sandhya Vandanams, are all praying to Lord Sun.

Mention has already been made of the Gayatri Mantra, entirely dedicated to Lord Sun. Next chapter is also about the same.

Thus ends 100 divine names on Lord *Sūrya* from 901 to 1,000.

*****

1001. *Oṃ Sāmrājyadānaniratāya Namaḥ* I
ॐ साम्राज्यदाननिरताय नमः ।

He is deeply engaged in or occupied with donating an empire.

1002. *Oṃ Samārādhanatoṣavate Namaḥ* । ॐ समाराधनतोषवते नमः ।

He is contented with Samaradhanai (giving food to Brahmins). He is too happy when his devotees offer food to others.

1003. *Oṃ Bhakta Duḥkhaḥ Kṣayakarāya Namaḥ* ।
ॐ भक्तदुःखक्षयकराय नमः ।

He alleviates the sorrows of his devotees.

He removes the sorrow and pain caused by worldly affairs.

The *Goutama sutrā* (I-22) says – *Tadatyarta Vomoko Pavarkaḥ* – Salvation is the complete release from that pain.

In *Veda* also – *Dukkhenātyanta Vimuktas Charati* – He lives completely free from pain.

Lalita Sahasranamam – 191st name – *Duḥkhahantrī* – Destroyer of Sorrows.

1004. *Oṃ Bhavasāgaratārakāya Namaḥ* । ॐ भवसागरतारकाय नमः ।

He helps his devotees to cross over the ocean of birth and death cycle and worldly affairs. He ensures liberation to his devotees.

It has to be construed that once we get the knowledge of Brahmam, the bonding to this world will automatically cut off.

1005. *Oṃ Bhayāpahartre Namaḥ* । ॐ भयापहर्त्रे नमः ।

He wards of fear or danger of his devotees.

Drives away all the fears from water and earth.

Veda says – *Ānandam Brahmaŋo Vidwan Na Bhibheti Kutaschana* – One who has reached eternal bliss knows no fear.

In the *Vāyu Purāŋa* also it is mentioned that when frightened the very thought of God alleviates all fears.

Viṣhŋu Sahasranāma – 935th name – *Bhayāpahaḥ* & 834th name – *Bhayanāshanaḥ* – He relieves the fear of cycle of birth and death. **He** destroys the fear for those who do follow the righteous path.

Lalita Sahasranamam – 121st name – *Bhayāpahā* – she dispels all fears.

1006. *Oṃ Bhagavate Namaḥ* | ॐ भगवते नमः ।

He is with complete wealth, charity, fame, liberation, etc.

707th, 886th and 944th names above may also be referred.

1007. *Oṃ Aprameyaparākramāya Namaḥ* | ॐ अप्रमेयपराक्रमाय नमः ।

He has unlimited energy and strength.

He cannot be perceived by sensual organs. He can be understood only through meditation.

Viṣhṇu Sahasranāma – 46th name – *Aprameyaḥ* & 248th name – *Aprameyātmā* – He is devoid of sense objects. He is an immeasurable self.

1008. *Oṃ Manusvāmine Namaḥ* | ॐ मनुस्वामिने नमः ।

He is lord of all human beings.

Next name may also be referred.

1009. *Oṃ Manupataye Namaḥ* | ॐ मनुपतये नमः ।

He is head of all human beings.

Previous name may also be compared.

1010. *Oṃ Mānyāya Namaḥ* | ॐ मान्याय नमः ।

He has to be adored.

Viṣhṇu Sahasranāma – 749th name – *Mānyāḥ* – By all means, he is the ruler of all.

1011. *Oṃ Manvantarādhipāya Namaḥ* | ॐ मन्वन्तराधिपाय नमः ।

He is the head of all *manvantaras*, in the form of *Manus*.

A *manvantara* is a cyclic period of time that represents the reign or age of one Manu, the progenitor of mankind. *Manvantaras* are a unit of time within a *Kalpa*, which is a day in the life of Brahma.

Thus ends 11 divine names on Lord *Sūrya* from 1,001 to 1,011.

*****

Generally, Sahasranama means 1,000 names. *Ashtotra* Sahasranama means 1,008 names. Amazingly, 1,011 names are given in this Sahasranama. All the Sahasranamas are available as verses in one or other Purana. Scholars will divide those shlokas into names. Thus, this Surya Sahasranama Stotra is given in 117 verses in Bhavishya Purana. When dividing these verses 1,011 names are available. It does not seem to be any particular reason for this.

From the comparisons and explanations given above, it is obvious that most of the names are same or conveying the same message with that Lalitā, Gāyatri, *Viṣṇu* and Shiva Sahasranamams and other Vedic statements, stressing the message that all are one and the same. This clearly evidences that all the Gods one and the same and that is *Brahmam*. On account of our ignorance, we create various Gods/ Goddesses and try to distinguish/ differentiate among them. Once we get matured, we will realise the single Brahmam, who is without any form neither any qualities.

An analysis of these 1,011 names reveals the below. There are;

- 55 names appearing 2 times
- 12 names appearing 3 times
- 4 names appearing 4 times
- 1 name appearing 5 times

Let us all understand the meanings and chant this sahasranamam and get the choicest blessings of Lord Sun.

*****

Gāyatri Mantra

Gāyatri mantra is mentioned as "*Gāyatrīm Chandasām Mātaḥ*" – *chandas* here means *Vedas* – *Gāyatri* is the mother of all *Vedas*.

In *Śrīmad Bhagavad Gīta* (10.34), Lord *Krişṇa* says "Among the *mantras*, I am in the form of *Gāyatri*". We used to have *Upanişats* about various Gods. We have two *Upanişats* about *Gāyatri* viz., *Gāyatrī Upanişat* and *Gāyatrī Rahasya Upanişat*. These illustrate the glory and majesty of *Gayatri* mantra very eloquently. Is the glory of *Gāyatri* be mentioned anything more?

Only after *Upanayana*, a boy becomes eligible to learn *Vedas* and other holy *mantras*. Before chanting any *mantra*, or before performing any *Pooja* or worship, *Gāyatri mantra* has to be chant first – else the other *mantra* or *Pooja* will not yield any result.

Gāyatri mantra is not about any particular God. In some schools, it is mentioned that *Gāyatri* is about Sun God. But it is not so. Some other schools say that this is about *Gāyatri*, one of the consorts of Lord *Brahma*. It is about *Brahmam*, the ultimate goal of the life. *Brahmam* and Lord *Brahma* are different. It is specified that only the nature is the greatest among all.

The *Gāyatri mantra* has 24 letters as;

Oṃ – the *Praṇava mantra* – prefixed with any *mantra*.

Bhūḥ Bhuvaḥ Svaḥ – *Vyāhruti mantras* – prefixed to add power/ strength.

Tatsavituḥ Vareṇyam Bargo Devasya Dhīmahi Dhiyo Yo Naḥ Pracodayāt

Normal apparent meaning of this is – let us meditate upon the *Brahmam* mentioned as *Savitā* and represented by *Praṇava mantra Oṃ*. It is that *Brahmam* indicated through the three *vyāhruti mantras*. It is the brightness of the divine nature. It is that *Brahmam* who create, protect and destroy the three worlds – Earth, space between heaven, called as the upper world and the intervening galaxy. Let that *Brahmam* direct and move our knowledge in the Right direction (towards him).

An ordinary ceiling fan with a speed of around 900 rotations per minute creates so much sound. In that case, the planets and other members of the Solar system have a speed of around 20,000 rotations per minute. Then what would be the decibel of the sound created – can we imagine?[6] That sound is the *praṇava mantra 'Oṃ'* – says *Gāyatri*. Sage *Viśwāmitra* realised this sound through his penance and taught to his students. They all unanimously named this sound as *'Oṃ'*. *Oṃ* is that *Brahmam*, since it is eternal in all the three tenses. This is the first revolutionary idea of naming the formless *Brahmam*. In *Śrīmad Bhagavad Gīta* also Lord *Krişṇa* says *"Omiti Ekākşaram Brahma"* (8-12).

The word *Gāyatri* means, whoever sings it, will be protected. *Veda* says; *"Gāyantam Trāyate Yasmāt Gāyatri Yabidhīyate"*. When it is said as sings, it does not mean that it is like singing a song. It is chanting with affection and focus. Whoever chants this *mantra* with devotion and love they will be protected. Hence this name.

Let us look at some more aspects of *Gāyatri mantra*.

Om Bhūḥ Bhuvaḥ Svaḥ –

- *Oṃ* – *praṇava mantra* prefixed with any *mantra*.
- *Bhūḥ* – the earth

---

[6] In mid-2010, astronomers at the University of Sheffield, with the support of NASA managed to record the vibrations (eerie musical harmonies) produced by the magnetic field in the outer atmosphere of Sun. Huge magnetic loops known as coronal loops were observed coiling away from the outer layer of the Sun's atmosphere, which behave like sound waves traveling through a wind instrument, *'Oṃ'* i.e. vibrate like strings on a musical instrument.

- *Bhuvaḥ* – the planets
- *Svaḥ* – the galaxy

Tatsavituḥ Vareṇyam –

- *Tat* – that (*Brahmam*)
- *Savituḥ* – Sun God (stars)
- *Vareṇyam* – worshipable or respectable

Once the name and form of a person is known, it is easy to search and find him. Sage *Viśwāmitra* says – it is easy to realise the formless *Brahmam* with the name *Oṃ* and with the lights of stars. For a mathematician, if the value of x is known as 2 then he will immediately find the value of y in the equation 2x + 2y = 0. Same case is *Viśwāmitra*'s. An unconfirmed news – this *Viśwāmitra* was the first person to teach the *Gāyatri mantra* to *Rāma* and *Lakşmaṇa*.

Bargo Devasya Dhīmahi –

- *Bargo* – light
- *Devasya* – God
- *Dhīmahi* – to be meditated upon

Sage further insists – search the formless *Brahmam* with the available light, through meditation. He further asserts to chant the *mantra Oṃ*. He also teaches us how to pray.

Dhiyo Yo Naḥ Pracodayāt –

- *Dhiyo* – knowledge
- *Yo* – who
- *Naḥ* – us all
- *Pracodayāt* – lead in the correct path

Oh! *Brahmam*, please lead our knowledge in the correct path to reach you.

The earth called *Bhūḥ*, the planets addressed as *Bhuvaḥ* and the entire galaxy termed as *Svaḥ*, are all rotating at enormous speed. The sound created on account of this rotation is *'Oṃ'* denoting the *Brahmam*. *Tat*, that *Brahmam*, *Savituḥ* – reveals in the light (*Bargo*) illuminated by the stars. We all need to worship (*Vareṇyam*) and meditate upon (*Dhīmahi*) him (*Devasya*). He (*Yo*) will take our (*Naḥ*) knowledge (*Dhiyo*) in the Right path (*Pracodayāt*) towards him.

One God is associated with each of the 24 letters in *Gāyatri mantra* as below;

#	Letters		God
1.	तत्	*Tat*	*Gaṇapati*
2.	स	*Sa*	*Narasimhar*
3.	वि	*Vi*	*Viṣṇu*
4.	तुः	*Tuḥ*	*Śiva*
5.	व	*Va*	*Kriśna*
6.	रे	*Re*	*Rādhā*
7.	णि	*Ni*	*Lakshmi*
8.	यं	*Yam*	*Agni*
9.	भः	*Bhaḥ*	*Indra*
10.	गो	*Go*	*Saraswati*
11.	दे	*De*	*Durgā*
12.	वः	*Vaḥ*	*Hanumān*
13.	य	*Ya*	*Prithvi*
14.	धी	*Dhee*	*Sūrya*
15.	म	*Ma*	*Rāma*
16.	हि	*Hi*	*Sīta*
17.	धि	*Dhi*	*Candra*
18.	यो	*Yo*	*Yama*
19.	यो	*Yo*	*Brahmā*
20.	नः	*Naḥ*	*Varuṇan*
21.	प्र	*Pra*	*Kāli*
22.	चो	*Co*	*Hayagrīva*
23.	द	*Da*	*Hamsa*
24.	यात्	*Yāt*	*Tulasi*

Lord *Agni* dwells in the face of *Gāyatri Devi*, *Brahmā* the creator dwells in the forehead, *Viṣṇu* the protector in the heart and the lord *Śiva* the destroyer in the top most part of head.
Thus, *Gāyatri Devi* and *Gāyatri Mantra* are conglomeration of all Gods.

There are two important aspects to note – first *Gāyatri mantra* should not be chant as any other verses (*shlokas*). This is a *Veda mantra*. The lifeline of *Veda* is *svara*. Hence, it has to be chant with appropriate *svaras*. Secondly, in the word *'Dhiyoyonaḥ'* the last syllable ('f' like sound) has to be apparent. Else it gives a negative meaning. Thus, having chant in an inappropriate manner and in an urgency, the *mantra* should not be blamed for not being generous in the resultant fruits. Hence, by learning it properly from an appropriate teacher, let us all chant, how much small quantity ever possible and reap the best results.

The importance of *Gāyatri Mantra*:

From the very words of *Kānchi Paramācārya* himself – Chanting of *Gāyatri mantra* is the primary task among those mentioned in *Śāstras*.

Tripam Evatu Vedebhyaḥ Pādam Pādamadūtuham – Manusmruti

Each *pāda* of *Gāyatri mantra* has been taken from three *Vedas* – says *Manu*. We have left most of the parts of *Vedas* – at least this should be continued – else what is the way out for us?

The *Gāyatri mantra* is the essence squeezed out by tightening the three *Vedas Ṛg, Yajur* and *Sāma*. That is the reason it is called as "*Tripāda Gāyatri*". *Atharva Veda* has a separate *Gāyatri mantra* of its own. When *Vedas* talk about *Gāyatri*, it is mentioned as the *Gāyatri mantra* including the power of all the other *mantras*. This is the one, which gives power to all other *mantras*. Without chanting this no other *mantra* is capable of blessing any fruit or result. For purification of body, we take bath. For purification of mind, we have to chant *Gāyatri mantra.*

Those who have left chanting *Gāyatri mantra* for three generations, will never get any welfare. *Taitrīya Àraṇyaka* says *"Sahasra Paramā Devī Śata Madyā Daśāvarā"* – chanting *Gāyatri mantra* 1,000 times is the best, at least 100 times have to be chant and least 10 times.

Whatever be the danger period, everyone should chant at least 12 times each of morning, noon and evening without fail. These three are the peace periods of a day. All these three periods have to be meditated and worshiped as *Gāyatri, Sāvitrī* and *Saraswatī.*

Gāyatri has to meditated in the morning in the form of *Brāhmī,* consort of *Brahma,* in the noon *Roudhrī,* consort of *Rudra* and in the evening *Vaiṣṇavī,* consort of *Viṣṇu.*

Recently, Dr. Howard Steingeria, an American Scientist, collected various *mantras,* hymns and invocations from different parts of the world and tested for the strength in his laboratory and found out that our *Gāyatri Mantra* produced 110,000 sound waves per second. This was the highest and was found to be the most powerful hymn in the world. Through the combination of sound or sound waves in a particular frequency, this *mantra* was capable of developing specific potentialities, which we call spiritual. The Hamburg University initiated this research both on the mental and physical plane of creation.

The *Gāyatri mantra* is broadcast daily from 7:00 to 7:15 p.m. over Radio Paramaribo, Surinam, South America for the past two years and in Amsterdam Holland for the past six months. They say that in the evening after hectic day's work, hearing this makes the life peaceful and also people get a quality sleep during night, so that they start fresh next day.

It is understood that people doing various things through hypnotism;

- The hypnotism that would lead us to liberation is *Gāyatri mantra.*
- The hypnotism viz., *Gāyatri mantra* is the one which will enable us to control all the desires and get the full fruit of taking this birth.

The *argya* (offering water) and the *Gāyatri mantra* are the important ones in *Sandyāvandana*. The other *mantras* are all around these and as limbs around the body. Even those who are unable to move, have to offer *argya* and chant minimum 12 *Gāyatris*. Okey – *paramācārya* himself has given liberty to do only these two – is not a consolation to all. It is the liberty given only to the extreme – the bed ridden, unmovable sick persons and not to everyone. If others also take this liberty, then probably, they may also become sick and bed ridden. Hence, everyone should follow this ritual at the appropriate time on a daily basis. During the *Mahābhārata* battle, where they could not get any pure water, the warriors performed *Sandhyāvandana* with dust (*dhūḷi*) instead of water. But they did not shirk off from performing the routine. Even for those who are unconscious or with heavy fever, it has been mentioned, that others can offer *argya* and *Gāyatri mantra* on their behalf by getting the vessel of water from their hands. And after performance of *argya*, a drop of water can be poured in the mouth. It is seemingly that we all have fallen unconscious or with fever on a daily basis – expecting other to do everything for us.

If anyone is suffering from fever or any disease it needs some medicine urgently. In the same manner the *ātma* is suffering from the disease called bondage and needs a medicine called *Gāyatri*. This should not be ignored at any point of time. There should not be any day missing out *Sandhyāvandanam*. Chanting of *Gāyatri mantra* is nothing impossible for anybody. Excepting water this does not need any other raw material. There is not also much of bodily efforts. A tool that can give so much benefits is easily available, which we should grab at the earliest.

The great power that drives the world is the Sun visible in the sky. But the power hidden within us is the new Sun. This new power is called Buddhi (intellect). Gayatri mantra is the power to strengthen this intellect.

Gāyatri should be imagined in the form of a mother and worshipped. Though God is available in all forms, the form of a mother so affectionate and pretty. *Vedas* affirm that *Gāyatri* is in that form of mother.

There are umpteen *mantras*. Before chanting them, we used to announce the desire for which that *mantra* is chant – *sankalpa* (solemn vow or determination to perform, desire in the heart or mind). But the desire for *Gāyatri mantra* is cleansing of the mind – removing the mental contamination. All other *mantras* lead to cleansing of mind at the end. But the immediate and the only result of *Gāyatri mantra* is removing the pollution in the mind.

Paramācārya has ordered three important areas:

1. Perform *Sandhyāvandam* all the three times daily without fail.
2. Chant *gāyatri* mantra for 1,000 times at all possible times – *sahasra gāyatri*
3. Follow fasting on all *Ekādaśi* days.

Significance of chanting *Gāyatri mantra* 12 times:

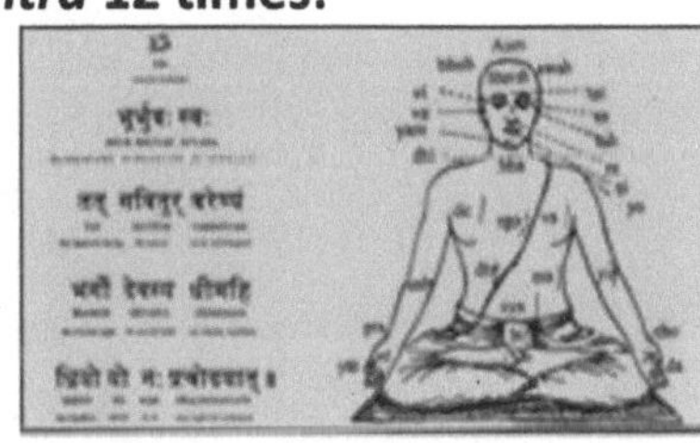

Chanting *Gāyatri mantra* 12 times has enormous implication. In every *Yajñopavīta*, the *brahma* knot has to be made by chanting *Gāyatri mantra* 12 times. Then only the *Yajñopavīta* gets vibration and holiness.

Again, whenever we change the *Yajñopavīta* one has to chant *Gāyatri mantra* for 12 times, before removing the old one. This is in a way handing over of charge – power transfer from the old one to the new one. This small piece of task is not in vogue with all, for the basic reason of ignorance.

In the same manner, when someone bows to the elders, the elder has to chant *Gāyatri mantra* for 12 times before blessing the other person. For instance, if *Lakşmaṇa* bows to *Rāma*, by the time *Lakşmaṇa* starts to bow, till he completes announcing *abhivādanam*, *Rāma* has to chant *Gāyatri mantra* for 12 times. Then he has to bless whatever is needed by *Lakşmaṇa*. With the power of *Gāyatri mantra* whatever be the legal desire, it will be satiated.

Hence, all are requested to chant *Gāyatri mantra* for 12 times at all possible times. Thus, the chanter will be benefitted with mammoth benefits.

These are all very small nuances, easily follow-able with very huge paybacks. People are ready to follow these, if properly taught. Only the unawareness is the cause.

If people want to achieve in their life, the primary requirement is knowledge and understanding. Chanting of Gāyatri mantra will purify the mind and improve the understanding capacity. Consequently, the knowledge has to develop and will be ready to face any challenging tasks. Let everyone be benefitted.

*****

Śrī Sūrya Sahasranāma Stotram

This Stotram contains 1,000 divine names of Lord Surya. This is part of *Bhaviṣya Purāṇam.*

Pūrva Bhagaḥ

Sumanturuvāca I

Māghe Māsi Site Pakṣe Saptamyāṅkurunandana I
Nirāhāro Ravimbhaktyā Pūjayedvidhinā Nṛpa II 1

Pūrvoktena Japejjapyandevasya Purataḥ Sthitaḥ I
Śuddhaikāgramanā Rājañjitakrodho Jitendriyaḥ II 2

Śatānīka Uvāca I

Kena Mantreṇa Japtena Darśanaṃ Bhagavānvrajet I
Stotreṇa Vāpi Savitā Tanme Kathaya Suvrata II 3

Sumanturuvāca I

Stuto Nāmasahasreṇa Yadā Bhaktimatā Mayā I
Tadā Me Darśanaṃ Yātaḥ Sākṣād Devo Divākaraḥ II 4

Śatānīka Uvāca I

Nāmnāṃ Sahasraṃ Savituḥ Śrotumiccāmi He Dvija I
Yena Te Darśanaṃ Yātaḥ Sākṣāddevo Divākaraḥ II 1

Sarvamaṅgalamaṅgalyaṃ Sarvapāpapraṇāśanam I
Stotrametanmahāpuṇyaṃ Sarvopadravanāśanam II 2

Na Tadasti Bhayaṃ Kiñcidyadanena Na Naśyati I
Jvarādyairmucyate Rājan Stotre'smin Paṭhite Naraḥ II 3

Anye Ca Rogāḥ Śāmyanti Paṭhataḥ Śṛṇvatastathā |
Sampadyante Yathā Kāmāḥ Sarva Eva Yathepsitāḥ || 4

Ya Etadāditaḥ Śrutvā Saṅgrāmaṃ Praviśennaraḥ |
Sa Jitvā Samare Śatrūnabhyeti Gṛhamakṣataḥ || 5

Vandhyānāṃ Putrajananaṃ Bhītānāṃ Bhayanāśanam |
Bhūtikāri Daridrāṇāṃ Kuṣṭhināṃ Paramauṣadham || 6

Bālānāṃ Caiva Sarveṣāṃ Graharakṣonivāraṇam |
Paṭhate Saṃyato Rājan Sa Śreyaḥ Paramāpnuyāt || 7

Sa Siddhaḥ Sarvasaṅkalpaḥ Sukhamatyantamaśnute |
Dharmārthibhirdharmalubdhaiḥ Sukhāya Ca Sukhārthibhiḥ || 8

Rājyāya Rājyakāmaiśca Paṭhitavyamidaṃ Naraiḥ |
Vidyāvahaṃ Tu Viprāṇāṃ Kṣatriyāṇāṃ Jayāvaham || 9

Paśvāvahaṃ Tu Vaiśyānāṃ Śūdrāṇāṃ Dharmavardhanam |
Paṭhatāṃ Śṛṇvatāmetadbhavatīti Na Saṃśayaḥ || 10

Taccṛṇuṣva Nṛpaśreṣṭha Prayatātmā Bravīmi Te |
Nāmnāṃ Sahasraṃ Vikhyātaṃ Devadevasya Dhīmataḥ || 11

Dhyānam

Dhyeyaḥ Sadā Savitṛmaṇḍalamadhyavartī
Nārāyaṇaḥ Sarasijāsanasanniviṣṭaḥ |
Keyūravān Makarakuṇḍalavān Kirīṭī
Hārī Hiraṇmayavapurdhṛtaśaṅkhacakraḥ ||

Atha Stotram

Oṃ Viśvavidviśvajitkartā Viśvātmā Viśvatomukhaḥ |
Viśveśvaro Viśvayonirniyatātmā Jitendriyaḥ || 1

Kālāśrayaḥ Kālakartā Kālahā Kālanāśanaḥ I

Mahāyogī Mahāsiddhirmahātmā Sumahābalaḥ II 2

Prabhurvibhurbhūtanātho Bhūtātmā Bhuvaneśvaraḥ I

Bhūtabhavyo Bhāvitātmā Bhūtāntaḥkaraṇaṃ Śivaḥ II 3

Śaraṇyaḥ Kamalānando Nandano Nandavardhanaḥ I

Vareṇyo Varado Yogī Susaṃyuktaḥ Prakāśakaḥ II 4

Prāptayānaḥ Paraprāṇaḥ Pūtātmā Prayataḥ Priyaḥ I

Nayaḥ Sahasrapāt Sādhurdivyakuṇḍalamaṇḍitaḥ II 5

Avyaṅgadhārī Dhīrātmā Savitā Vāyuvāhanaḥ I

Samāhitamatirdātā Vidhātā Kṛtamaṅgalaḥ II 6

Kapardī Kalpapādrudraḥ Sumanā Dharmavatsalaḥ I

Samāyukto Vimuktātmā Kṛtātmā Kṛtināṃ Varaḥ II 7

Avicintyavapuḥ Śreṣṭho Mahāyogī Maheśvaraḥ I

Kāntaḥ Kāmārirādityo Niyatātmā Nirākulaḥ II 8

Kāmaḥ Kāruṇikaḥ Kartā Kamalākarabodhanaḥ I

Saptasaptiracintyātmā Mahākāruṇikottamaḥ II 9

Sañjīvano Jīvanātho Jayo Jīvo Jagatpatiḥ I

Ayukto Viśvanilayaḥ Saṃvibhāgī Vṛṣadhvajaḥ II 10

Vṛṣākapiḥ Kalpakartā Kalpāntakaraṇo Raviḥ I

Ekacakraratho Maunī Suratho Rathināṃ Varaḥ II 11

Sakrodhano Raśmimālī Tejorāśirvibhāvasuḥ I

Divyakṛddinakṛddevo Devadevo Divaspatiḥ II 12

Dīnanātho Haro Hotā Divyabāhurdivākaraḥ ।
Yajño Yajñapatiḥ Pūṣā Svarṇaretāḥ Parāvaraḥ ॥ 13

Parāparajñastaraṇiraṃśumālī Manoharaḥ ।
Prājñaḥ Prājñapatiḥ Sūryaḥ Savitā Viṣṇuraṃśumān ॥ 14

Sadāgatirgandhavaho Vihito Vidhirāśugaḥ ।
Pataṅgaḥ Patagaḥ Sthāṇurvihaṅgo Vihago Varaḥ ॥ 15

Haryaśvo Haritāśvaśca Haridaśvo Jagatpriyaḥ ।
Tryambakaḥ Sarvadamano Bhāvitātmā Bhiṣagvaraḥ ॥ 16

Ālokakṛllokanātho Lokālokanamaskṛtaḥ ।
Kālaḥ Kalpāntako Vahnistapanaḥ Saṃpratāpanaḥ ॥ 17

Virocano Virūpākṣaḥ Sahasrākṣaḥ Purandaraḥ ।
Sahasraraśmirmihiro Vividhāmbarabhūṣaṇaḥ ॥ 18

Khagaḥ Pratardano Dhanyo Hayago Vāgviśāradaḥ ।
Śrīmānaśiśiro Vāgmī Śrīpatiḥ Śrīniketanaḥ ॥ 19

Śrīkaṇṭhaḥ Śrīdharaḥ Śrīmān Śrīnivāso Vasupradaḥ ।
Kāmacārī Mahāmāyo Mahogro'viditāmayaḥ ॥ 20

Tīrthakriyāvān Sunayo Vibhakto Bhaktavatsalaḥ ।
Kīrtiḥ Kīrtikaro Nityaḥ Kuṇḍalī Kavacī Rathī ॥ 21

Hiraṇyaretāḥ Saptāśvaḥ Prayatātmā Parantapaḥ ।
Buddhimānamaraśreṣṭho Rociṣṇuḥ Pākaśāsanaḥ ॥ 22

Samudro Dhanado Dhātā Māndhātā Kaśmalāpahaḥ ।
Tamoghno Dhvāntahā Vahnirhotā'ntaḥkaraṇo Guhaḥ ॥ 23

Paśumān Prayatānando Bhūteśaḥ Śrīmatāṃ Varaḥ I
Nityo'dito Nityarathaḥ Sureśaḥ Surapūjitaḥ II 24

Ajito Vijito Jetā Jaṅgamasthāvarātmakaḥ I
Jīvānando Nityagāmī Vijetā Vijayapradaḥ II 25

Parjanyo'gniḥ Sthitiḥ Stheyaḥ Sthaviro'tha Nirañjanaḥ I
Pradyotano Rathārūḍhaḥ Sarvalokaprakāśakaḥ II 26

Dhruvo Meṣī Mahāvīryo Haṃsaḥ Saṃsāratārakaḥ I
Sṛṣṭikartā Kriyāheturmārtaṇḍo Marutāṃ Patiḥ II 27

Marutvān Dahanastvaṣṭā Bhago Bhargo'ryamā Kapiḥ I
Varuṇeśo Jagannāthaḥ Kṛtakṛtyaḥ Sulocanaḥ II 28

Vivasvān Bhānumān Kāryaḥ Kāraṇastejasāṃ Nidhiḥ I
Asaṅgagāmī Tigmāṃśurgharmāṃśurdīptadīdhitiḥ II 29

Sahasradīdhitirbradhnaḥ Sahasrāṃśurdivākaraḥ I
Gabhastimān Dīdhitimān Sragvī Maṇikuladyutiḥ II 30

Bhāskaraḥ Surakāryajñaḥ Sarvajñastīkṣṇadīdhitiḥ I
Surajyeṣṭhaḥ Surapatirbahujño Vacasāṃ Patiḥ II 31

Tejonidhirbṛhattejā Bṛhatkīrtirbṛhaspatiḥ I
Ahimānūrjito Dhīmānāmuktaḥ Kīrtivardhanaḥ II 32

Mahāvaidyo Gaṇapatirdhaneśo Gaṇanāyakaḥ I
Tīvrapratāpanastāpī Tāpano Viśvatāpanaḥ II 33

Kārtasvaro Hṛṣīkeśaḥ Padmānando'tinanditaḥ I
Padmanābho'mṛtāhāraḥ Sthitimān Ketumān Nabhaḥ II 34

Anādyanto'cyuto Viśvo Viśvāmitro Ghṛṇirvirāṭ I
Āmuktakavaco Vāgmī Kañcukī Viśvabhāvanaḥ II 35

Animittagatiḥ Śreṣṭhaḥ Śaraṇyaḥ Sarvatomukhaḥ I
Vigāhī Veṇurasahaḥ Samāyuktaḥ Samākratuḥ II 36

Dharmaketurdharmaratiḥ Saṃhartā Saṃyamo Yamaḥ I
Praṇatārtiharo Vāyuḥ Siddhakāryo Janeśvaraḥ II 37

Nabho Vigāhanaḥ Satyaḥ Savitātmā Manoharaḥ I
Hārī Harirharo Vāyurṛtuḥ Kālānaladyutiḥ II 38

Sukhasevyo Mahātejā Jagatāmekakāraṇam I
Mahendro Viṣṭutaḥ Stotraṃ Stutihetuḥ Prabhākaraḥ II 39

Sahasrakara Āyuṣmān Aroṣaḥ Sukhadaḥ Sukhī I
Vyādhihā Sukhadaḥ Saukhyaṃ Kalyāṇaḥ Kalatāṃ Varaḥ II 40

Ārogyakāraṇaṃ Siddhirṛddhirvṛddhirbṛhaspatiḥ I
Hiraṇyaretā Ārogyaṃ Vidvān Bradhno Budho Mahān II 41

Prāṇavān Dhṛtimān Gharmo Gharmakartā Rucipradaḥ I
Sarvapriyaḥ Sarvasahaḥ Sarvaśatruvināśanaḥ II 42

Prāṃśurvidyotano Dyotaḥ Sahasrakiraṇaḥ Kṛtī I
Keyūrī Bhūṣaṇodbhāsī Bhāsito Bhāsano'nalaḥ II 43

Śaraṇyārtiharo Hotā Khadyotaḥ Khagasattamaḥ I
Sarvadyoto Bhavadyotaḥ Sarvadyutikaro Mataḥ II 44

Kalyāṇaḥ Kalyāṇakaraḥ Kalyaḥ Kalyakaraḥ Kaviḥ I
Kalyāṇakṛt Kalyavapuḥ Sarvakalyāṇabhājanam II 45

Śāntipriyaḥ Prasannātmā Praśāntaḥ Praśamapriyaḥ I
Udārakarmā Sunayaḥ Suvarcā Varcasojjvalaḥ II 46

Varcasvī Varcasāmīśastrailokyeśo Vaśānugaḥ I
Tejasvī Suyaśā Varṣmī Varṇādhyakṣo Balipriyaḥ II 47

Yaśasvī Tejonilayastejasvī Prakṛtisthitaḥ I
Ākāśagaḥ Śīghragatirāśugo Gatimān Khagaḥ II 48

Gopatirgrahadeveśo Gomānekaḥ Prabhañjanaḥ I
Janitā Prajano Jīvo Dīpaḥ Sarvaprakāśakaḥ II 49

Sarvasākṣī Yoganityo Nabhasvānasurāntakaḥ I
Rakṣoghno Vighnaśamanaḥ Kirīṭī Sumanaḥpriyaḥ II 50

Marīcimālī Sumatiḥ Kṛtābhikhyaviśeṣakaḥ I
Śiṣṭācāraḥ Śubhākāraḥ Svacārācāratatparaḥ II 51

Mandāro Māṭharo Veṇuḥ Kṣudhāpaḥ Kṣmāpatirguruḥ I
Suviśiṣṭo Viśiṣṭātmā Vidheyo Jñānaśobhanaḥ II 52

Mahāśvetaḥ Priyo Jñeyaḥ Sāmago Mokṣadāyakaḥ I
Sarvavedapragītātmā Sarvavedalayo Mahān II 53

Vedamūrtiścaturvedo Vedabhṛdvedapāragaḥ I
Kriyāvānasito Jiṣṇurvarīyāṃśurvarapradaḥ II 54

Vratacārī Vratadharo Lokabandhuralaṅkṛtaḥ I
Alaṅkārākṣaro Vedyo Vidyāvān Viditāśayaḥ II 55

Ākāro Bhūṣaṇo Bhūṣyo Bhūṣṇurbhuvanapūjitaḥ I
Cakrapāṇirdhvajadharaḥ Sureśo Lokavatsalaḥ II 56

Vāgmipatirmahābāhuḥ Prakṛtirvikṛtirguṇaḥ I
Andhakārāpahaḥ Śreṣṭho Yugāvarto Yugādikṛt II 57

Aprameyaḥ Sadāyogī Nirahaṅkāra Īśvaraḥ I
Śubhapradaḥ Śubhaḥ Śāstā Śubhakarmā Śubhapradaḥ II 58

Satyavān Śrutimānuccairnakāro Vṛddhido'nalaḥ I
Balabhṛdbalado Bandhurmatimān Balināṃ Varaḥ II 59

Anaṅgo Nāgarājendraḥ Padmayonirgaṇeśvaraḥ I
Saṃvatsara Ṛturnetā Kālacakrapravartakaḥ II 60

Padmekṣaṇaḥ Padmayoniḥ Prabhāvānamaraḥ Prabhuḥ I
Sumūrtiḥ Sumatiḥ Somo Govindo Jagadādijaḥ II 61

Pītavāsāḥ Kṛṣṇavāsā Digvāsāstvindriyātigaḥ I
Atīndriyo'nekarūpaḥ Skandaḥ Parapurañjayaḥ II 62

Śaktimāñjaladhṛgbhāsvān Mokṣaheturayonijaḥ I
Sarvadarśī Jitādarśo Duḥsvapnāśubhanāśanaḥ II 63

Māṅgalyakartā Taraṇirvegavān Kaśmalāpahaḥ I
Spaṣṭākṣaro Mahāmantro Viśākho Yajanapriyaḥ II 64

Viśvakarmā Mahāśaktirdyutirīśo Vihaṅgamaḥ I
Vicakṣaṇo Dakṣa Indraḥ Pratyūṣaḥ Priyadarśanaḥ II 65

Akhinno Vedanilayo Vedavidviditāśayaḥ I
Prabhākaro Jitaripuḥ Sujano'ruṇasārathiḥ II 66

Kunāśī Surataḥ Skando Mahito'bhimato Guruḥ I
Graharājo Grahapatirgrahanakṣatramaṇḍalaḥ II 67

Bhāskaraḥ Satatānando Nandano Naravāhanaḥ I
Maṅgalo'tha Maṅgalavān Māṅgalyo Maṅgalāvahaḥ II 68

Maṅgalyacārucaritaḥ Śīrṇaḥ Sarvavrato Vratī I
Caturmukhaḥ Padmamālī Pūtātmā Praṇatārtihā II 69

Akiñcanaḥ Satāmīśo Nirguṇo Guṇavāñcuciḥ I
Sampūrṇaḥ Puṇḍarīkākṣo Vidheyo Yogatatparaḥ II 70

Sahasrāṃśuḥ Kratumatiḥ Sarvajñaḥ Sumatiḥ Suvāk I
Suvāhano Mālyadāmā Kṛtāhāro Haripriyaḥ II 71

Brahmā Pracetāḥ Prathitaḥ Prayatātmā Sthirātmakaḥ I
Śatavinduḥ Śatamukho Garīyānanalaprabhaḥ II 72

Dhıro Mahattaro Vipraḥ Purāṇapuruṣottamaḥ I
Vidyārājādhirājo Hi Vidyāvān Bhūtidaḥ Sthitaḥ II 73

Anirdeśyavapuḥ Śrīmān Vipāpmā Bahumaṅgalaḥ I
Svaḥsthitaḥ Surathaḥ Svarṇo Mokṣado Baliketanaḥ II 74

Nirdvandvo Dvandvahā Sargaḥ Sarvagaḥ Saṃprakāśakaḥ I
Dayāluḥ Sūkṣmadhīḥ Kṣāntiḥ Kṣemākṣemasthitipriyaḥ II 75

Bhūdharo Bhūpatirvaktā Pavitrātmā Trilocanaḥ I
Mahāvarāhaḥ Priyakṛddātā Bhoktā'bhayapradaḥ II 76

Cakravartī Dhṛtikaraḥ Sampūrṇo'tha Maheśvaraḥ I
Caturvedadharo'cintyo Vinindyo Vividhāśanaḥ II 77

Vicitraratha Ekākī Saptasaptiḥ Parātparaḥ I
Sarvodadhisthitikaraḥ Sthitistheyaḥ Sthitipriyaḥ II 78

Niṣkalaḥ Puṣkalo Vibhurvasumān Vāsavapriyaḥ I
Paśumān Vāsavasvāmī Vasudhāmā Vasupradaḥ II 79

Balavān Jñānavāṃstattvamoṅkārastriṣu Saṃsthitaḥ I
Saṅkalpayonirdinakṛdbhagavān Kāraṇāpahaḥ II 80

Nīlakaṇṭho Dhanādhyakṣaścaturvedapriyaṃvadaḥ I
Vaṣaṭkārodgātā Hotā Svāhākāro Hutāhutiḥ II 81

Janārdano Janānando Naro Nārāyaṇo'mbudaḥ I
Sandehanāśano Vāyurdhanvī Suranamaskṛtaḥ II 82

Vigrahī Vimalo Vindurviśoko Vimaladyutiḥ I
Dyutimān Dyotano Vidyudvidyāvān Vidito Balī II 83

Gharmado Himado Hāsaḥ Kṛṣṇavartmā Sutājitaḥ I
Sāvitrībhāvito Rājā Viśvāmitro Ghṛṇirvirāṭ II 84

Saptārciḥ Saptaturagaḥ Saptalokanamaskṛtaḥ I
Sampūrṇo'tha Jagannāthaḥ Sumanāḥ Śobhanapriyaḥ II 85

Sarvātmā Sarvakṛt Sṛṣṭiḥ Saptimān Saptamīpriyaḥ I
Sumedhā Medhiko Medhyo Medhāvī Madhusūdanaḥ II 86

Aṅgiraḥpatiḥ Kālajño Dhūmaketuḥ Suketanaḥ I
Sukhī Sukhapradaḥ Saukhyaṃ Kāmī Kāntipriyo Muniḥ II 87

Santāpanaḥ Santapana Ātapastapasāṃ Patiḥ I
Umāpatiḥ Sahasrāṃśuḥ Priyakārī Priyaṅkaraḥ II 88

Prītirvimanyurambhotthaḥ Khañjano Jagatāṃ Patiḥ I
Jagatpitā Prītamanāḥ Sarvaḥ Kharvo Guho'calaḥ II 89

Sarvago Jagadānando Jagannetā Surārihā I
Śreyaḥ Śreyaskaro Jyāyān Mahānuttama Udbhavaḥ II 90

Uttamo Merumeyo'tha Dharaṇo Dharaṇīdharaḥ I
Dharādhyakṣo Dharmarājo Dharmādharmapravartakaḥ II 91

Rathādhyakṣo Rathagatistaruṇastanito'nalaḥ I
Uttaro'nuttarastāpī Avākpatirapāṃ Patiḥ II 92

Puṇyasaṅkīrtanaḥ Puṇyo Heturlokatrayāśrayaḥ I
Svarbhānurvigatānando Viśiṣṭotkṛṣṭakarmakṛt II 93

Vyādhipraṇāśanaḥ Kṣemaḥ Śūraḥ Sarvajitāṃ Varaḥ I
Ekaratho Rathādhīśaḥ Pitā Śanaiścarasya Hi II 94

Vaivasvatagururmṛtyurdharmanityo Mahāvrataḥ I
Pralambahārāsañcārī Pradyoto Dyotitānalaḥ II 95

Santāpahṛt Paro Mantro Mantramūrtirmahābalaḥ I
Śreṣṭhātmā Supriyaḥ Śambhurmarutāmīśvareśvaraḥ II 96

Saṃsāragativiccettā Saṃsārārṇavatārakaḥ I
Saptajihvaḥ Sahasrārcī Ratnagarbho'parājitaḥ II 97

Dharmaketurameyātmā Dharmādharmavarapradaḥ I
Lokasākṣī Lokagururlokeśaścaṇḍavāhanaḥ II 98

Dharmayūpo Yūpavṛkṣo Dhanuṣpāṇirdhanurdharaḥ I
Pinākadhṛṅmahotsāho Mahāmāyo Mahāśanaḥ II 99

Vīraḥ Śaktimatāṃ Śreṣṭhaḥ Sarvaśastrabhṛtāṃ Varaḥ I
Jñānagamyo Durārādhyo Lohitāṅgo Vivardhanaḥ II 100

Khago'ndho Dharmado Nityo Dharmakṛccitravikramaḥ I
Bhagavānātmavān Mantrastryakṣaro Nīlalohitaḥ II 101

Eko'nekastrayī Kālaḥ Savitā Samitiñjayaḥ I
Śārṅgadhanvā'nalo Bhīmaḥ Sarvapraharaṇāyudhaḥ II 102

Sukarmā Parameṣṭhī Ca Nākapālī Divisthitaḥ I
Vadānyo Vāsukirvaidya Ātreyo'tha Parākramaḥ II 103

Dvāparaḥ Paramodāraḥ Paramo Brahmacaryavān I
Udīcyaveṣo Mukuṭī Padmahasto Himāṃśubhṛt II 104

Sitaḥ Prasannavadanaḥ Padmodaranibhānanaḥ I
Sāyaṃ Divā Divyavapuranirdeśyo Mahālayaḥ II 105

Mahāratho Mahānīśaḥ Śeṣaḥ Sattvarajastamaḥ I
Dhṛtātapatrapratimo Vimarṣī Nirṇayaḥ Sthitaḥ II 106

Ahiṃsakaḥ Śuddhamatiradvitīyo Vivardhanaḥ I
Sarvado Dhanado Mokṣo Vihārī Bahudāyakaḥ II 107

Cārurātriharo Nātho Bhagavān Sarvago'vyayaḥ I
Manoharavapuḥ Śubhraḥ Śobhanaḥ Suprabhāvanaḥ II 108

Suprabhāvaḥ Supratāpaḥ Sunetro Digvidikpatiḥ I
Rājñīpriyaḥ Śabdakaro Graheśastimirāpahaḥ II 109

Saiṃhikeyaripurdevo Varado Varanāyakaḥ I
Caturbhujo Mahāyogī Yogīśvarapatistathā II 110

Anādirūpo'ditijo Ratnakāntiḥ Prabhāmayaḥ I
Jagatpradīpo Vistīrṇo Mahāvistīrṇamaṇḍalaḥ II 111

Ekacakrarathaḥ Svarṇarathaḥ Svarṇaśarīradhṛk I
Nirālambo Gaganago Dharmakarmaprabhāvakṛt II 112

Dharmātmā Karmaṇāṃ Sākṣī Pratyakṣaḥ Parameśvaraḥ I
Merusevī Sumedhāvī Merurakṣākaro Mahān II 113

Ādhārabhūto Ratimāṃstathā Ca Dhanadhānyakṛt I
Pāpasantāpahartā Ca Manovāñcitadāyakaḥ II 114

Rogahartā Rājyadāyī Ramaṇīyaguṇo'nṛṇī I
Kālatrayānantarūpo Munivṛndanamaskṛtaḥ II 115

Sandhyārāgakaraḥ Siddhaḥ Sandhyāvandanavanditaḥ I
Sāmrājyadānanirataḥ Samārādhanatoṣavān II 116

Bhaktaduḥkhakṣayakaro Bhavasāgaratārakaḥ
Bhayāpahartā Bhagavānaprameyaparākramaḥ I
Manusvāmī Manupatirmānyo Manvantarādhipaḥ II 117

Phalaśrutiḥ

Etatte Sarvamākhyātaṃ Yanmāṃ Tvaṃ Paripṛccasi I
Nāmnāṃ Sahasraṃ Savituḥ Pārāśaryo Yadāha Me II 1

Dhanyaṃ Yaśasyamāyuṣyaṃ Duḥkhaduḥsvapnanāśanam I
Bandhamokṣakaraṃ Caiva Bhānornāmānukīrtanāt II 2

Yastvidaṃ Śṛṇuyānnityaṃ Paṭhedvā Prayato Naraḥ I
Akṣayaṃ Sukhamannādyaṃ Bhavettasyopasādhitam II 3

Nṛpāgnitaskarabhayaṃ Vyādhito Na Bhayaṃ Bhavet I
Vijayī Ca Bhavennityamāśrayaṃ Paramāpnuyāt II 4

Kīrtimān Subhago Vidvān Sa Sukhī Priyadarśanaḥ I
Jīvedvarṣaśatāyuśca Sarvavyādhivivarjitaḥ II 5

Nāmnāṃ Sahasramidamaṃśumataḥ Paṭhedyaḥ
Prātaḥ Śucirniyamavān Susamṛddhiyuktaḥ ।
Dūreṇa Taṃ Pariharanti Sadaiva Rogāḥ
Bhūtāḥ Suparṇamiva Sarvamahoragendrāḥ ॥ 6

॥ *Iti Śrī Bhaviṣyapurāṇe Saptamakalpe Śrī Bhagavat Sūryasya Sahasranāma Stotraṃ Sampūrṇam* ॥

श्रीसूर्यसहस्रनामस्तोत्रम्

पूर्व भागः

सुमन्तुरुवाच।

माघे मासि सिते पक्षे सप्तम्याङ्कुरुनन्दन ।
निराहारो रविम्भक्त्या पूजयेद्विधिना नृप ॥ १

पूर्वोक्तेन जपेज्जप्यन्देवस्य पुरतः स्थितः ।
शुद्धैकाग्रमना राजञ्जितक्रोधो जितेन्द्रियः ॥ २

शतानीक उवाच ।

केन मन्त्रेण जप्तेन दर्शनं भगवान्व्रजेत् ।
स्तोत्रेण वापि सविता तन्मे कथय सुव्रत ॥ ३

सुमन्तुरुवाच।

स्तुतो नामसहस्रेण यदा भक्तिमता मया ।
तदा मे दर्शनं यातः साक्षाद् देवो दिवाकरः ॥ ४

शतानीक उवाच ।

नाम्नां सहस्रं सवितुः श्रोतुमिच्चामि हे द्विज ।
येन ते दर्शनं यातः साक्षाद्देवो दिवाकरः ॥ १

सर्वमङ्गलमङ्गल्यं सर्वपापप्रणाशनम् ।
स्तोत्रमेतन्महापुण्यं सर्वोपद्रवनाशनम् ॥ २

न तदस्ति भयं किञ्चिद्यदनेन न नश्यति।
ज्वराद्यैर्मुच्यते राजन् स्तोत्रेऽस्मिन् पठिते नरः ॥ ३

अन्ये च रोगाः शाम्यन्ति पठतः शृण्वतस्तथा।
सम्पद्यन्ते यथा कामाः सर्व एव यथेप्सिताः ॥ ४

य एतदादितः श्रुत्वा सङ्ग्रामं प्रविशेन्नरः।
स जित्वा समरे शत्रूनभ्येति गृहमक्षतः ॥ ५

वन्ध्यानां पुत्रजननं भीतानां भयनाशनम्।
भूतिकारि दरिद्राणां कुष्ठिनां परमौषधम् ॥ ६

बालानां चैव सर्वेषां ग्रहरक्षोनिवारणम्।
पठते संयतो राजन् स श्रेयः परमाप्नुयात् ॥ ७

स सिद्धः सर्वसङ्कल्पः सुखमत्यन्तमश्नुते।
धर्मार्थिभिर्धर्मलुब्धैः सुखाय च सुखार्थिभिः ॥ ८

राज्याय राज्यकामैश्च पठितव्यमिदं नरैः।
विद्यावहं तु विप्राणां क्षत्रियाणां जयावहम् ॥ ९

पश्वावहं तु वैश्यानां शूद्राणां धर्मवर्धनम्।
पठतां शृण्वतामेतद्भवतीति न संशयः ॥ १०

तच्छृणुष्व नृपश्रेष्ठ प्रयतात्मा ब्रवीमि ते।
नाम्नां सहस्रं विख्यातं देवदेवस्य धीमतः ॥ ११

ध्यानम्

ध्येयः सदा सवितृमण्डलमध्यवर्ती नारायणः सरसिजासनसन्निविष्टः।
केयूरवान् मकरकुण्डलवान् किरीटीहारी हिरण्मयवपुर्धृतशङ्खचक्रः ॥

अथ स्तोत्रम्

ॐ विश्वविद्विश्वजित्कर्ता विश्वात्मा विश्वतोमुखः।
विश्वेश्वरो विश्वयोनिर्नियतात्मा जितेन्द्रियः ॥ १

कालाश्रयः कालकर्ता कालहा कालनाशनः ।
महायोगी महासिद्धिर्महात्मा सुमहाबलः ॥ २

प्रभुर्विभुर्भूतनाथो भूतात्मा भुवनेश्वरः ।
भूतभव्यो भावितात्मा भूतान्तःकरणं शिवः ॥ ३

शरण्यः कमलानन्दो नन्दनो नन्दवर्धनः ।
वरेण्यो वरदो योगी सुसंयुक्तः प्रकाशकः ॥ ४

प्राप्तयानः परप्राणः पूतात्मा प्रयतः प्रियः ।
नयः सहस्रपात् साधुर्दिव्यकुण्डलमण्डितः ॥ ५

अव्यङ्गधारी धीरात्मा सविता वायुवाहनः ।
समाहितमतिर्दाता विधाता कृतमङ्गलः ॥ ६

कपर्दी कल्पपाद्रुद्रः सुमना धर्मवत्सलः ।
समायुक्तो विमुक्तात्मा कृतात्मा कृतिनां वरः ॥ ७

अविचिन्त्यवपुः श्रेष्ठो महायोगी महेश्वरः ।
कान्तः कामारिरादित्यो नियतात्मा निराकुलः ॥ ८

कामः कारुणिकः कर्ता कमलाकरबोधनः ।
सप्तसप्तिरचिन्त्यात्मा महाकारुणिकोत्तमः ॥ ९

सञ्जीवनो जीवनाथो जयो जीवो जगत्पतिः ।
अयुक्तो विश्वनिलयः संविभागी वृषध्वजः ॥ १०

वृषाकपिः कल्पकर्ता कल्पान्तकरणो रविः ।
एकचक्ररथो मौनी सुरथो रथिनां वरः ॥ ११

सक्रोधनो रश्मिमाली तेजोराशिर्विभावसुः ।
दिव्यकृद्दिनकृद्देवो देवदेवो दिवस्पतिः ॥ १२

दीननाथो हरो होता दिव्यबाहुर्दिवाकरः ।
यज्ञो यज्ञपतिः पूषा स्वर्णरेताः परावरः ॥ १३

परापरज्ञस्तरणिरंशुमाली मनोहरः ।
प्राज्ञः प्राज्ञपतिः सूर्यः सविता विष्णुरंशुमान् ॥ १४

सदागतिर्गन्धवहो विहितो विधिराशुगः ।
पतङ्गः पतगः स्थाणुर्विहङ्गो विहगो वरः ॥ १५

हर्यश्वो हरिताश्वश्च हरिदश्वो जगत्प्रियः ।
त्र्यम्बकः सर्वदमनो भावितात्मा भिषग्वरः ॥ १६

आलोककृल्लोकनाथो लोकालोकनमस्कृतः ।
कालः कल्पान्तको वह्निस्तपनः संप्रतापनः ॥ १७

विरोचनो विरूपाक्षः सहस्राक्षः पुरन्दरः ।
सहस्ररश्मिर्मिहिरो विविधाम्बरभूषणः ॥ १८

खगः प्रतर्दनो धन्यो हयगो वाग्विशारदः ।
श्रीमानशिशिरो वाग्मी श्रीपतिः श्रीनिकेतनः ॥ १९

श्रीकण्ठः श्रीधरः श्रीमान् श्रीनिवासो वसुप्रदः ।
कामचारी महामायो महोग्रोऽविदितामयः ॥ २०

तीर्थक्रियावान् सुनयो विभक्तो भक्तवत्सलः ।
कीर्तिः कीर्तिकरो नित्यः कुण्डली कवची रथी ॥ २१

हिरण्यरेताः सप्ताश्वः प्रयतात्मा परन्तपः ।
बुद्धिमानमरश्रेष्ठो रोचिष्णुः पाकशासनः ॥ २२

समुद्रो धनदो धाता मान्धाता कश्मलापहः ।
तमोघ्नो ध्वान्तहा वह्निर्होताऽन्तःकरणो गुहः ॥ २३

पशुमान् प्रयतानन्दो भूतेशः श्रीमतां वरः ।
नित्योऽदितो नित्यरथः सुरेशः सुरपूजितः ॥ २४

अजितो विजितो जेता जङ्गमस्थावरात्मकः ।
जीवानन्दो नित्यगामी विजेता विजयप्रदः ॥ २५

पर्जन्योऽग्निः स्थितिः स्थेयः स्थविरोऽथ निरञ्जनः ।
प्रद्योतनो रथारूढः सर्वलोकप्रकाशकः ॥ २६

ध्रुवो मेषी महावीर्यो हंसः संसारतारकः ।
सृष्टिकर्ता क्रियाहेतुर्मार्तण्डो मरुतां पतिः ॥ २७

मरुत्वान् दहनस्त्वष्टा भगो भर्गोऽर्यमा कपिः ।
वरुणेशो जगन्नाथः कृतकृत्यः सुलोचनः ॥ २८

विवस्वान् भानुमान् कार्यः कारणस्तेजसां निधिः ।
असङ्गगामी तिग्मांशुर्घर्मांशुर्दीप्तदीधितिः ॥ २९

सहस्रदीधितिर्ब्रध्नः सहस्रांशुर्दिवाकरः ।
गभस्तिमान् दीधितिमान् स्रग्वी मणिकुलद्युतिः ॥ ३०

भास्करः सुरकार्यज्ञः सर्वज्ञस्तीक्ष्णदीधितिः ।
सुरज्येष्ठः सुरपतिर्बहुज्ञो वचसां पतिः ॥ ३१

तेजोनिधिर्बृहत्तेजा बृहत्कीर्तिर्बृहस्पतिः ।
अहिमानूर्जितो धीमानामुक्तः कीर्तिवर्धनः ॥ ३२

महावैद्यो गणपतिर्धनेशो गणनायकः ।
तीव्रप्रतापनस्तापी तापनो विश्वतापनः ॥ ३३

कार्तस्वरो हृषीकेशः पद्मानन्दोऽतिनन्दितः ।
पद्मनाभोऽमृताहारः स्थितिमान् केतुमान् नभः ॥ ३४

अनाद्यन्तोऽच्युतो विश्वो विश्वामित्रो घृणिर्विराट् ।
आमुक्तकवचो वाग्मी कञ्चुकी विश्वभावनः ॥ ३५

अनिमित्तगतिः श्रेष्ठः शरण्यः सर्वतोमुखः ।
विगाही वेणुरसहः समायुक्तः समाक्रतुः ॥ ३६

धर्मकेतुर्धर्मरतिः संहर्ता संयमो यमः ।
प्रणतार्तिहरो वायुः सिद्धकार्यो जनेश्वरः ॥ ३७

नभो विगाहनः सत्यः सवितात्मा मनोहरः ।
हारी हरिर्हरो वायुरृतुः कालानलद्युतिः ॥ ३८

सुखसेव्यो महातेजा जगतामेककारणम् ।
महेन्द्रो विष्टुतः स्तोत्रं स्तुतिहेतुः प्रभाकरः ॥ ३९

सहस्रकर आयुष्मान् अरोषः सुखदः सुखी ।
व्याधिहा सुखदः सौख्यं कल्याणः कलतां वरः ॥ ४०

आरोग्यकारणं सिद्धिरृद्धिर्वृद्धिर्बृहस्पतिः ।
हिरण्यरेता आरोग्यं विद्वान् ब्रध्नो बुधो महान् ॥ ४१

प्राणवान् धृतिमान् घर्मो घर्मकर्ता रुचिप्रदः ।
सर्वप्रियः सर्वसहः सर्वशत्रुविनाशनः ॥ ४२

प्रांशुर्विद्योतनो द्योतः सहस्रकिरणः कृती ।
केयूरी भूषणोद्भासी भासितो भासनोऽनलः ॥ ४३

शरण्यार्तिहरो होता खद्योतः खगसत्तमः ।
सर्वद्योतो भवद्योतः सर्वद्युतिकरो मतः ॥ ४४

कल्याणः कल्याणकरः कल्यः कल्यकरः कविः ।
कल्याणकृत् कल्यवपुः सर्वकल्याणभाजनम् ॥ ४५

शान्तिप्रियः प्रसन्नात्मा प्रशान्तः प्रशमप्रियः ।
उदारकर्मा सुनयः सुवर्चा वर्चसोज्ज्वलः ॥ ४६

वर्चस्वी वर्चसामीशस्त्रैलोक्येशो वशानुगः ।
तेजस्वी सुयशा वर्ष्मी वर्णाध्यक्षो बलिप्रियः ॥ ४७

यशस्वी तेजोनिलयस्तेजस्वी प्रकृतिस्थितः ।
आकाशगः शीघ्रगतिराशुगो गतिमान् खगः ॥ ४८

गोपतिर्ग्रहदेवेशो गोमानेकः प्रभञ्जनः ।
जनिता प्रजनो जीवो दीपः सर्वप्रकाशकः ॥ ४९

सर्वसाक्षी योगनित्यो नभस्वानसुरान्तकः ।
रक्षोघ्नो विघ्नशमनः किरीटी सुमनःप्रियः ॥ ५०

मरीचिमाली सुमतिः कृताभिख्यविशेषकः ।
शिष्टाचारः शुभाकारः स्वचाराचारतत्परः ॥ ५१

मन्दारो माठरो वेणुः क्षुधापः क्ष्मापतिर्गुरुः ।
सुविशिष्टो विशिष्टात्मा विधेयो ज्ञानशोभनः ॥ ५२

महाश्वेतः प्रियो ज्ञेयः सामगो मोक्षदायकः ।
सर्व्ववेदप्रगीतात्मा सर्व्ववेदलयो महान् ॥ ५३

वेदमूर्तिश्चतुर्वेदो वेदभृद्वेदपारगः ।
क्रियावानसितो जिष्णुर्वरीयांशुर्वरप्रदः ॥ ५४

व्रतचारी व्रतधरो लोकबन्धुरलङ्कृतः ।
अलङ्काराक्षरो वेद्यो विद्यावान् विदिताशयः ॥ ५५

आकारो भूषणो भूष्यो भूष्णुर्भुवनपूजितः ।
चक्रपाणिर्ध्वजधरः सुरेशो लोकवत्सलः ॥ ५६

वाग्मिपतिर्महाबाहुः प्रकृतिर्विकृतिर्गुणः ।
अन्धकारापहः श्रेष्ठो युगावर्तो युगादिकृत् ॥ ५७

अप्रमेयः सदायोगी निरहङ्कार ईश्वरः ।
शुभप्रदः शुभः शास्ता शुभकर्मा शुभप्रदः ॥ ५८

सत्यवान् श्रुतिमानुच्चैर्नकारो वृद्धिदोऽनलः ।
बलभृद्बलदो बन्धुर्मतिमान् बलिनां वरः ॥ ५९

अनङ्गो नागराजेन्द्रः पद्मयोनिर्गणेश्वरः ।
संवत्सर ऋतुर्नेता कालचक्रप्रवर्तकः ॥ ६०

पद्मेक्षणः पद्मयोनिः प्रभावानमरः प्रभुः ।
सुमूर्तिः सुमतिः सोमो गोविन्दो जगदादिजः ॥ ६१

पीतवासाः कृष्णवासा दिग्वासास्त्विन्द्रियातिगः ।
अतीन्द्रियोऽनेकरूपः स्कन्दः परपुरञ्जयः ॥ ६२

शक्तिमाञ्जलधृग्भास्वान् मोक्षहेतुरयोनिजः ।
सर्वदर्शी जितादर्शो दुःस्वप्नाशुभनाशनः ॥ ६३

माङ्गल्यकर्ता तरणिर्वेगवान् कश्मलापहः ।
स्पष्टाक्षरो महामन्त्रो विशाखो यजनप्रियः ॥ ६४

विश्वकर्मा महाशक्तिर्द्युतिरीशो विहङ्गमः ।
विचक्षणो दक्ष इन्द्रः प्रत्यूषः प्रियदर्शनः ॥ ६५

अखिन्नो वेदनिलयो वेदविद्विदिताशयः ।
प्रभाकरो जितरिपुः सुजनोऽरुणसारथिः ॥ ६६

कुनाशी सुरतः स्कन्दो महितोऽभिमतो गुरुः ।
ग्रहराजो ग्रहपतिर्ग्रहनक्षत्रमण्डलः ॥ ६७

भास्करः सततानन्दो नन्दनो नरवाहनः ।
मङ्गलोऽथ मङ्गलवान् माङ्गल्यो मङ्गलावहः ॥ ६८

मङ्गल्यचारुचरितः शीर्णः सर्वव्रतो व्रती ।
चतुर्मुखः पद्ममाली पूतात्मा प्रणतार्तिहा ॥ ६९

अकिञ्चनः सतामीशो निर्गुणो गुणवाञ्छुचिः ।
सम्पूर्णः पुण्डरीकाक्षो विधेयो योगतत्परः ॥ ७०

सहस्रांशुः क्रतुमतिः सर्वज्ञः सुमतिः सुवाक् ।
सुवाहनो माल्यदामा कृताहारो हरिप्रियः ॥ ७१

ब्रह्मा प्रचेताः प्रथितः प्रयतात्मा स्थिरात्मकः ।
शतविन्दुः शतमुखो गरीयाननलप्रभः ॥ ७२

धीरो महत्तरो विप्रः पुराणपुरुषोत्तमः ।
विद्याराजाधिराजो हि विद्यावान् भूतिदः स्थितः ॥ ७३

अनिर्देश्यवपुः श्रीमान् विपाप्मा बहुमङ्गलः ।
स्वःस्थितः सुरथः स्वर्णो मोक्षदो बलिकेतनः ॥ ७४

निर्द्वन्द्वो द्वन्द्वहा सर्गः सर्वगः संप्रकाशकः ।
दयालुः सूक्ष्मधीः क्षान्तिः क्षेमाक्षेमस्थितिप्रियः ॥ ७५

भूधरो भूपतिर्वक्ता पवित्रात्मा त्रिलोचनः ।
महावराहः प्रियकृद्दाता भोक्ताऽभयप्रदः ॥ ७६

चक्रवर्ती धृतिकरः सम्पूर्णोऽथ महेश्वरः ।
चतुर्वेदधरोऽचिन्त्यो विनिन्द्यो विविधाशनः ॥ ७७

विचित्ररथ एकाकी सप्तसप्तिः परात्परः ।
सर्वोदधिस्थितिकरः स्थितिस्थेयः स्थितिप्रियः ॥ ७८

निष्कलः पुष्कलो विभुर्वसुमान् वासवप्रियः ।
पशुमान् वासवस्वामी वसुधामा वसुप्रदः ॥ ७९

बलवान् ज्ञानवांस्तत्त्वमोङ्कारस्त्रिषु संस्थितः ।
सङ्कल्पयोनिर्दिनकृद्भगवान् कारणापहः ॥ ८०

नीलकण्ठो धनाध्यक्षश्चतुर्वेदप्रियंवदः ।
वषट्कारोद्गाता होता स्वाहाकारो हुताहुतिः ॥ ८१

जनार्दनो जनानन्दो नरो नारायणोऽम्बुदः ।
सन्देहनाशनो वायुर्धन्वी सुरनमस्कृतः ॥ ८२

विग्रही विमलो विन्दुर्विशोको विमलद्युतिः ।
द्युतिमान् द्योतनो विद्युद्विद्यावान् विदितो बली ॥ ८३

घर्मदो हिमदो हासः कृष्णवर्त्मा सुताजितः ।
सावित्रीभावितो राजा विश्वामित्रो घृणिर्विराट् ॥ ८४

सप्तार्चिः सप्ततुरगः सप्तलोकनमस्कृतः ।
सम्पूर्णोऽथ जगन्नाथः सुमनाः शोभनप्रियः ॥ ८५

सर्वात्मा सर्वकृत् सृष्टिः सप्तिमान् सप्तमीप्रियः ।
सुमेधा मेधिको मेध्यो मेधावी मधुसूदनः ॥ ८६

अङ्गिरःपतिः कालज्ञो धूमकेतुः सुकेतनः ।
सुखी सुखप्रदः सौख्यं कामी कान्तिप्रियो मुनिः ॥ ८७

सन्तापनः सन्तपन आतपस्तपसां पतिः ।
उमापतिः सहस्रांशुः प्रियकारी प्रियङ्करः ॥ ८८

प्रीतिर्विमन्युरम्भोत्थः खञ्जनो जगतां पतिः ।
जगत्पिता प्रीतमनाः सर्वः खर्वो गुहोऽचलः ॥ ८९

सर्वगो जगदानन्दो जगन्नेता सुरारिहा ।
श्रेयः श्रेयस्करो ज्यायान् महानुत्तम उद्भवः ॥ ९०

उत्तमो मेरुमेयोऽथ धरणो धरणीधरः ।
धराध्यक्षो धर्मराजो धर्माधर्मप्रवर्तकः ॥ ९१

रथाध्यक्षो रथगतिस्तरुणस्तनितोऽनलः ।
उत्तरोऽनुत्तरस्तापी अवाक्पतिरपां पतिः ॥ ९२

पुण्यसङ्कीर्तनः पुण्यो हेतुर्लोकत्रयाश्रयः ।
स्वर्भानुर्विगतानन्दो विशिष्टोत्कृष्टकर्मकृत् ॥ ९३

व्याधिप्रणाशनः क्षेमः शूरः सर्वजितां वरः ।
एकरथो रथाधीशः पिता शनैश्चरस्य हि ॥ ९४

वैवस्वतगुरुर्मृत्युर्धर्मनित्यो महाव्रतः ।
प्रलम्बहारासञ्चारी प्रद्योतो द्योतितानलः ॥ ९५

सन्तापहृत् परो मन्त्रो मन्त्रमूर्तिर्महाबलः ।
श्रेष्ठात्मा सुप्रियः शम्भुर्मरुतामीश्वरेश्वरः ॥ ९६

संसारगतिविच्छेत्ता संसारार्णवतारकः ।
सप्तजिह्वः सहस्रार्ची रत्नगर्भोऽपराजितः ॥ ९७

धर्मकेतुरमेयात्मा धर्माधर्मवरप्रदः ।
लोकसाक्षी लोकगुरुर्लोकेशश्चण्डवाहनः ॥ ९८

धर्मयूपो यूपवृक्षो धनुष्पाणिर्धनुर्धरः ।
पिनाकधृङ्महोत्साहो महामायो महाशनः ॥ ९९

वीरः शक्तिमतां श्रेष्ठः सर्वशस्त्रभृतां वरः ।
ज्ञानगम्यो दुराराध्यो लोहिताङ्गो विवर्धनः ॥ १००

खगोऽन्धो धर्मदो नित्यो धर्मकृच्चित्रविक्रमः ।
भगवानात्मवान् मन्त्रस्त्र्यक्षरो नीललोहितः ॥ १०१

एकोऽनेकस्त्रयी कालः सविता समितिञ्जयः ।
शार्ङ्गधन्वाऽनलो भीमः सर्वप्रहरणायुधः ॥ १०२

सुकर्मा परमेष्ठी च नाकपाली दिविस्थितः ।
वदान्यो वासुकिर्वैद्य आत्रेयोऽथ पराक्रमः ॥ १०३

द्वापरः परमोदारः परमो ब्रह्मचर्यवान् ।
उदीच्यवेषो मुकुटी पद्महस्तो हिमांशुभृत् ॥ १०४

सितः प्रसन्नवदनः पद्मोदरनिभाननः ।
सायं दिवा दिव्यवपुरनिर्देश्यो महालयः ॥ १०५

महारथो महानीशः शेषः सत्त्वरजस्तमः ।
धृतातपत्रप्रतिमो विमर्षी निर्णयः स्थितः ॥ १०६

अहिंसकः शुद्धमतिरद्वितीयो विवर्धनः ।
सर्वदो धनदो मोक्षो विहारी बहुदायकः ॥ १०७

चारुरात्रिहरो नाथो भगवान् सर्वगोऽव्ययः ।
मनोहरवपुः शुभ्रः शोभनः सुप्रभावनः ॥ १०८

सुप्रभावः सुप्रतापः सुनेत्रो दिग्विदिक्पतिः ।
राज्ञीप्रियः शब्दकरो ग्रहेशस्तिमिरापहः ॥ १०९

सैंहिकेयरिपुर्देवो वरदो वरनायकः ।
चतुर्भुजो महायोगी योगीश्वरपतिस्तथा ॥ ११०

अनादिरूपोऽदितिजो रत्नकान्तिः प्रभामयः ।
जगत्प्रदीपो विस्तीर्णो महाविस्तीर्णमण्डलः ॥ १११

एकचक्ररथः स्वर्णरथः स्वर्णशरीरधृक् ।
निरालम्बो गगनगो धर्मकर्मप्रभावकृत् ॥ ११२

धर्मात्मा कर्मणां साक्षी प्रत्यक्षः परमेश्वरः ।
मेरुसेवी सुमेधावी मेरुरक्षाकरो महान् ॥ ११३

आधारभूतो रतिमांस्तथा च धनधान्यकृत् ।
पापसन्तापहर्ता च मनोवाञ्छितदायकः ॥ ११४

रोगहर्ता राज्यदायी रमणीयगुणोऽनृणी ।
कालत्रयानन्तरूपो मुनिवृन्दनमस्कृतः ॥ ११५

सन्ध्यारागकरः सिद्धः सन्ध्यावन्दनवन्दितः ।
साम्राज्यदाननिरतः समाराधनतोषवान् ॥ ११६

भक्तदुःखक्षयकरो भवसागरतारकः
भयापहर्ता भगवानप्रमेयपराक्रमः ।
मनुस्वामी मनुपतिर्मान्यो मन्वन्तराधिपः ॥ ११७

फलश्रुतिः

एतत्ते सर्वमाख्यातं यन्मां त्वं परिपृच्चसि ।
नाम्नां सहस्रं सवितुः पाराशर्यो यदाह मे ॥ १

धन्यं यशस्यमायुष्यं दुःखदुःस्वप्ननाशनम् ।
बन्धमोक्षकरं चैव भानोर्नामानुकीर्तनात् ॥ २

यस्त्विदं शृणुयान्नित्यं पठेद्वा प्रयतो नरः ।
अक्षयं सुखमन्नाद्यं भवेत्तस्योपसाधितम् ॥ ३

नृपाग्नितस्करभयं व्याधितो न भयं भवेत् ।
विजयी च भवेन्नित्यमाश्रयं परमाप्नुयात् ॥ ४

कीर्तिमान् सुभगो विद्वान् स सुखी प्रियदर्शनः ।
जीवेद्वर्षशतायुश्च सर्वव्याधिविवर्जितः ॥ ५

नाम्नां सहस्रमिदमंशुमतः पठेद्यःप्रातः शुचिर्नियमवान् सुसमृद्धियुक्तः ।
दूरेण तं परिहरन्ति सदैव रोगाः भूताः सुपर्णमिव सर्वमहोरगेन्द्राः ॥ ६

॥ इति श्री भविष्यपुराणे सप्तमकल्पे श्री भगवत्सूर्यस्य सहस्र नाम स्तोत्रं सम्पूर्णम् ॥

*****

Śrī Sūrya Sahasranāmāmāvalī
(श्री सूर्य सहस्र नामावली)

One thousand holy names of Lord Surya taken from Bhavishya Puranam.

Dhyānam

Dhyeyaḥ Sadā Savitṛmaṇḍalamadhyavartī
Nārāyaṇaḥ Sarasijāsanasanniviṣṭaḥ ।
Keyūravān Makarakuṇḍalavān Kirīṭī
Hārī Hiraṇmayavapurdhṛtaśaṅkhacakraḥ ॥

ध्यानम्

ध्येयः सदा सवितृमण्डलमध्यवर्ती नारायणः सरसिजासनसन्निविष्टः ।
केयूरवान् मकरकुण्डलवान् किरीटीहारी हिरण्मयवपुर्धृतशङ्खचक्रः ॥

1.	*Oṃ Viśvavide Namaḥ* ।	ॐ विश्वविदे नमः ।
2.	*Oṃ Viśvajite Namaḥ* ।	ॐ विश्वजिते नमः ।
3.	*Oṃ Viśvakartre Namaḥ* ।	ॐ विश्वकर्त्रे नमः ।
4.	*Oṃ Viśvātmane Namaḥ* ।	ॐ विश्वात्मने नमः ।
5.	*Oṃ Viśvatomukhāya Namaḥ*	ॐ विश्वतोमुखाय नमः ।
6.	*Oṃ Viśveśvarāya Namaḥ* ।	ॐ विश्वेश्वराय नमः ।
7.	*Oṃ Viśvayonaye Namaḥ* ।	ॐ विश्वयोनये नमः ।
8.	*Oṃ Niyatātmane Namaḥ* ।	ॐ नियतात्मने नमः ।
9.	*Oṃ Jitendriyāya Namaḥ* ।	ॐ जितेन्द्रियाय नमः ।
10.	*Oṃ Kālāśrayāya Namaḥ* ।	ॐ कालाश्रयाय नमः ।
11.	*Oṃ Kālakartre Namaḥ* ।	ॐ कालकर्त्रे नमः ।
12.	*Oṃ Kālaghne Namaḥ* ।	ॐ कालघ्ने नमः ।
13.	*Oṃ Kālanāśanāya Namaḥ* ।	ॐ कालनाशनाय नमः ।
14.	*Oṃ Mahāyogine Namaḥ* ।	ॐ महायोगिने नमः ।
15.	*Oṃ Mahāsiddhaye Namaḥ* ।	ॐ महासिद्धये नमः ।

16.	*Oṃ Mahātmane Namaḥ* I	ॐ महात्मने नमः ।
17.	*Oṃ Sumahābalāya Namaḥ* I	ॐ सुमहाबलाय नमः ।
18.	*Oṃ Prabhave Namaḥ* I	ॐ प्रभवे नमः ।
19.	*Oṃ Vibhave Namaḥ* I	ॐ विभवे नमः ।
20.	*Oṃ Bhūtanāthāya Namaḥ* I	ॐ भूतनाथाय नमः ।
21.	*Oṃ Bhūtātmane Namaḥ* I	ॐ भूतात्मने नमः ।
22.	*Oṃ Bhuvaneśvarāya Namaḥ*	ॐ भुवनेश्वराय नमः ।
23.	*Oṃ Bhūtabhavyāya Namaḥ* I	ॐ भूतभव्याय नमः ।
24.	*Oṃ Bhāvitātmane Namaḥ* I	ॐ भावितात्मने नमः ।
25.	*Oṃ Bhūtāntaḥkaraṇāya Namaḥ* I	ॐ भूतान्तःकरणाय नमः ।
26.	*Oṃ Śivāya Namaḥ* I	ॐ शिवाय नमः ।
27.	*Oṃ Śaraṇyāya Namaḥ* I	ॐ शरण्याय नमः ।
28.	*Oṃ Kamalānandāya Namaḥ* I	ॐ कमलानन्दाय नमः ।
29.	*Oṃ Nandanāya Namaḥ* I	ॐ नन्दनाय नमः ।
30.	*Oṃ Nandavardhanāya Namaḥ* I	ॐ नन्दवर्धनाय नमः ।
31.	*Oṃ Vareṇyāya Namaḥ* I	ॐ वरेण्याय नमः ।
32.	*Oṃ Varadāya Namaḥ* I	ॐ वरदाय नमः ।
33.	*Oṃ Yogine Namaḥ* I	ॐ योगिने नमः ।
34.	*Oṃ Susaṃyuktāya Namaḥ* I	ॐ सुसंयुक्ताय नमः ।
35.	*Oṃ Prakāśakāya Namaḥ* I	ॐ प्रकाशकाय नमः ।
36.	*Oṃ Prāptayānāya Namaḥ* I	ॐ प्राप्तयानाय नमः ।
37.	*Oṃ Paraprāṇāya Namaḥ* I	ॐ परप्राणाय नमः ।
38.	*Oṃ Pūtātmane Namaḥ* I	ॐ पूतात्मने नमः ।
39.	*Oṃ Prayatāya Namaḥ* I	ॐ प्रयताय नमः ।
40.	*Oṃ Priyāya Namaḥ* I	ॐ प्रियाय नमः ।

41.	*Oṃ Nayāya Namaḥ* I	ॐ नयाय नमः ।
42.	*Oṃ Sahasrapāde Namaḥ* I	ॐ सहस्रपदे नमः ।
43.	*Oṃ Sādhave Namaḥ* I	ॐ साधवे नमः ।
44.	*Oṃ Divyakuṇḍalamaṇḍitāya Namaḥ* I	ॐ दिव्यकुण्डलमण्डिताय नमः ।
45.	*Oṃ Avyaṅgadhāriṇe Namaḥ* I	ॐ अव्यङ्गधारिणे नमः ।
46.	*Oṃ Dhīrātmane Namaḥ* I	ॐ धीरात्मने नमः ।
47.	*Oṃ Savitre Namaḥ* I	ॐ सवित्रे नमः ।
48.	*Oṃ Vāyuvāhanāya Namaḥ* I	ॐ वायुवाहनाय नमः ।
49.	*Oṃ Samāhitamataye Namaḥ*	ॐ समाहितमतये नमः ।
50.	*Oṃ Dātre Namaḥ* I	ॐ दात्रे नमः ।
51.	*Oṃ Vidhātre Namaḥ* I	ॐ विधात्रे नमः ।
52.	*Oṃ Kṛtamaṅgalāya Namaḥ* I	ॐ कृतमङ्गलाय नमः ।
53.	*Oṃ Kapardine Namaḥ* I	ॐ कपर्दिने नमः ।
54.	*Oṃ Kalpapāde Namaḥ* I	ॐ कल्पपादे नमः ।
55.	*Oṃ Rudrāya Namaḥ* I	ॐ रुद्राय नमः ।
56.	*Oṃ Sumanāya Namaḥ* I	ॐ सुमनाय नमः ।
57.	*Oṃ Dharmavatsalāya Namaḥ* I	ॐ धर्मवत्सलाय नमः ।
58.	*Oṃ Samāyuktāya Namaḥ* I	ॐ समायुक्ताय नमः ।
59.	*Oṃ Vimuktātmane Namaḥ* I	ॐ विमुक्तात्मने नमः ।
60.	*Oṃ Kṛtātmane Namaḥ* I	ॐ कृतात्मने नमः ।
61.	*Oṃ Kṛtināṃ Varāya Namaḥ* I	ॐ कृतिनां वराय नमः ।
62.	*Oṃ Avicintyavapave Namaḥ* I	ॐ अविचिन्त्यवपवे नमः ।
63.	*Oṃ Śreṣṭhāya Namaḥ* I	ॐ श्रेष्ठाय नमः ।
64.	*Oṃ Mahāyogine Namaḥ* I	ॐ महायोगिने नमः ।
65.	*Oṃ Maheśvarāya Namaḥ* I	ॐ महेश्वराय नमः ।

66.	*Oṃ Kāntāya Namaḥ* |	ॐ कान्ताय नमः ।
67.	*Oṃ Kāmāraye Namaḥ* |	ॐ कामारये नमः ।
68.	*Oṃ Ādityāya Namaḥ* |	ॐ आदित्याय नमः ।
69.	*Oṃ Niyatātmane Namaḥ* |	ॐ नियतात्मने नमः ।
70.	*Oṃ Nirākulāya Namaḥ* |	ॐ निराकुलाय नमः ।
71.	*Oṃ Kāmāya Namaḥ* |	ॐ कामाय नमः ।
72.	*Oṃ Kāruṇikāya Namaḥ* |	ॐ कारुणिकाय नमः ।
73.	*Oṃ Kartre Namaḥ* |	ॐ कर्त्रे नमः ।
74.	*Oṃ Kamalākarabodhanāya Namaḥ* |	ॐ कमलाकरबोधनाय नमः ।
75.	*Oṃ Saptasaptaye Namaḥ* |	ॐ सप्तसप्तये नमः ।
76.	*Oṃ Acintyātmane Namaḥ* |	ॐ अचिन्त्यात्मने नमः ।
77.	*Oṃ Mahākāruṇikottamāya Namaḥ* |	ॐ महाकारुणिकोत्तमाय नमः ।
78.	*Oṃ Sañjīvanāya Namaḥ* |	ॐ सञ्जीवनाय नमः ।
79.	*Oṃ Jīvanāthāya Namaḥ* |	ॐ जीवनाथाय नमः ।
80.	*Oṃ Jayāya Namaḥ* |	ॐ जयाय नमः ।
81.	*Oṃ Jīvāya Namaḥ* |	ॐ जीवाय नमः ।
82.	*Oṃ Jagatpataye Namaḥ* |	ॐ जगत्पतये नमः ।
83.	*Oṃ Ayuktāya Namaḥ* |	ॐ अयुक्ताय नमः ।
84.	*Oṃ Viśvanilayāya Namaḥ* |	ॐ विश्वनिलयाय नमः ।
85.	*Oṃ Saṃvibhāgine Namaḥ* |	ॐ संविभागिने नमः ।
86.	*Oṃ Vṛṣadhvajāya Namaḥ* |	ॐ वृषध्वजाय नमः ।
87.	*Oṃ Vṛṣākapaye Namaḥ* |	ॐ वृषाकपये नमः ।
88.	*Oṃ Kalpakartre Namaḥ* |	ॐ कल्पकर्त्रे नमः ।
89.	*Oṃ Kalpāntakaraṇāya Namaḥ* |	ॐ कल्पान्तकरणाय नमः ।
90.	*Oṃ Ravaye Namaḥ* |	ॐ रवये नमः ।

91.	*Oṃ Ekacakrarathāya Namaḥ*	ॐ एकचक्ररथाय नमः ।
92.	*Oṃ Maunine Namaḥ* ।	ॐ मौनिने नमः ।
93.	*Oṃ Surathāya Namaḥ* ।	ॐ सुरथाय नमः ।
94.	*Oṃ Rathināṃ Varāya Namaḥ* ।	ॐ रथिनां वराय नमः ।
95.	*Oṃ Sakrodhanāya Namaḥ* ।	ॐ सक्रोधनाय नमः ।
96.	*Oṃ Raśmimāline Namaḥ* ।	ॐ रश्मिमालिने नमः ।
97.	*Oṃ Tejorāśaye Namaḥ* ।	ॐ तेजोराशये नमः ।
98.	*Oṃ Vibhāvasave Namaḥ* ।	ॐ विभावसवे नमः ।
99.	*Oṃ Divyakṛte Namaḥ* ।	ॐ दिव्यकृते नमः ।
100.	*Oṃ Dinakṛte Namaḥ* ।	ॐ दिनकृते नमः ।
101.	*Oṃ Devāya Namaḥ* ।	ॐ देवाय नमः ।
102.	*Oṃ Devadevāya Namaḥ* ।	ॐ देवदेवाय नमः ।
103.	*Oṃ Divaspataye Namaḥ* ।	ॐ दिवस्पतये नमः ।
104.	*Oṃ Dīnanāthāya Namaḥ* ।	ॐ दीननाथाय नमः ।
105.	*Oṃ Harāya Namaḥ* ।	ॐ हराय नमः ।
106.	*Oṃ Hotre Namaḥ* ।	ॐ होत्रे नमः ।
107.	*Oṃ Divyabāhave Namaḥ* ।	ॐ दिव्यबाहवे नमः ।
108.	*Oṃ Divākarāya Namaḥ* ।	ॐ दिवाकराय नमः ।
109.	*Oṃ Yajñāya Namaḥ* ।	ॐ यज्ञाय नमः ।
110.	*Oṃ Yajñapataye Namaḥ* ।	ॐ यज्ञपतये नमः ।
111.	*Oṃ Pūṣṇe Namaḥ* ।	ॐ पूष्णे नमः ।
112.	*Oṃ Svarṇaretase Namaḥ* ।	ॐ स्वर्णरेतसे नमः ।
113.	*Oṃ Parāvarāya Namaḥ* ।	ॐ परावराय नमः ।
114.	*Oṃ Parāparajñāya Namaḥ* ।	ॐ परापरज्ञाय नमः ।
115.	*Oṃ Taraṇaye Namaḥ* ।	ॐ तरणये नमः ।
116.	*Oṃ Aṃśumāline Namaḥ* ।	ॐ अंशुमालिने नमः ।

117.	*Oṃ Manoharāya Namaḥ* |	ॐ मनोहराय नमः ।
118.	*Oṃ Prājñāya Namaḥ* |	ॐ प्राज्ञाय नमः ।
119.	*Oṃ Prājñapataye Namaḥ* |	ॐ प्राज्ञपतये नमः ।
120.	*Oṃ Sūryāya Namaḥ* |	ॐ सूर्याय नमः ।
121.	*Oṃ Savitre Namaḥ* |	ॐ सवित्रे नमः ।
122.	*Oṃ Viṣṇave Namaḥ* |	ॐ विष्णवे नमः ।
123.	*Oṃ Aṃśumate Namaḥ* |	ॐ अंशुमते नमः ।
124.	*Oṃ Sadāgataye Namaḥ* |	ॐ सदागतये नमः ।
125.	*Oṃ Gandhavahāya Namaḥ* |	ॐ गन्धवहाय नमः ।
126.	*Oṃ Vihitāya Namaḥ* |	ॐ विहिताय नमः ।
127.	*Oṃ Vidhaye Namaḥ* |	ॐ विधये नमः ।
128.	*Oṃ Āśugāya Namaḥ* |	ॐ आशुगाय नमः ।
129.	*Oṃ Pataṅgāya Namaḥ* |	ॐ पतङ्गाय नमः ।
130.	*Oṃ Patagāya Namaḥ* |	ॐ पतगाय नमः ।
131.	*Oṃ Sthāṇave Namaḥ* |	ॐ स्थाणवे नमः ।
132.	*Oṃ Vihaṅgāya Namaḥ* |	ॐ विहङ्गाय नमः ।
133.	*Oṃ Vihagāya Namaḥ* |	ॐ विहगाय नमः ।
134.	*Oṃ Varāya Namaḥ* |	ॐ वराय नमः ।
135.	*Oṃ Haryaśvāya Namaḥ* |	ॐ हर्यश्वाय नमः ।
136.	*Oṃ Haritāśvāya Namaḥ* |	ॐ हरिताश्वाय नमः ।
137.	*Oṃ Haridaśvāya Namaḥ* |	ॐ हरिदश्वाय नमः ।
138.	*Oṃ Jagatpriyāya Namaḥ* |	ॐ जगत्प्रियाय नमः ।
139.	*Oṃ Tryambakāya Namaḥ* |	ॐ त्र्यम्बकाय नमः ।
140.	*Oṃ Sarvadamanāya Namaḥ* |	ॐ सर्वदमनाय नमः ।
141.	*Oṃ Bhāvitātmane Namaḥ* |	ॐ भावितात्मने नमः ।
142.	*Oṃ Bhiṣagvarāya Namaḥ* |	ॐ भिषग्वराय नमः ।

143.	*Oṃ Ālokakṛte Namaḥ* I	ॐ आलोककृते नमः ।
144.	*Oṃ Lokanāthāya Namaḥ* I	ॐ लोकनाथाय नमः ।
145.	*Oṃ Lokālokanamaskṛtāya Namaḥ* I	ॐ लोकालोकनमस्कृताय नमः ।
146.	*Oṃ Kālāya Namaḥ* I	ॐ कालाय नमः ।
147.	*Oṃ Kalpāntakāya Namaḥ* I	ॐ कल्पान्तकाय नमः ।
148.	*Oṃ Vahnaye Namaḥ* I	ॐ वह्नये नमः ।
149.	*Oṃ Tapanāya Namaḥ* I	ॐ तपनाय नमः ।
150.	*Oṃ Sampratāpanāya Namaḥ*	ॐ संप्रतापनाय नमः ।
151.	*Oṃ Virocanāya Namaḥ* I	ॐ विरोचनाय नमः ।
152.	*Oṃ Virūpākṣāya Namaḥ* I	ॐ विरूपाक्षाय नमः ।
153.	*Oṃ Sahasrākṣāya Namaḥ* I	ॐ सहस्राक्षाय नमः ।
154.	*Oṃ Purandarāya Namaḥ* I	ॐ पुरन्दराय नमः ।
155.	*Oṃ Sahasraraśmaye Namaḥ*	ॐ सहस्ररश्मये नमः ।
156.	*Oṃ Mihirāya Namaḥ* I	ॐ मिहिराय नमः ।
157.	*Oṃ Vividhāmbarabhūṣaṇāya Namaḥ* I	ॐ विविधाम्बरभूषणाय नमः ।
158.	*Oṃ Khagāya Namaḥ* I	ॐ खगाय नमः ।
159.	*Oṃ Pratardanāya Namaḥ* I	ॐ प्रतर्दनाय नमः ।
160.	*Oṃ Dhanyāya Namaḥ* I	ॐ धन्याय नमः ।
161.	*Oṃ Hayagāya Namaḥ* I	ॐ हयगाय नमः ।
162.	*Oṃ Vāgviśāradāya Namaḥ* I	ॐ वाग्विशारदाय नमः ।
163.	*Oṃ Śrīmate Namaḥ* I	ॐ श्रीमते नमः ।
164.	*Oṃ Aśiśirāya Namaḥ* I	ॐ अशिशिराय नमः ।
165.	*Oṃ Vāgmine Namaḥ* I	ॐ वाग्मिने नमः ।
166.	*Oṃ Śrīpataye Namaḥ* I	ॐ श्रीपतये नमः ।
167.	*Oṃ Śrīniketanāya Namaḥ* I	ॐ श्रीनिकेतनाय नमः ।
168.	*Oṃ Śrīkaṇṭhāya Namaḥ* I	ॐ श्रीकण्ठाय नमः ।

169.	*Oṃ Śrīdharāya Namaḥ* I	ॐ श्रीधराय नमः ।
170.	*Oṃ Śrīmate Namaḥ* I	ॐ श्रीमते नमः ।
171.	*Oṃ Śrīnivāsāya Namaḥ* I	ॐ श्रीनिवासाय नमः ।
172.	*Oṃ Vasupradāya Namaḥ* I	ॐ वसुप्रदाय नमः ।
173.	*Oṃ Kāmacāriṇe Namaḥ* I	ॐ कामचारिणे नमः ।
174.	*Oṃ Mahāmāyāya Namaḥ* I	ॐ महामायाय नमः ।
175.	*Oṃ Mahogrāya Namaḥ* I	ॐ महोग्राय नमः ।
176.	*Oṃ Aviditāmayāya Namaḥ* I	ॐ अविदितामयाय नमः ।
177.	*Oṃ Tīrthakriyāvate Namaḥ* I	ॐ तीर्थक्रियावते नमः ।
178.	*Oṃ Sunayāya Namaḥ* I	ॐ सुनयाय नमः ।
179.	*Oṃ Vibhaktāya Namaḥ* I	ॐ विभक्ताय नमः ।
180.	*Oṃ Bhaktavatsalāya Namaḥ*	ॐ भक्तवत्सलाय नमः ।
181.	*Oṃ Kīrtaye Namaḥ* I	ॐ कीर्तये नमः ।
182.	*Oṃ Kīrtikarāya Namaḥ* I	ॐ कीर्तिकराय नमः ।
183.	*Oṃ Nityāya Namaḥ* I	ॐ नित्याय नमः ।
184.	*Oṃ Kuṇḍaline Namaḥ* I	ॐ कुण्डलिने नमः ।
185.	*Oṃ Kavacine Namaḥ* I	ॐ कवचिने नमः ।
186.	*Oṃ Rathine Namaḥ* I	ॐ रथिने नमः ।
187.	*Oṃ Hiraṇyaretase Namaḥ* I	ॐ हिरण्यरेतसे नमः ।
188.	*Oṃ Saptāśvāya Namaḥ* I	ॐ सप्ताश्वाय नमः ।
189.	*Oṃ Prayatātmane Namaḥ* I	ॐ प्रयतात्मने नमः ।
190.	*Oṃ Parantapāya Namaḥ* I	ॐ परन्तपाय नमः।
191.	*Oṃ Buddhimate Namaḥ* I	ॐ बुद्धिमते नमः ।
192.	*Oṃ Amaraśreṣṭhāya Namaḥ*	ॐ अमरश्रेष्ठाय नमः ।
193.	*Oṃ Rociṣṇave Namaḥ* I	ॐ रोचिष्णवे नमः ।
194.	*Oṃ Pākaśāsanāya Namaḥ* I	ॐ पाकशासनाय नमः ।

195.	*Oṃ Samudrāya Namaḥ* ।	ॐ समुद्राय नमः ।
196.	*Oṃ Dhanadāya Namaḥ* ।	ॐ धनदाय नमः ।
197.	*Oṃ Dhātre Namaḥ* ।	ॐ धात्रे नमः ।
198.	*Oṃ Māndhātre Namaḥ* ।	ॐ मान्धात्रे नमः ।
199.	*Oṃ Kaśmalāpahāya Namaḥ* ।	ॐ कश्मलापहाय नमः ।
200.	*Oṃ Tamoghnāya Namaḥ* ।	ॐ तमोघ्नाय नमः ।
201.	*Oṃ Dhvāntaghne Namaḥ* ।	ॐ ध्वान्तघ्ने नमः ।
202.	*Oṃ Vahnaye Namaḥ* ।	ॐ वह्नये नमः ।
203.	*Oṃ Hotre Namaḥ* ।	ॐ होत्रे नमः ।
204.	*Oṃ Antaḥkaraṇāya Namaḥ* ।	ॐ अन्तःकरणाय नमः ।
205.	*Oṃ Guhāya Namaḥ* ।	ॐ गुहाय नमः ।
206.	*Oṃ Paśumate Namaḥ* ।	ॐ पशुमते नमः ।
207.	*Oṃ Prayatānandāya Namaḥ*	ॐ प्रयतानन्दाय नमः ।
208.	*Oṃ Bhūteśāya Namaḥ* ।	ॐ भूतेशाय नमः ।
209.	*Oṃ Śrīmatāṃ Varāya Namaḥ* ।	ॐ श्रीमतां वराय नमः ।
210.	*Oṃ Nityāya Namaḥ* ।	ॐ नित्याय नमः ।
211.	*Oṃ Aditāya Namaḥ* ।	ॐ अदिताय नमः ।
212.	*Oṃ Nityarathāya Namaḥ* ।	ॐ नित्यरथाय नमः ।
213.	*Oṃ Sureśāya Namaḥ* ।	ॐ सुरेशाय नमः ।
214.	*Oṃ Surapūjitāya Namaḥ* ।	ॐ सुरपूजिताय नमः ।
215.	*Oṃ Ajitāya Namaḥ* ।	ॐ अजिताय नमः ।
216.	*Oṃ Vijitāya Namaḥ* ।	ॐ विजिताय नमः ।
217.	*Oṃ Jetre Namaḥ* ।	ॐ जेत्रे नमः ।
218.	*Oṃ Jaṅgama Sthāvarātmakāya Namaḥ* ।	ॐ जङ्गमस्थावरात्मकाय नमः ।
219.	*Oṃ Jīvānandāya Namaḥ* ।	ॐ जीवानन्दाय नमः ।

220.	*Oṃ Nityagāmine Namaḥ* |	ॐ नित्यगामिने नमः ।
221.	*Oṃ Vijetre Namaḥ* |	ॐ विजेत्रे नमः ।
222.	*Oṃ Vijayapradāya Namaḥ* |	ॐ विजयप्रदाय नमः ।
223.	*Oṃ Parjanyāya Namaḥ* |	ॐ पर्जन्याय नमः ।
224.	*Oṃ Agnaye Namaḥ* |	ॐ अग्नये नमः ।
225.	*Oṃ Sthitaye Namaḥ* |	ॐ स्थितये नमः ।
226.	*Oṃ Stheyāya Namaḥ* |	ॐ स्थेयाय नमः ।
227.	*Oṃ Sthavirāya Namaḥ* |	ॐ स्थविराय नमः ।
228.	*Oṃ Nirañjanāya Namaḥ* |	ॐ निरञ्जनाय नमः ।
229.	*Oṃ Pradyotanāya Namaḥ* |	ॐ प्रद्योतनाय नमः ।
230.	*Oṃ Rathārūḍhāya Namaḥ* |	ॐ रथारूढाय नमः ।
231.	*Oṃ Sarvalokaprakāśakāya Namaḥ* |	ॐ सर्वलोकप्रकाशकाय नमः ।
232.	*Oṃ Dhruvāya Namaḥ* |	ॐ ध्रुवाय नमः ।
233.	*Oṃ Meṣine Namaḥ* |	ॐ मेषिने नमः ।
234.	*Oṃ Mahāvīryāya Namaḥ* |	ॐ महावीर्याय नमः ।
235.	*Oṃ Haṃsāya Namaḥ* |	ॐ हंसाय नमः ।
236.	*Oṃ Saṃsāratārakāya Namaḥ* |	ॐ संसारतारकाय नमः ।
237.	*Oṃ Sṛṣṭikartre Namaḥ* |	ॐ सृष्टिकर्त्रे नमः ।
238.	*Oṃ Kriyāhetave Namaḥ* |	ॐ क्रियाहेतवे नमः ।
239.	*Oṃ Mārtaṇḍāya Namaḥ* |	ॐ मार्तण्डाय नमः ।
240.	*Oṃ Marutāṃ Namaḥ* |	ॐ मरुतां नमः ।
241.	*Oṃ Pataye Namaḥ* |	ॐ पतये नमः ।
242.	*Oṃ Marutvate Namaḥ* |	ॐ मरुत्वते नमः ।
243.	*Oṃ Dahanāya Namaḥ* |	ॐ दहनाय नमः ।

244.	*Oṃ Tvaṣṭre Namaḥ* |	ॐ त्वष्ट्रे नमः ।
245.	*Oṃ Bhagāya Namaḥ* |	ॐ भगाय नमः ।
246.	*Oṃ Bhargāya Namaḥ* |	ॐ भर्गाय नमः ।
247.	*Oṃ Aryamṇe Namaḥ* |	ॐ अर्यम्णे नमः ।
248.	*Oṃ Kapaye Namaḥ* |	ॐ कपये नमः ।
249.	*Oṃ Varuṇeśāya Namaḥ* |	ॐ वरुणेशाय नमः ।
250.	*Oṃ Jagannāthāya Namaḥ* |	ॐ जगन्नाथाय नमः ।
251.	*Oṃ Kṛtakṛtyāya Namaḥ* |	ॐ कृतकृत्याय नमः ।
252.	*Oṃ Sulocanāya Namaḥ* |	ॐ सुलोचनाय नमः ।
253.	*Oṃ Vivasvate Namaḥ* |	ॐ विवस्वते नमः ।
254.	*Oṃ Bhānumate Namaḥ* |	ॐ भानुमते नमः ।
255.	*Oṃ Kāryāya Namaḥ* |	ॐ कार्याय नमः ।
256.	*Oṃ Kāraṇāya Namaḥ* |	ॐ कारणाय नमः ।
257.	*Oṃ Tejasāṃ Nidhaye Namaḥ*	ॐ तेजसां निधये नमः ।
258.	*Oṃ Asaṅgagāmine Namaḥ* |	ॐ असङ्गगामिने नमः ।
259.	*Oṃ Tigmāṃśave Namaḥ* |	ॐ तिग्मांशवे नमः ।
260.	*Oṃ Dharmāṃśave Namaḥ* |	ॐ धर्मांशवे नमः ।
261.	*Oṃ Dīptadīdhitaye Namaḥ* |	ॐ दीप्तदीधितये नमः ।
262.	*Oṃ Sahasradīdhitaye Namaḥ*	ॐ सहस्रदीधितये नमः ।
263.	*Oṃ Bradhnāya Namaḥ* |	ॐ ब्रध्नाय नमः ।
264.	*Oṃ Sahasrāṃśave Namaḥ* |	ॐ सहस्रांशवे नमः ।
265.	*Oṃ Divākarāya Namaḥ* |	ॐ दिवाकराय नमः ।
266.	*Oṃ Gabhastimate Namaḥ* |	ॐ गभस्तिमते नमः ।
267.	*Oṃ Dīdhitimate Namaḥ* |	ॐ दीधितिमते नमः ।
268.	*Oṃ Sragviṇe Namaḥ* |	ॐ स्रग्विणे नमः ।
269.	*Oṃ Maṇikuladyutaye Namaḥ*	ॐ मणिकुलद्युतये नमः ।
270.	*Oṃ Bhāskarāya Namaḥ* |	ॐ भास्कराय नमः ।

271.	*Oṃ Surakāryajñāya Namaḥ* I	ॐ सुरकार्यज्ञाय नमः ।
272.	*Oṃ Sarvajñāya Namaḥ* I	ॐ सर्वज्ञाय नमः ।
273.	*Oṃ Tīkṣṇadīdhitaye Namaḥ* I	ॐ तीक्ष्णदीधितये नमः ।
274.	*Oṃ Surajyeṣṭhāya Namaḥ* I	ॐ सुरज्येष्ठाय नमः ।
275.	*Oṃ Surapataye Namaḥ* I	ॐ सुरपतये नमः ।
276.	*Oṃ Bahujñāya Namaḥ* I	ॐ बहुज्ञाय नमः ।
277.	*Oṃ Vacasāṃ Pataye Namaḥ*	ॐ वचसां पतये नमः ।
278.	*Oṃ Tejonidhaye Namaḥ* I	ॐ तेजोनिधये नमः ।
279.	*Oṃ Bṛhattejase Namaḥ* I	ॐ बृहत्तेजसे नमः ।
280.	*Oṃ Bṛhatkīrtaye Namaḥ* I	ॐ बृहत्कीर्तये नमः ।
281.	*Oṃ Bṛhaspataye Namaḥ* I	ॐ बृहस्पतये नमः ।
282.	*Oṃ Ahimate Namaḥ* I	ॐ अहिमते नमः ।
283.	*Oṃ Ūrjitāya Namaḥ* I	ॐ ऊर्जिताय नमः ।
284.	*Oṃ Dhīmate Namaḥ* I	ॐ धीमते नमः ।
285.	*Oṃ Āmuktāya Namaḥ* I	ॐ आमुक्ताय नमः ।
286.	*Oṃ Kīrtivardhanāya Namaḥ* I	ॐ कीर्तिवर्धनाय नमः ।
287.	*Oṃ Mahāvaidyāya Namaḥ* I	ॐ महावैद्याय नमः ।
288.	*Oṃ Gaṇapataye Namaḥ* I	ॐ गणपतये नमः ।
289.	*Oṃ Dhaneśāya Namaḥ* I	ॐ धनेशाय नमः ।
290.	*Oṃ Gaṇanāyakāya Namaḥ* I	ॐ गणनायकाय नमः ।
291.	*Oṃ Tīvrapratāpanāya Namaḥ* I	ॐ तीव्रप्रतापनाय नमः ।
292.	*Oṃ Tāpine Namaḥ* I	ॐ तापिने नमः ।
293.	*Oṃ Tāpanāya Namaḥ* I	ॐ तापनाय नमः ।
294.	*Oṃ Viśvatāpanāya Namaḥ* I	ॐ विश्वतापनाय नमः ।
295.	*Oṃ Kārtasvarāya Namaḥ* I	ॐ कार्तस्वराय नमः ।
296.	*Oṃ Hṛṣīkeśāya Namaḥ* I	ॐ हृषीकेशाय नमः ।

297.	Oṃ Padmānandāya Namaḥ ।	ॐ पद्मानन्दाय नमः ।
298.	Oṃ Atinanditāya Namaḥ ।	ॐ अतिनन्दिताय नमः ।
299.	Oṃ Padmanābhāya Namaḥ ।	ॐ पद्मनाभाय नमः ।
300.	Oṃ Amṛtāhārāya Namaḥ ।	ॐ अमृताहाराय नमः ।
301.	Oṃ Sthitimate Namaḥ ।	ॐ स्थितिमते नमः ।
302.	Oṃ Ketumate Namaḥ ।	ॐ केतुमते नमः ।
303.	Oṃ Nabhase Namaḥ ।	ॐ नभसे नमः ।
304.	Oṃ Anādyantāya Namaḥ ।	ॐ अनाद्यन्ताय नमः ।
305.	Oṃ Acyutāya Namaḥ ।	ॐ अच्युताय नमः ।
306.	Oṃ Viśvāya Namaḥ ।	ॐ विश्वाय नमः ।
307.	Oṃ Viśvāmitrāya Namaḥ ।	ॐ विश्वामित्राय नमः ।
308.	Oṃ Ghṛṇaye Namaḥ ।	ॐ घृणये नमः ।
309.	Oṃ Virāje Namaḥ ।	ॐ विराजे नमः ।
310.	Oṃ Āmuktakavacāya Namaḥ	ॐ आमुक्तकवचाय नमः ।
311.	Oṃ Vāgmine Namaḥ ।	ॐ वाग्मिने नमः ।
312.	Oṃ Kañcukine Namaḥ ।	ॐ कञ्चुकिने नमः ।
313.	Oṃ Viśvabhāvanāya Namaḥ।	ॐ विश्वभावनाय नमः ।
314.	Oṃ Animittagataye Namaḥ ।	ॐ अनिमित्तगतये नमः ।
315.	Oṃ Śreṣṭhāya Namaḥ ।	ॐ श्रेष्ठाय नमः ।
316.	Oṃ Śaraṇyāya Namaḥ ।	ॐ शरण्याय नमः ।
317.	Oṃ Sarvatomukhāya Namaḥ	ॐ सर्वतोमुखाय नमः ।
318.	Oṃ Vigāhine Namaḥ ।	ॐ विगाहिने नमः ।
319.	Oṃ Veṇurasahāya Namaḥ ।	ॐ वेणुरसहाय नमः ।
320.	Oṃ Samāyuktāya Namaḥ ।	ॐ समायुक्ताय नमः ।
321.	Oṃ Samākratave Namaḥ ।	ॐ समाक्रतवे नमः ।
322.	Oṃ Dharmaketave Namaḥ ।	ॐ धर्मकेतवे नमः ।

323.	*Oṃ Dharmarataye Namaḥ* I	ॐ धर्मरतये नमः ।
324.	*Oṃ Saṃhartre Namaḥ* I	ॐ संहर्त्रे नमः ।
325.	*Oṃ Saṃyamāya Namaḥ* I	ॐ संयमाय नमः ।
326.	*Oṃ Yamāya Namaḥ* I	ॐ यमाय नमः ।
327.	*Oṃ Praṇatārtiharāya Namaḥ*	ॐ प्रणतार्तिहराय नमः ।
328.	*Oṃ Vāyave Namaḥ* I	ॐ वायवे नमः ।
329.	*Oṃ Siddhakāryāya Namaḥ* I	ॐ सिद्धकार्याय नमः ।
330.	*Oṃ Janeśvarāya Namaḥ* I	ॐ जनेश्वराय नमः ।
331.	*Oṃ Nabhase Namaḥ* I	ॐ नभसे नमः ।
332.	*Oṃ Vigāhanāya Namaḥ* I	ॐ विगाहनाय नमः ।
333.	*Oṃ Satyāya Namaḥ* I	ॐ सत्याय नमः ।
334.	*Oṃ Savitre Namaḥ* I	ॐ सवित्रे नमः ।
335.	*Oṃ Ātmane Namaḥ* I	ॐ आत्मने नमः ।
336.	*Oṃ Manoharāya Namaḥ* I	ॐ मनोहराय नमः ।
337.	*Oṃ Hāriṇe Namaḥ* I	ॐ हारिणे नमः ।
338.	*Oṃ Haraye Namaḥ* I	ॐ हरये नमः ।
339.	*Oṃ Harāya Namaḥ* I	ॐ हराय नमः ।
340.	*Oṃ Vāyave Namaḥ* I	ॐ वायवे नमः ।
341.	*Oṃ Ṛtave Namaḥ* I	ॐ ऋतवे नमः ।
342.	*Oṃ Kālānaladyutaye Namaḥ*	ॐ कालानलद्युतये नमः ।
343.	*Oṃ Sukhasevyāya Namaḥ* I	ॐ सुखसेव्याय नमः ।
344.	*Oṃ Mahātejase Namaḥ* I	ॐ महातेजसे नमः ।
345.	*Oṃ Jagatāmekakāraṇāya Namaḥ* I	ॐ जगतामेककारणाय नमः ।
346.	*Oṃ Mahendrāya Namaḥ* I	ॐ महेन्द्राय नमः ।
347.	*Oṃ Viṣṭutāya Namaḥ* I	ॐ विष्टुताय नमः ।
348.	*Oṃ Stotrāya Namaḥ* I	ॐ स्तोत्राय नमः ।

349.	Oṃ Stutihetave Namaḥ I	ॐ स्तुतिहेतवे नमः ।
350.	Oṃ Prabhākarāya Namaḥ I	ॐ प्रभाकराय नमः ।
351.	Oṃ Sahasrakarāya Namaḥ I	ॐ सहस्रकराय नमः ।
352.	Oṃ Āyuṣmate Namaḥ I	ॐ आयुष्मते नमः ।
353.	Oṃ Aroṣāya Namaḥ I	ॐ अरोषाय नमः ।
354.	Oṃ Sukhadāya Namaḥ I	ॐ सुखदाय नमः ।
355.	Oṃ Sukhine Namaḥ I	ॐ सुखिने नमः ।
356.	Oṃ Vyādhighne Namaḥ I	ॐ व्याधिघ्ने नमः ।
357.	Oṃ Sukhadāya Namaḥ I	ॐ सुखदाय नमः ।
358.	Oṃ Saukhyāya Namaḥ I	ॐ सौख्याय नमः ।
359.	Oṃ Kalyāṇāya Namaḥ I	ॐ कल्याणाय नमः ।
360.	Oṃ Kalatāṃ Varāya Namaḥ I	ॐ कलतां वराय नमः ।
361.	Oṃ Ārogyakāraṇāya Namaḥ	ॐ आरोग्यकारणाय नमः ।
362.	Oṃ Siddhaye Namaḥ I	ॐ सिद्धये नमः ।
363.	Oṃ Ṛddhaye Namaḥ I	ॐ ऋद्धये नमः ।
364.	Oṃ Vṛddhaye Namaḥ I	ॐ वृद्धये नमः ।
365.	Oṃ Bṛhaspataye Namaḥ I	ॐ बृहस्पतये नमः ।
366.	Oṃ Hiraṇyaretase Namaḥ I	ॐ हिरण्यरेतसे नमः ।
367.	Oṃ Ārogyāya Namaḥ I	ॐ आरोग्याय नमः ।
368.	Oṃ Viduṣe Namaḥ I	ॐ विदुषे नमः ।
369.	Oṃ Bradhnāya Namaḥ I	ॐ ब्रध्नाय नमः ।
370.	Oṃ Budhāya Namaḥ I	ॐ बुधाय नमः ।
371.	Oṃ Mahate Namaḥ I	ॐ महते नमः ।
372.	Oṃ Prāṇavate Namaḥ I	ॐ प्राणवते नमः ।
373.	Oṃ Dhṛtimate Namaḥ I	ॐ धृतिमते नमः ।
374.	Oṃ Gharmāya Namaḥ I	ॐ घर्माय नमः ।
375.	Oṃ Gharmakartre Namaḥ I	ॐ घर्मकर्त्रे नमः ।

376.	*Oṃ Rucipradāya Namaḥ* ।	ॐ रुचिप्रदाय नमः ।
377.	*Oṃ Sarvapriyāya Namaḥ* ।	ॐ सर्वप्रियाय नमः ।
378.	*Oṃ Sarvasahāya Namaḥ* ।	ॐ सर्वसहाय नमः ।
379.	*Oṃ Sarvaśatruvināśanāya Namaḥ* ।	ॐ सर्वशत्रुविनाशनाय नमः ।
380.	*Oṃ Prāṃśave Namaḥ* ।	ॐ प्रांशवे नमः ।
381.	*Oṃ Vidyotanāya Namaḥ* ।	ॐ विद्योतनाय नमः ।
382.	*Oṃ Dyotāya Namaḥ* ।	ॐ द्योताय नमः ।
383.	*Oṃ Sahasrakiraṇāya Namaḥ*	ॐ सहस्रकिरणाय नमः ।
384.	*Oṃ Kṛtine Namaḥ* ।	ॐ कृतिने नमः ।
385.	*Oṃ Keyūriṇe Namaḥ* ।	ॐ केयूरिणे नमः ।
386.	*Oṃ Bhūṣaṇodbhāsine Namaḥ* ।	ॐ भूषणोद्भासिने नमः ।
387.	*Oṃ Bhāsitāya Namaḥ* ।	ॐ भासिताय नमः ।
388.	*Oṃ Bhāsanāya Namaḥ* ।	ॐ भासनाय नमः ।
389.	*Oṃ Analāya Namaḥ* ।	ॐ अनलाय नमः ।
390.	*Oṃ Śaraṇyārtiharāya Namaḥ*	ॐ शरण्यार्तिहराय नमः ।
391.	*Oṃ Hotre Namaḥ* ।	ॐ होत्रे नमः ।
392.	*Oṃ Khadyotāya Namaḥ* ।	ॐ खद्योताय नमः ।
393.	*Oṃ Khagasattamāya Namaḥ*	ॐ खगसत्तमाय नमः ।
394.	*Oṃ Sarvadyotāya Namaḥ* ।	ॐ सर्वद्योताय नमः ।
395.	*Oṃ Bhavadyotāya Namaḥ* ।	ॐ भवद्योताय नमः ।
396.	*Oṃ Sarvadyutikarāya Namaḥ* ।	ॐ सर्वद्युतिकराय नमः ।
397.	*Oṃ Matāya Namaḥ* ।	ॐ मताय नमः ।
398.	*Oṃ Kalyāṇāya Namaḥ* ।	ॐ कल्याणाय नमः ।
399.	*Oṃ Kalyāṇakarāya Namaḥ* ।	ॐ कल्याणकराय नमः ।
400.	*Oṃ Kalyāya Namaḥ* ।	ॐ कल्याय नमः ।

401.	Oṃ Kalyakarāya Namaḥ ।	ॐ कल्यकराय नमः ।
402.	Oṃ Kavaye Namaḥ ।	ॐ कवये नमः ।
403.	Oṃ Kalyāṇakṛte Namaḥ ।	ॐ कल्याणकृते नमः ।
404.	Oṃ Kalyavapave Namaḥ ।	ॐ कल्यवपवे नमः ।
405.	Oṃ Sarvakalyāṇabhājanāya Namaḥ ।	ॐ सर्वकल्याणभाजनाय नमः ।
406.	Oṃ Śāntipriyāya Namaḥ ।	ॐ शान्तिप्रियाय नमः ।
407.	Oṃ Prasannātmane Namaḥ ।	ॐ प्रसन्नात्मने नमः ।
408.	Oṃ Praśāntāya Namaḥ ।	ॐ प्रशान्ताय नमः ।
409.	Oṃ Praśamapriyāya Namaḥ ।	ॐ प्रशमप्रियाय नमः ।
410.	Oṃ Udārakarmaṇe Namaḥ ।	ॐ उदारकर्मणे नमः ।
411.	Oṃ Sunayāya Namaḥ ।	ॐ सुनयाय नमः ।
412.	Oṃ Suvarcase Namaḥ ।	ॐ सुवर्चसे नमः ।
413.	Oṃ Varcasojjvalāya Namaḥ ।	ॐ वर्चसोज्ज्वलाय नमः ।
414.	Oṃ Varcasvine Namaḥ ।	ॐ वर्चस्विने नमः ।
415.	Oṃ Varcasāmīśāya Namaḥ ।	ॐ वर्चसामीशाय नगः ।
416.	Oṃ Trailokyeśāya Namaḥ ।	ॐ त्रैलोक्येशाय नमः ।
417.	Oṃ Vaśānugāya Namaḥ ।	ॐ वशानुगाय नमः ।
418.	Oṃ Tejasvine Namaḥ ।	ॐ तेजस्विने नमः ।
419.	Oṃ Suyaśase Namaḥ ।	ॐ सुयशसे नमः ।
420.	Oṃ Varṣmiṇe Namaḥ ।	ॐ वर्ष्मिणे नमः ।
421.	Oṃ Varṇādhyakṣāya Namaḥ	ॐ वर्णाध्यक्षाय नमः ।
422.	Oṃ Balipriyāya Namaḥ ।	ॐ बलिप्रियाय नमः ।
423.	Oṃ Yaśasvine Namaḥ ।	ॐ यशस्विने नमः ।
424.	Oṃ Tejonilayāya Namaḥ ।	ॐ तेजोनिलयाय नमः ।
425.	Oṃ Tejasvine Namaḥ ।	ॐ तेजस्विने नमः ।
426.	Oṃ Prakṛtisthitāya Namaḥ ।	ॐ प्रकृतिस्थिताय नमः ।

427.	*Oṃ Ākāśagāya Namaḥ* I	ॐ आकाशगाय नमः ।
428.	*Oṃ Śīghragataye Namaḥ* I	ॐ शीघ्रगतये नमः ।
429.	*Oṃ Āśugāya Namaḥ* I	ॐ आशुगाय नमः ।
430.	*Oṃ Gatimate Namaḥ* I	ॐ गतिमते नमः ।
431.	*Oṃ Khagāya Namaḥ* I	ॐ खगाय नमः ।
432.	*Oṃ Gopataye Namaḥ* I	ॐ गोपतये नमः ।
433.	*Oṃ Grahadeveśāya Namaḥ* I	ॐ ग्रहदेवेशाय नमः ।
434.	*Oṃ Gomate Namaḥ* I	ॐ गोमते नमः ।
435.	*Oṃ Ekāya Namaḥ* I	ॐ एकाय नमः ।
436.	*Oṃ Prabhañjanāya Namaḥ* I	ॐ प्रभञ्जनाय नमः ।
437.	*Oṃ Janitre Namaḥ* I	ॐ जनित्रे नमः ।
438.	*Oṃ Prajanāya Namaḥ* I	ॐ प्रजनाय नमः ।
439.	*Oṃ Jīvāya Namaḥ* I	ॐ जीवाय नमः ।
440.	*Oṃ Dīpāya Namaḥ* I	ॐ दीपाय नमः ।
441.	*Oṃ Sarvaprakāśakāya Namaḥ* I	ॐ सर्वप्रकाशकाय नमः ।
442.	*Oṃ Sarvasākṣine Namaḥ* I	ॐ सर्वसाक्षिने नमः ।
443.	*Oṃ Yoganityāya Namaḥ* I	ॐ योगनित्याय नमः ।
444.	*Oṃ Nabhasvate Namaḥ* I	ॐ नभस्वते नमः ।
445.	*Oṃ Asurāntakāya Namaḥ* I	ॐ असुरान्तकाय नमः ।
446.	*Oṃ Rakṣoghnāya Namaḥ* I	ॐ रक्षोघ्नाय नमः ।
447.	*Oṃ Vighnaśamanāya Namaḥ*	ॐ विघ्नशमनाय नमः ।
448.	*Oṃ Kirīṭine Namaḥ* I	ॐ किरीटिने नमः ।
449.	*Oṃ Sumanaḥpriyāya Namaḥ*	ॐ सुमनःप्रियाय नमः ।
450.	*Oṃ Marīcimāline Namaḥ* I	ॐ मरीचिमालिने नमः ।
451.	*Oṃ Sumataye Namaḥ* I	ॐ सुमतये नमः ।
452.	*Oṃ Kṛtābhikhyaviśeṣakāya Namaḥ* I	ॐ कृताभिख्यविशेषकाय नमः ।

453.	*Oṃ Śiṣṭācārāya Namaḥ* I	ॐ शिष्टाचाराय नमः ।
454.	*Oṃ Śubhākārāya Namaḥ* I	ॐ शुभाकाराय नमः ।
455.	*Oṃ Svacārācāratatparāya Namaḥ* I	ॐ स्वचाराचारतत्पराय नमः ।
456.	*Oṃ Mandārāya Namaḥ* I	ॐ मन्दाराय नमः ।
457.	*Oṃ Māṭharāya Namaḥ* I	ॐ माठराय नमः ।
458.	*Oṃ Veṇave Namaḥ* I	ॐ वेणवे नमः ।
459.	*Oṃ Kṣudhāpāya Namaḥ* I	ॐ क्षुधापाय नमः ।
460.	*Oṃ Kṣmāpataye Namaḥ* I	ॐ क्ष्मापतये नमः ।
461.	*Oṃ Gurave Namaḥ* I	ॐ गुरवे नमः ।
462.	*Oṃ Suviśiṣṭāya Namaḥ* I	ॐ सुविशिष्टाय नमः ।
463.	*Oṃ Viśiṣṭātmane Namaḥ* I	ॐ विशिष्टात्मने नमः ।
464.	*Oṃ Vidheyāya Namaḥ* I	ॐ विधेयाय नमः ।
465.	*Oṃ Jñānaśobhanāya Namaḥ*	ॐ ज्ञानशोभनाय नमः ।
466.	*Oṃ Mahāśvetāya Namaḥ* I	ॐ महाश्वेताय नमः ।
467.	*Oṃ Priyāya Namaḥ* I	ॐ प्रियाय नमः ।
468.	*Oṃ Jñeyāya Namaḥ* I	ॐ ज्ञेयाय नमः ।
469.	*Oṃ Sāmagāya Namaḥ* I	ॐ सामगाय नमः ।
470.	*Oṃ Mokṣadāyakāya Namaḥ* I	ॐ मोक्षदायकाय नमः ।
471.	*Oṃ Sarvavedapragītātmane Namaḥ* I	ॐ सर्ववेदप्रगीतात्मने नमः ।
472.	*Oṃ Sarvavedalayāya Namaḥ*	ॐ सर्ववेदलयाय नमः ।
473.	*Oṃ Mahate Namaḥ* I	ॐ महते नमः ।
474.	*Oṃ Vedamūrtaye Namaḥ* I	ॐ वेदमूर्तये नमः ।
475.	*Oṃ Caturvedāya Namaḥ* I	ॐ चतुर्वेदाय नमः ।
476.	*Oṃ Vedabhṛte Namaḥ* I	ॐ वेदभृते नमः ।
477.	*Oṃ Vedapāragāya Namaḥ* I	ॐ वेदपारगाय नमः ।

478.	*Oṃ Kriyāvate Namaḥ* I	ॐ क्रियावते नमः ।
479.	*Oṃ Asitāya Namaḥ* I	ॐ असिताय नमः ।
480.	*Oṃ Jiṣṇave Namaḥ* I	ॐ जिष्णवे नमः ।
481.	*Oṃ Varīyāṃśave Namaḥ* I	ॐ वरीयांशवे नमः ।
482.	*Oṃ Varapradāya Namaḥ* I	ॐ वरप्रदाय नमः ।
483.	*Oṃ Vratacāriṇe Namaḥ* I	ॐ व्रतचारिणे नमः ।
484.	*Oṃ Vratadharāya Namaḥ* I	ॐ व्रतधराय नमः ।
485.	*Oṃ Lokabandhave Namaḥ* I	ॐ लोकबन्धवे नमः ।
486.	*Oṃ Alaṅkṛtāya Namaḥ* I	ॐ अलङ्कृताय नमः ।
487.	*Oṃ Alaṅkārākṣarāya Namaḥ*	ॐ अलङ्काराक्षराय नमः ।
488.	*Oṃ Vedyāya Namaḥ* I	ॐ वेद्याय नमः ।
489.	*Oṃ Vidyāvate Namaḥ* I	ॐ विद्यावते नमः ।
490.	*Oṃ Viditāśayāya Namaḥ* I	ॐ विदिताशयाय नमः ।
491.	*Oṃ Ākārāya Namaḥ* I	ॐ आकाराय नमः ।
492.	*Oṃ Bhūṣaṇāya Namaḥ* I	ॐ भूषणाय नमः ।
493.	*Oṃ Bhūṣyāya Namaḥ* I	ॐ भूष्याय नमः ।
494.	*Oṃ Bhūṣṇave Namaḥ* I	ॐ भूष्णवे नमः ।
495.	*Oṃ Bhuvanapūjitāya Namaḥ*	ॐ भुवनपूजिताय नमः ।
496.	*Oṃ Cakrapāṇaye Namaḥ* I	ॐ चक्रपाणये नमः ।
497.	*Oṃ Dhvajadharāya Namaḥ* I	ॐ ध्वजधराय नमः ।
498.	*Oṃ Sureśāya Namaḥ* I	ॐ सुरेशाय नमः ।
499.	*Oṃ Lokavatsalāya Namaḥ* I	ॐ लोकवत्सलाय नमः ।
500.	*Oṃ Vāgmipataye Namaḥ* I	ॐ वाग्मिपतये नमः ।
501.	*Oṃ Mahābāhave Namaḥ* I	ॐ महाबाहवे नमः ।
502.	*Oṃ Prakṛtaye Namaḥ* I	ॐ प्रकृतये नमः ।
503.	*Oṃ Vikṛtaye Namaḥ* I	ॐ विकृतये नमः ।

504.	*Oṃ Guṇāya Namaḥ* I	ॐ गुणाय नमः ।
505.	*Oṃ Andhakārāpahāya Namaḥ* I	ॐ अन्धकारापहाय नमः ।
506.	*Oṃ Śreṣṭhāya Namaḥ* I	ॐ श्रेष्ठाय नमः ।
507.	*Oṃ Yugāvartāya Namaḥ* I	ॐ युगावर्ताय नमः ।
508.	*Oṃ Yugādikṛte Namaḥ* I	ॐ युगादिकृते नमः ।
509.	*Oṃ Aprameyāya Namaḥ* I	ॐ अप्रमेयाय नमः ।
510.	*Oṃ Sadāyogine Namaḥ* I	ॐ सदायोगिने नमः ।
511.	*Oṃ Nirahaṅkārāya Namaḥ* I	ॐ निरहङ्काराय नमः ।
512.	*Oṃ Īśvarāya Namaḥ* I	ॐ ईश्वराय नमः ।
513.	*Oṃ Śubhapradāya Namaḥ* I	ॐ शुभप्रदाय नमः ।
514.	*Oṃ Śubhāya Namaḥ* I	ॐ शुभाय नमः ।
515.	*Oṃ Śāstre Namaḥ* I	ॐ शास्त्रे नमः ।
516.	*Oṃ Śubhakarmaṇe Namaḥ* I	ॐ शुभकर्मणे नमः ।
517.	*Oṃ Śubhapradāya Namaḥ* I	ॐ शुभप्रदाय नमः ।
518.	*Oṃ Satyavate Namaḥ* I	ॐ सत्यवते नमः ।
519.	*Oṃ Śrutimate Namaḥ* I	ॐ श्रुतिमते नमः ।
520.	*Oṃ Uccairnakārāya Namaḥ* I	ॐ उच्चैर्नकाराय नमः ।
521.	*Oṃ Vṛddhidāya Namaḥ* I	ॐ वृद्धिदाय नमः ।
522.	*Oṃ Analāya Namaḥ* I	ॐ अनलाय नमः ।
523.	*Oṃ Balabhṛte Namaḥ* I	ॐ बलभृते नमः ।
524.	*Oṃ Baladāya Namaḥ* I	ॐ बलदाय नमः ।
525.	*Oṃ Bandhave Namaḥ* I	ॐ बन्धवे नमः ।
526.	*Oṃ Matimate Namaḥ* I	ॐ मतिमते नमः ।
527.	*Oṃ Balināṃ Varāya Namaḥ* I	ॐ बलिनां वराय नमः ।
528.	*Oṃ Anaṅgāya Namaḥ* I	ॐ अनङ्गाय नमः ।
529.	*Oṃ Nāgarājendrāya Namaḥ* I	ॐ नागराजेन्द्राय नमः ।

530.	*Oṃ Padmayonaye Namaḥ* |	ॐ पद्मयोनये नमः।
531.	*Oṃ Gaṇeśvarāya Namaḥ* |	ॐ गणेश्वराय नमः।
532.	*Oṃ Saṃvatsarāya Namaḥ* |	ॐ संवत्सराय नमः।
533.	*Oṃ Ṛtave Namaḥ* |	ॐ ऋतवे नमः।
534.	*Oṃ Netre Namaḥ* |	ॐ नेत्रे नमः।
535.	*Oṃ Kālacakrapravartakāya Namaḥ* |	ॐ कालचक्रप्रवर्तकाय नमः।
536.	*Oṃ Padmekṣaṇāya Namaḥ* |	ॐ पद्मेक्षणाय नमः।
537.	*Oṃ Padmayonaye Namaḥ* |	ॐ पद्मयोनये नमः।
538.	*Oṃ Prabhāvate Namaḥ* |	ॐ प्रभावते नमः।
539.	*Oṃ Amarāya Namaḥ* |	ॐ अमराय नमः।
540.	*Oṃ Prabhave Namaḥ* |	ॐ प्रभवे नमः।
541.	*Oṃ Sumūrtaye Namaḥ* |	ॐ सुमूर्तयेनमः।
542.	*Oṃ Sumataye Namaḥ* |	ॐ सुमतये नमः।
543.	*Oṃ Somāya Namaḥ* |	ॐ सोमाय नमः।
544.	*Oṃ Govindāya Namaḥ* |	ॐ गोविन्दाय नमः।
545.	*Oṃ Jagadādijāya Namaḥ* |	ॐ जगदादिजाय नमः।
546.	*Oṃ Pītavāsase Namaḥ* |	ॐ पीतवाससे नमः।
547.	*Oṃ Kṛṣṇavāsase Namaḥ* |	ॐ कृष्णवाससे नमः।
548.	*Oṃ Digvāsase Namaḥ* |	ॐ दिग्वाससे नमः।
549.	*Oṃ Indriyātigāya Namaḥ* |	ॐ इन्द्रियातिगाय नमः।
550.	*Oṃ Atīndriyāya Namaḥ* |	ॐ अतीन्द्रियाय नमः।
551.	*Oṃ Anekarūpāya Namaḥ* |	ॐ अनेकरूपाय नमः।
552.	*Oṃ Skandāya Namaḥ* |	ॐ स्कन्दाय नमः।
553.	*Oṃ Parapurañjayāya Namaḥ*	ॐ परपुरञ्जयाय नमः।
554.	*Oṃ Śaktimate Namaḥ* |	ॐ शक्तिमते नमः।
555.	*Oṃ Jaladhṛge Namaḥ* |	ॐ जलधृगे नमः।

556.	*Oṃ Bhāsvate Namaḥ* |	ॐ भास्वते नमः ।
557.	*Oṃ Mokṣahetave Namaḥ* |	ॐ मोक्षहेतवे नमः ।
558.	*Oṃ Ayonijāya Namaḥ* |	ॐ अयोनिजाय नमः ।
559.	*Oṃ Sarvadarśine Namaḥ* |	ॐ सर्वदर्शिने नमः ।
560.	*Oṃ Jitādarśāya Namaḥ* |	ॐ जितादर्शाय नमः ।
561.	*Oṃ Duḥsvapnā Śubhanāśanāya Namaḥ* |	ॐ दुःस्वप्नाशुभनाशनाय नमः ।
562.	*Oṃ Māṅgalyakartre Namaḥ* |	ॐ माङ्गल्यकर्त्रे नमः ।
563.	*Oṃ Taraṇaye Namaḥ* |	ॐ तरणये नमः ।
564.	*Oṃ Vegavate Namaḥ* |	ॐ वेगवते नमः ।
565.	*Oṃ Kaśmalāpahāya Namaḥ* |	ॐ कश्मलापहाय नमः ।
566.	*Oṃ Spaṣṭākṣarāya Namaḥ* |	ॐ स्पष्टाक्षराय नमः ।
567.	*Oṃ Mahāmantrāya Namaḥ* |	ॐ महामन्त्राय नमः ।
568.	*Oṃ Viśākhāya Namaḥ* |	ॐ विशाखाय नमः ।
569.	*Oṃ Yajanapriyāya Namaḥ* |	ॐ यजनप्रियाय नमः ।
570.	*Oṃ Viśvakarmaṇe Namaḥ* |	ॐ विश्वकर्मणे नमः ।
571.	*Oṃ Mahāśaktaye Namaḥ* |	ॐ महाशक्तये नमः ।
572.	*Oṃ Dyutaye Namaḥ* |	ॐ द्युतये नमः ।
573.	*Oṃ Īśāya Namaḥ* |	ॐ ईशाय नमः ।
574.	*Oṃ Vihaṅgamāya Namaḥ* |	ॐ विहङ्गमाय नमः ।
575.	*Oṃ Vicakṣaṇāya Namaḥ* |	ॐ विचक्षणाय नमः ।
576.	*Oṃ Dakṣāya Namaḥ* |	ॐ दक्षाय नमः ।
577.	*Oṃ Indrāya Namaḥ* |	ॐ इन्द्राय नमः ।
578.	*Oṃ Pratyūṣāya Namaḥ* |	ॐ प्रत्यूषाय नमः ।
579.	*Oṃ Priyadarśanāya Namaḥ* |	ॐ प्रियदर्शनाय नमः ।
580.	*Oṃ Akhinnāya Namaḥ* |	ॐ अखिन्नाय नमः ।

581.	*Oṃ Vedanilayāya Namaḥ* |	ॐ वेदनिलयाय नमः ।
582.	*Oṃ Vedavide Namaḥ* |	ॐ वेदविदे नमः ।
583.	*Oṃ Viditāśayāya Namaḥ* |	ॐ विदिताशयाय नमः ।
584.	*Oṃ Prabhākarāya Namaḥ* |	ॐ प्रभाकराय नमः ।
585.	*Oṃ Jitaripave Namaḥ* |	ॐ जितरिपवे नमः ।
586.	*Oṃ Sujanāya Namaḥ* |	ॐ सुजनाय नमः ।
587.	*Oṃ Aruṇasārathaye Namaḥ* |	ॐ अरुणसारथये नमः ।
588.	*Oṃ Kunāśine Namaḥ* |	ॐ कुनाशिने नमः ।
589.	*Oṃ Suratāya Namaḥ* |	ॐ सुरताय नमः ।
590.	*Oṃ Skandāya Namaḥ* |	ॐ स्कन्दाय नमः ।
591.	*Oṃ Mahitāya Namaḥ* |	ॐ महिताय नमः ।
592.	*Oṃ Abhimatāya Namaḥ* |	ॐ अभिमताय नमः ।
593.	*Oṃ Gurave Namaḥ* |	ॐ गुरवे नमः ।
594.	*Oṃ Graharājāya Namaḥ* |	ॐ ग्रहराजाय नमः ।
595.	*Oṃ Grahapataye Namaḥ* |	ॐ ग्रहपतये नमः ।
596.	*Oṃ Graha Nakṣatra Maṇḍalāya Namaḥ* |	ॐ ग्रहनक्षत्रमण्डलाय नमः ।
597.	*Oṃ Bhāskarāya Namaḥ* |	ॐ भास्कराय नमः ।
598.	*Oṃ Satatānandāya Namaḥ* |	ॐ सततानन्दाय नमः ।
599.	*Oṃ Nandanāya Namaḥ* |	ॐ नन्दनाय नमः ।
600.	*Oṃ Naravāhanāya Namaḥ* |	ॐ नरवाहनाय नमः ।
601.	*Oṃ Maṅgalāya Namaḥ* |	ॐ मङ्गलाय नमः ।
602.	*Oṃ Maṅgalavate Namaḥ* |	ॐ मङ्गलवते नमः ।
603.	*Oṃ Māṅgalyāya Namaḥ* |	ॐ माङ्गल्याय नमः ।
604.	*Oṃ Maṅgalāvahāya Namaḥ* |	ॐ मङ्गलावहाय नमः ।
605.	*Oṃ Maṅgalyacārucaritāya Namaḥ* |	ॐ मङ्गल्यचारुचरिताय नमः ।

606.	*Oṃ Śīrṇāya Namaḥ* |	ॐ शीर्णाय नमः ।
607.	*Oṃ Sarvavratāya Namaḥ* |	ॐ सर्वव्रताय नमः ।
608.	*Oṃ Vratine Namaḥ* |	ॐ व्रतिने नमः ।
609.	*Oṃ Caturmukhāya Namaḥ* |	ॐ चतुर्मुखाय नमः ।
610.	*Oṃ Padmamāline Namaḥ* |	ॐ पद्ममालिने नमः ।
611.	*Oṃ Pūtātmane Namaḥ* |	ॐ पूतात्मने नमः ।
612.	*Oṃ Praṇatārtighne Namaḥ* |	ॐ प्रणतार्तिघ्ने नमः ।
613.	*Oṃ Akiñcanāya Namaḥ* |	ॐ अकिञ्चनाय नमः ।
614.	*Oṃ Satāmīśāya Namaḥ* |	ॐ सतामीशाय नमः ।
615.	*Oṃ Nirguṇāya Namaḥ* |	ॐ निर्गुणाय नमः ।
616.	*Oṃ Guṇavate Namaḥ* |	ॐ गुणवते नमः ।
617.	*Oṃ Śucaye Namaḥ* |	ॐ शुचये नमः ।
618.	*Oṃ Sampūrṇāya Namaḥ* |	ॐ सम्पूर्णाय नमः ।
619.	*Oṃ Puṇḍarīkākṣāya Namaḥ* |	ॐ पुण्डरीकाक्षाय नमः ।
620.	*Oṃ Vidheyāya Namaḥ* |	ॐ विधेयाय नमः ।
621.	*Oṃ Yogatatparāya Namaḥ* |	ॐ योगतत्पराय नमः ।
622.	*Oṃ Sahasrāṃśave Namaḥ* |	ॐ सहस्रांशवे नमः ।
623.	*Oṃ Kratumataye Namaḥ* |	ॐ क्रतुमतये नमः ।
624.	*Oṃ Sarvajñāya Namaḥ* |	ॐ सर्वज्ञाय नमः ।
625.	*Oṃ Sumataye Namaḥ* |	ॐ सुमतये नमः ।
626.	*Oṃ Suvāce Namaḥ* |	ॐ सुवाचे नमः ।
627.	*Oṃ Suvāhanāya Namaḥ* |	ॐ सुवाहनाय नमः ।
628.	*Oṃ Mālyadāmne Namaḥ* |	ॐ माल्यदाम्ने नमः ।
629.	*Oṃ Kṛtāhārāya Namaḥ* |	ॐ कृताहाराय नमः ।
630.	*Oṃ Haripriyāya Namaḥ* |	ॐ हरिप्रियाय नमः ।
631.	*Oṃ Brahmaṇe Namaḥ* |	ॐ ब्रह्मणे नमः ।
632.	*Oṃ Pracetase Namaḥ* |	ॐ प्रचेतसे नमः ।

633.	*Oṃ Prathitāya Namaḥ* |	ॐ प्रथिताय नमः ।
634.	*Oṃ Prayatātmane Namaḥ* |	ॐ प्रयतात्मने नमः ।
635.	*Oṃ Sthirātmakāya Namaḥ* |	ॐ स्थिरात्मकाय नमः ।
636.	*Oṃ Śatavindave Namaḥ* |	ॐ शतविन्दवे नमः ।
637.	*Oṃ Śatamukhāya Namaḥ* |	ॐ शतमुखाय नमः ।
638.	*Oṃ Garīyase Namaḥ* |	ॐ गरीयसे नमः ।
639.	*Oṃ Analaprabhāya Namaḥ* |	ॐ अनलप्रभाय नमः ।
640.	*Oṃ Dhīrāya Namaḥ* |	ॐ धीराय नमः ।
641.	*Oṃ Mahattarāya Namaḥ* |	ॐ महत्तराय नमः ।
642.	*Oṃ Viprāya Namaḥ* |	ॐ विप्राय नमः ।
643.	*Oṃ Purāṇapuruṣottamāya Namaḥ* |	ॐ पुराणपुरुषोत्तमाय नमः ।
644.	*Oṃ Vidyārājādhirājāya Namaḥ* |	ॐ विद्याराजाधिराजाय नमः ।
645.	*Oṃ Vidyāvate Namaḥ* |	ॐ विद्यावते नमः ।
646.	*Oṃ Bhūtidāya Namaḥ* |	ॐ भूतिदाय नमः ।
647.	*Oṃ Sthitāya Namaḥ* |	ॐ स्थिताय नमः ।
648.	*Oṃ Anirdeśyavapave Namaḥ*	ॐ अनिर्देश्यवपवे नमः ।
649.	*Oṃ Śrīmate Namaḥ* |	ॐ श्रीमते नमः ।
650.	*Oṃ Vipāpmane Namaḥ* |	ॐ विपाप्मने नमः ।
651.	*Oṃ Bahumaṅgalāya Namaḥ* |	ॐ बहुमङ्गलाय नमः ।
652.	*Oṃ Svaḥsthitāya Namaḥ* |	ॐ स्वःस्थिताय नमः ।
653.	*Oṃ Surathāya Namaḥ* |	ॐ सुरथाय नमः ।
654.	*Oṃ Svarṇāya Namaḥ* |	ॐ स्वर्णाय नमः ।
655.	*Oṃ Mokṣadāya Namaḥ* |	ॐ मोक्षदाय नमः ।
656.	*Oṃ Baliketanāya Namaḥ* |	ॐ बलिकेतनाय नमः ।
657.	*Oṃ Nirdvandvāya Namaḥ* |	ॐ निर्द्वन्द्वाय नमः ।

658.	*Oṃ Dvandvaghne Namaḥ* ।	ॐ द्वन्द्वघ्ने नमः ।
659.	*Oṃ Sargāya Namaḥ* ।	ॐ सर्गाय नमः ।
660.	*Oṃ Sarvagāya Namaḥ* ।	ॐ सर्वगाय नमः ।
661.	*Oṃ Saṃprakāśakāya Namaḥ*	ॐ संप्रकाशकाय नमः ।
662.	*Oṃ Dayālave Namaḥ* ।	ॐ दयालवे नमः ।
663.	*Oṃ Sūkṣmadhiye Namaḥ* ।	ॐ सूक्ष्मधिये नमः ।
664.	*Oṃ Kṣāntaye Namaḥ* ।	ॐ क्षान्तये नमः ।
665.	*Oṃ Kṣemā Kṣema Sthiti Priyāya Namaḥ* ।	ॐ क्षेमाक्षेमस्थितिप्रियाय नमः ।
666.	*Oṃ Bhūdharāya Namaḥ* ।	ॐ भूधराय नमः ।
667.	*Oṃ Bhūpataye Namaḥ* ।	ॐ भूपतये नमः ।
668.	*Oṃ Vaktre Namaḥ* ।	ॐ वक्त्रे नमः ।
669.	*Oṃ Pavitrātmane Namaḥ* ।	ॐ पवित्रात्मने नमः ।
670.	*Oṃ Trilocanāya Namaḥ* ।	ॐ त्रिलोचनाय नमः ।
671.	*Oṃ Mahāvarāhāya Namaḥ* ।	ॐ महावराहाय नमः ।
672.	*Oṃ Priyakṛte Namaḥ* ।	ॐ प्रियकृते नमः ।
673.	*Oṃ Dātre Namaḥ* ।	ॐ दात्रे नमः ।
674.	*Oṃ Bhoktre Namaḥ* ।	ॐ भोक्त्रे नमः ।
675.	*Oṃ Abhayapradāya Namaḥ*।	ॐ अभयप्रदाय नमः ।
676.	*Oṃ Cakravartine Namaḥ* ।	ॐ चक्रवर्तिने नमः ।
677.	*Oṃ Dhṛtikarāya Namaḥ* ।	ॐ धृतिकराय नमः ।
678.	*Oṃ Sampūrṇāya Namaḥ* ।	ॐ सम्पूर्णाय नमः ।
679.	*Oṃ Maheśvarāya Namaḥ* ।	ॐ महेश्वराय नमः ।
680.	*Oṃ Caturvedadharāya Namaḥ* ।	ॐ चतुर्वेदधराय नमः ।
681.	*Oṃ Acintyāya Namaḥ* ।	ॐ अचिन्त्याय नमः ।
682.	*Oṃ Vinindyāya Namaḥ* ।	ॐ विनिन्द्याय नमः ।

683.	Oṃ Vividhāśanāya Namaḥ I	ॐ विविधाशनाय नमः ।
684.	Oṃ Vicitrarathāya Namaḥ I	ॐ विचित्ररथाय नमः ।
685.	Oṃ Ekākine Namaḥ I	ॐ एकाकिने नमः ।
686.	Oṃ Saptasaptaye Namaḥ I	ॐ सप्तसप्तये नमः ।
687.	Oṃ Parātparāya Namaḥ I	ॐ परात्पराय नमः ।
688.	Oṃ Sarvodadhisthitikarāya Namaḥ I	ॐ सर्वोदधिस्थितिकराय नमः ।
689.	Oṃ Sthitistheyāya Namaḥ I	ॐ स्थितिस्थेयाय नमः ।
690.	Oṃ Sthitipriyāya Namaḥ I	ॐ स्थितिप्रियाय नमः ।
691.	Oṃ Niṣkalāya Namaḥ I	ॐ निष्कलाय नमः ।
692.	Oṃ Puṣkalāya Namaḥ I	ॐ पुष्कलाय नमः ।
693.	Oṃ Vibhave Namaḥ I	ॐ विभवे नमः ।
694.	Oṃ Vasumate Namaḥ I	ॐ वसुमते नमः ।
695.	Oṃ Vāsavapriyāya Namaḥ I	ॐ वासवप्रियाय नमः ।
696.	Oṃ Paśumate Namaḥ I	ॐ पशुमते नमः ।
697.	Oṃ Vāsavasvāmine Namaḥ I	ॐ वासवस्वामिने नमः ।
698.	Oṃ Vasudhāmne Namaḥ I	ॐ वसुधाम्ने नमः ।
699.	Oṃ Vasupradāya Namaḥ I	ॐ वसुप्रदाय नमः ।
700.	Oṃ Balavate Namaḥ I	ॐ बलवते नमः ।
701.	Oṃ Jñānavate Namaḥ I	ॐ ज्ञानवते नमः ।
702.	Oṃ Tattvāya Namaḥ I	ॐ तत्त्वाय नमः ।
703.	Oṃ Oṃṅkārāya Namaḥ I	ॐ ओङ्काराय नमः ।
704.	Oṃ Triṣu Saṃsthitāya Namaḥ I	ॐ त्रिषु संस्थिताय नमः ।
705.	Oṃ Saṅkalpayonaye Namaḥ I	ॐ सङ्कल्पयोनये नमः ।
706.	Oṃ Dinakṛte Namaḥ I	ॐ दिनकृते नमः ।
707.	Oṃ Bhagavate Namaḥ I	ॐ भगवते नमः ।

708.	*Oṃ Kāraṇāpahāya Namaḥ* I	ॐ कारणापहाय नमः ।
709.	*Oṃ Nīlakaṇṭhāya Namaḥ* I	ॐ नीलकण्ठाय नमः ।
710.	*Oṃ Dhanādhyakṣāya Namaḥ*	ॐ धनाध्यक्षाय नमः ।
711.	*Oṃ Caturvedapriyaṃvadāya Namaḥ* I	ॐ चतुर्वेदप्रियंवदाय नमः ।
712.	*Oṃ Vaṣaṭkārāya Namaḥ* I	ॐ वषट्काराय नमः ।
713.	*Oṃ Udgātre Namaḥ* I	ॐ उद्गात्रे नमः ।
714.	*Oṃ Hotre Namaḥ* I	ॐ होत्रे नमः ।
715.	*Oṃ Svāhākārāya Namaḥ* I	ॐ स्वाहाकाराय नमः ।
716.	*Oṃ Hutāhutaye Namaḥ* I	ॐ हुताहुतये नमः ।
717.	*Oṃ Janārdanāya Namaḥ* I	ॐ जनार्दनाय नमः ।
718.	*Oṃ Janānandāya Namaḥ* I	ॐ जनानन्दाय नमः ।
719.	*Oṃ Narāya Namaḥ* I	ॐ नराय नमः ।
720.	*Oṃ Nārāyaṇāya Namaḥ* I	ॐ नारायणाय नमः ।
721.	*Oṃ Ambudāya Namaḥ* I	ॐ अम्बुदाय नमः ।
722.	*Oṃ Sandehanāśanāya Namaḥ* I	ॐ सन्देहनाशनाय नमः ।
723.	*Oṃ Vāyave Namaḥ* I	ॐ वायवे नमः ।
724.	*Oṃ Dhanvine Namaḥ* I	ॐ धन्विने नमः ।
725.	*Oṃ Suranamaskṛtāya Namaḥ* I	ॐ सुरनमस्कृताय नमः ।
726.	*Oṃ Vigrahine Namaḥ* I	ॐ विग्रहिने नमः ।
727.	*Oṃ Vimalāya Namaḥ* I	ॐ विमलाय नमः ।
728.	*Oṃ Vindave Namaḥ* I	ॐ विन्दवे नमः ।
729.	*Oṃ Viśokāya Namaḥ* I	ॐ विशोकाय नमः ।
730.	*Oṃ Vimaladyutaye Namaḥ* I	ॐ विमलद्युतये नमः ।
731.	*Oṃ Dyutimate Namaḥ* I	ॐ द्युतिमते नमः ।
732.	*Oṃ Dyotanāya Namaḥ* I	ॐ द्योतनाय नमः ।

733.	*Oṃ Vidyute Namaḥ* I	ॐ विद्युते नमः ।
734.	*Oṃ Vidyāvate Namaḥ* I	ॐ विद्यावते नमः ।
735.	*Oṃ Viditāya Namaḥ* I	ॐ विदिताय नमः ।
736.	*Oṃ Baline Namaḥ* I	ॐ बलिने नमः ।
737.	*Oṃ Gharmadāya Namaḥ* I	ॐ घर्मदाय नमः ।
738.	*Oṃ Himadāya Namaḥ* I	ॐ हिमदाय नमः ।
739.	*Oṃ Hāsāya Namaḥ* I	ॐ हासाय नमः ।
740.	*Oṃ Kṛṣṇavartmane Namaḥ* I	ॐ कृष्णवर्त्मने नमः ।
741.	*Oṃ Sutājitāya Namaḥ* I	ॐ सुताजिताय नमः ।
742.	*Oṃ Sāvitrībhāvitāya Namaḥ* I	ॐ सावित्रीभाविताय नमः ।
743.	*Oṃ Rājñe Namaḥ* I	ॐ राज्ञे नमः ।
744.	*Oṃ Viśvāmitrāya Namaḥ* I	ॐ विश्वामित्राय नमः ।
745.	*Oṃ Ghṛṇaye Namaḥ* I	ॐ घृणये नमः ।
746.	*Oṃ Virāje Namaḥ* I	ॐ विराजे नमः ।
747.	*Oṃ Saptārciṣe Namaḥ* I	ॐ सप्तार्चिषे नमः ।
748.	*Oṃ Saptaturagāya Namaḥ* I	ॐ सप्ततुरगाय नमः ।
749.	*Oṃ Saptalokanamaskṛtāya Namaḥ* I	ॐ सप्तलोकनमस्कृताय नमः ।
750.	*Oṃ Sampūrṇāya Namaḥ* I	ॐ सम्पूर्णाय नमः ।
751.	*Oṃ Jagannāthāya Namaḥ* I	ॐ जगन्नाथाय नमः ।
752.	*Oṃ Sumanase Namaḥ* I	ॐ सुमनसे नमः ।
753.	*Oṃ Śobhanapriyāya Namaḥ* I	ॐ शोभनप्रियाय नमः ।
754.	*Oṃ Sarvātmane Namaḥ* I	ॐ सर्वात्मने नमः ।
755.	*Oṃ Sarvakṛte Namaḥ* I	ॐ सर्वकृते नमः ।
756.	*Oṃ Sṛṣṭaye Namaḥ* I	ॐ सृष्टये नमः ।
757.	*Oṃ Saptimate Namaḥ* I	ॐ सप्तिमते नमः ।
758.	*Oṃ Saptamīpriyāya Namaḥ* I	ॐ सप्तमीप्रियाय नमः ।

759.	Oṃ Sumedhase Namaḥ I	ॐ सुमेधसे नमः ।
760.	Oṃ Medhikāya Namaḥ I	ॐ मेधिकाय नमः ।
761.	Oṃ Medhyāya Namaḥ I	ॐ मेध्याय नमः ।
762.	Oṃ Medhāvine Namaḥ I	ॐ मेधाविने नमः ।
763.	Oṃ Madhusūdanāya Namaḥ	ॐ मधुसूदनाय नमः ।
764.	Oṃ Aṅgiraḥpataye Namaḥ I	ॐ अङ्गिरःपतये नमः ।
765.	Oṃ Kālajñāya Namaḥ I	ॐ कालज्ञाय नमः ।
766.	Oṃ Dhūmaketave Namaḥ I	ॐ धूमकेतवे नमः ।
767.	Oṃ Suketanāya Namaḥ I	ॐ सुकेतनाय नमः ।
768.	Oṃ Sukhine Namaḥ I	ॐ सुखिने नमः ।
769.	Oṃ Sukhapradāya Namaḥ I	ॐ सुखप्रदाय नमः ।
770.	Oṃ Saukhyāya Namaḥ I	ॐ सौख्याय नमः ।
771.	Oṃ Kāmine Namaḥ I	ॐ कामिने नमः ।
772.	Oṃ Kāntaye Namaḥ I	ॐ कान्तये नमः ।
773.	Oṃ Kāntipriyāya Namaḥ I	ॐ कान्तिप्रियाय नमः ।
774.	Oṃ Munaye Namaḥ I	ॐ मुनये नमः ।
775.	Oṃ Santāpanāya Namaḥ I	ॐ सन्तापनाय नमः ।
776.	Oṃ Santapanāya Namaḥ I	ॐ सन्तपनाय नमः ।
777.	Oṃ Ātapāya Namaḥ I	ॐ आतपाय नमः ।
778.	Oṃ Tapasāṃ Pataye Namaḥ	ॐ तपसां पतये नमः ।
779.	Oṃ Umāpataye Namaḥ I	ॐ उमापतये नमः ।
780.	Oṃ Sahasrāṃśave Namaḥ I	ॐ सहस्रांशवे नमः ।
781.	Oṃ Priyakāriṇe Namaḥ I	ॐ प्रियकारिणे नमः ।
782.	Oṃ Priyaṅkarāya Namaḥ I	ॐ प्रियङ्कराय नमः ।
783.	Oṃ Prītaye Namaḥ I	ॐ प्रीतये नमः ।
784.	Oṃ Vimanyave Namaḥ I	ॐ विमन्यवे नमः ।

785.	*Oṃ Ambhotthāya Namaḥ* |	ॐ अम्भोत्थाय नमः ।
786.	*Oṃ Khañjanāya Namaḥ* |	ॐ खञ्जनाय नमः ।
787.	*Oṃ Jagatāṃ Pataye Namaḥ* |	ॐ जगतां पतये नमः ।
788.	*Oṃ Jagatpitre Namaḥ* |	ॐ जगत्पित्रे नमः ।
789.	*Oṃ Prītamanase Namaḥ* |	ॐ प्रीतमनसे नमः ।
790.	*Oṃ Sarvāya Namaḥ* |	ॐ सर्वाय नमः ।
791.	*Oṃ Kharvāya Namaḥ* |	ॐ खर्वाय नमः ।
792.	*Oṃ Guhāya Namaḥ* |	ॐ गुहाय नमः ।
793.	*Oṃ Acalāya Namaḥ* |	ॐ अचलाय नमः ।
794.	*Oṃ Sarvagāya Namaḥ* |	ॐ सर्वगाय नमः ।
795.	*Oṃ Jagadānandāya Namaḥ* |	ॐ जगदानन्दाय नमः ।
796.	*Oṃ Jagannetre Namaḥ* |	ॐ जगन्नेत्रे नमः ।
797.	*Oṃ Surārighne Namaḥ* |	ॐ सुरारिघ्ने नमः ।
798.	*Oṃ Śreyase Namaḥ* |	ॐ श्रेयसे नमः ।
799.	*Oṃ Śreyaskarāya Namaḥ* |	ॐ श्रेयस्कराय नमः ।
800.	*Oṃ Jyāyase Namaḥ* |	ॐ ज्यायसे नमः ।
801.	*Oṃ Mahate Namaḥ* |	ॐ महते नमः ।
802.	*Oṃ Uttamāya Namaḥ* |	ॐ उत्तमाय नमः ।
803.	*Oṃ Udbhavāya Namaḥ* |	ॐ उद्भवाय नमः ।
804.	*Oṃ Uttamāya Namaḥ* |	ॐ उत्तमाय नमः ।
805.	*Oṃ Merumeyāya Namaḥ* |	ॐ मेरुमेयाय नमः ।
806.	*Oṃ Athāya Namaḥ* |	ॐ अथाय नमः ।
807.	*Oṃ Dharaṇāya Namaḥ* |	ॐ धरणाय नमः ।
808.	*Oṃ Dharaṇīdharāya Namaḥ* |	ॐ धरणीधराय नमः ।
809.	*Oṃ Dharādhyakṣāya Namaḥ*	ॐ धराध्यक्षाय नमः ।
810.	*Oṃ Dharmarājāya Namaḥ* |	ॐ धर्मराजाय नमः ।

811.	*Oṃ Dharmā Dharma Pravartakāya Namaḥ* ।	ॐ धर्माधर्मप्रवर्तकाय नमः ।
812.	*Oṃ Rathādhyakṣāya Namaḥ*	ॐ रथाध्यक्षाय नमः ।
813.	*Oṃ Rathagataye Namaḥ* ।	ॐ रथगतये नमः ।
814.	*Oṃ Taruṇāya Namaḥ* ।	ॐ तरुणाय नमः ।
815.	*Oṃ Tanitāya Namaḥ* ।	ॐ तनिताय नमः ।
816.	*Oṃ Analāya Namaḥ* ।	ॐ अनलाय नमः ।
817.	*Oṃ Uttarāya Namaḥ* ।	ॐ उत्तराय नमः ।
818.	*Oṃ Anuttarastāpine Namaḥ* ।	ॐ अनुत्तरस्तापिने नमः ।
819.	*Oṃ Avākpataye Namaḥ* ।	ॐ अवाक्पतये नमः ।
820.	*Oṃ Apāṃ Pataye Namaḥ* ।	ॐ अपां पतये नमः ।
821.	*Oṃ Puṇyasaṅkīrtanāya Namaḥ* ।	ॐ पुण्यसङ्कीर्तनाय नमः ।
822.	*Oṃ Puṇyāya Namaḥ* ।	ॐ पुण्याय नमः ।
823.	*Oṃ Hetave Namaḥ* ।	ॐ हेतवे नमः ।
824.	*Oṃ Lokatrayāśrayāya Namaḥ* ।	ॐ लोकत्रयाश्रयाय नमः ।
825.	*Oṃ Svarbhānave Namaḥ* ।	ॐ स्वर्भानवे नमः ।
826.	*Oṃ Vigatānandāya Namaḥ* ।	ॐ विगतानन्दाय नमः ।
827.	*Oṃ Viśiṣṭotkṛṣṭakarmakṛte Namaḥ* ।	ॐ विशिष्टोत्कृष्टकर्मकृते नमः ।
828.	*Oṃ Vyādhipraṇāśanāya Namaḥ* ।	ॐ व्याधिप्रणाशनाय नमः ।
829.	*Oṃ Kṣemāya Namaḥ* ।	ॐ क्षेमाय नमः ।
830.	*Oṃ Śūrāya Namaḥ* ।	ॐ शूराय नमः ।
831.	*Oṃ Sarvajitāṃ Varāya Namaḥ* ।	ॐ सर्वजितां वराय नमः ।
832.	*Oṃ Ekarathāya Namaḥ* ।	ॐ एकरथाय नमः ।
833.	*Oṃ Rathādhīśāya Namaḥ* ।	ॐ रथाधीशाय नमः ।

834.	Oṃ Śanaiścarasyanamaḥ |	ॐ शनैश्चरस्यनमः।
835.	Oṃ Pitre Namaḥ |	ॐ पित्रे नमः।
836.	Oṃ Vaivasvatagurave Namaḥ |	ॐ वैवस्वतगुरवे नमः।
837.	Oṃ Mṛtyave Namaḥ |	ॐ मृत्यवे नमः।
838.	Oṃ Dharmanityāya Namaḥ |	ॐ धर्मनित्याय नमः।
839.	Oṃ Mahāvratāya Namaḥ |	ॐ महाव्रताय नमः।
840.	Oṃ Pralambahārasañcāriṇe Namaḥ |	ॐ प्रलम्बहारसञ्चारिणे नमः।
841.	Oṃ Pradyotāya Namaḥ |	ॐ प्रद्योताय नमः।
842.	Oṃ Dyotitānalāya Namaḥ |	ॐ द्योतितानलाय नमः।
843.	Oṃ Santāpahṛte Namaḥ |	ॐ सन्तापहृते नमः।
844.	Oṃ Parasmai Namaḥ |	ॐ परस्मै नमः।
845.	Oṃ Mantrāya Namaḥ |	ॐ मन्त्राय नमः।
846.	Oṃ Mantramūrtaye Namaḥ|	ॐ मन्त्रमूर्तये नमः।
847.	Oṃ Mahābalāya Namaḥ |	ॐ महाबलाय नमः।
848.	Oṃ Śreṣṭhātmane Namaḥ |	ॐ श्रेष्ठात्मने नमः।
849.	Oṃ Supriyāya Namaḥ |	ॐ सुप्रियाय नमः।
850.	Oṃ Śambhave Namaḥ |	ॐ शम्भवे नमः।
851.	Oṃ Marutāmīśvareśvarāya Namaḥ |	ॐ मरुतामीश्वरेश्वराय नमः।
852.	Oṃ Saṃsāragativicchettre Namaḥ |	ॐ संसारगतिविच्छेत्त्रे नमः।
853.	Oṃ Saṃsārārṇavatārakāya Namaḥ |	ॐ संसारार्णवतारकाय नमः।
854.	Oṃ Saptajihvāya Namaḥ |	ॐ सप्तजिह्वाय नमः।
855.	Oṃ Sahasrārciṣe Namaḥ |	ॐ सहस्रार्चिषे नमः।
856.	Oṃ Ratnagarbhāya Namaḥ |	ॐ रत्नगर्भाय नमः।

857.	*Oṃ Aparājitāya Namaḥ* |	ॐ अपराजिताय नमः ।
858.	*Oṃ Dharmaketave Namaḥ* |	ॐ धर्मकेतवे नमः ।
859.	*Oṃ Ameyātmane Namaḥ* |	ॐ अमेयात्मने नमः ।
860.	*Oṃ Dharmā Dharmavara Pradāya Namaḥ* |	ॐ धर्माधर्मवरप्रदाय नमः ।
861.	*Oṃ Lokasākṣiṇe Namaḥ* |	ॐ लोकसाक्षिणे नमः ।
862.	*Oṃ Lokagurave Namaḥ* |	ॐ लोकगुरवे नमः ।
863.	*Oṃ Lokeśāya Namaḥ* |	ॐ लोकेशाय नमः ।
864.	*Oṃ Caṇḍavāhanāya Namaḥ* |	ॐ चण्डवाहनाय नमः ।
865.	*Oṃ Dharmayūpāya Namaḥ* |	ॐ धर्मयूपाय नमः ।
866.	*Oṃ Yūpavṛkṣāya Namaḥ* |	ॐ यूपवृक्षाय नमः ।
867.	*Oṃ Dhanuṣpāṇaye Namaḥ* |	ॐ धनुष्पाणये नमः ।
868.	*Oṃ Dhanurdharāya Namaḥ* |	ॐ धनुर्धराय नमः ।
869.	*Oṃ Pinākadhṛte Namaḥ* |	ॐ पिनाकधृते नमः ।
870.	*Oṃ Mahotsāhāya Namaḥ* |	ॐ महोत्साहाय नमः ।
871.	*Oṃ Mahāmāyāya Namaḥ* |	ॐ महामायाय नमः ।
872.	*Oṃ Mahāśanāya Namaḥ* |	ॐ महाशनाय नमः ।
873.	*Oṃ Vīrāya Namaḥ* |	ॐ वीराय नमः ।
874.	*Oṃ Śaktimatāṃ Śreṣṭhāya Namaḥ* |	ॐ शक्तिमतां श्रेष्ठाय नमः ।
875.	*Oṃ Sarvaśastrabhṛtāṃ Varāya Namaḥ* |	ॐ सर्वशस्त्रभृतां वराय नमः ।
876.	*Oṃ Jñānagamyāya Namaḥ* |	ॐ ज्ञानगम्याय नमः ।
877.	*Oṃ Durārādhyāya Namaḥ* |	ॐ दुराराध्याय नमः ।
878.	*Oṃ Lohitāṅgāya Namaḥ* |	ॐ लोहिताङ्गाय नमः ।
879.	*Oṃ Vivardhanāya Namaḥ* |	ॐ विवर्धनाय नमः ।
880.	*Oṃ Khagāya Namaḥ* |	ॐ खगाय नमः ।

881.	*Oṃ Andhāya Namaḥ* I	ॐ अन्धाय नमः ।
882.	*Oṃ Dharmadāya Namaḥ* I	ॐ धर्मदाय नमः ।
883.	*Oṃ Nityāya Namaḥ* I	ॐ नित्याय नमः ।
884.	*Oṃ Dharmakṛte Namaḥ* I	ॐ धर्मकृते नमः ।
885.	*Oṃ Citravikramāya Namaḥ* I	ॐ चित्रविक्रमाय नमः ।
886.	*Oṃ Bhagavate Namaḥ* I	ॐ भगवते नमः ।
887.	*Oṃ Ātmavate Namaḥ* I	ॐ आत्मवते नमः ।
888.	*Oṃ Mantrāya Namaḥ* I	ॐ मन्त्राय नमः ।
889.	*Oṃ Tryakṣarāya Namaḥ* I	ॐ त्र्यक्षराय नमः ।
890.	*Oṃ Nīlalohitāya Namaḥ* I	ॐ नीललोहिताय नमः ।
891.	*Oṃ Ekāya Namaḥ* I	ॐ एकाय नमः ।
892.	*Oṃ Anekāya Namaḥ* I	ॐ अनेकाय नमः ।
893.	*Oṃ Trayine Namaḥ* I	ॐ त्रयिने नमः ।
894.	*Oṃ Kālāya Namaḥ* I	ॐ कालाय नमः ।
895.	*Oṃ Savitre Namaḥ* I	ॐ सवित्रे नमः ।
896.	*Oṃ Samitiñjayāya Namaḥ* I	ॐ समितिञ्जयाय नमः ।
897.	*Oṃ Śārṅgadhanvane Namaḥ*	ॐ शार्ङ्गधन्वने नमः ।
898.	*Oṃ Analāya Namaḥ* I	ॐ अनलाय नमः ।
899.	*Oṃ Bhīmāya Namaḥ* I	ॐ भीमाय नमः ।
900.	*Oṃ Sarvapraharaṇāyudhāya Namaḥ* I	ॐ सर्वप्रहरणायुधाय नमः ।
901.	*Oṃ Sukarmaṇe Namaḥ* I	ॐ सुकर्मणे नमः ।
902.	*Oṃ Parameṣṭhine Namaḥ* I	ॐ परमेष्ठिने नमः ।
903.	*Oṃ Nākapāline Namaḥ* I	ॐ नाकपालिने नमः ।
904.	*Oṃ Divisthitāya Namaḥ* I	ॐ दिविस्थिताय नमः ।
905.	*Oṃ Vadānyāya Namaḥ* I	ॐ वदान्याय नमः ।
906.	*Oṃ Vāsukaye Namaḥ* I	ॐ वासुकये नमः ।

907.	*Oṃ Vaidyāya Namaḥ* I	ॐ वैद्याय नमः ।
908.	*Oṃ Ātreyāya Namaḥ* I	ॐ आत्रेयाय नमः ।
909.	*Oṃ Parākramāya Namaḥ* I	ॐ पराक्रमाय नमः ।
910.	*Oṃ Dvāparāya Namaḥ* I	ॐ द्वापराय नमः ।
911.	*Oṃ Paramodārāya Namaḥ* I	ॐ परमोदाराय नमः ।
912.	*Oṃ Paramāya Namaḥ* I	ॐ परमाय नमः ।
913.	*Oṃ Brahmacaryavate Namaḥ* I	ॐ ब्रह्मचर्यवते नमः ।
914.	*Oṃ Udīcyaveṣāya Namaḥ* I	ॐ उदीच्यवेषाय नमः ।
915.	*Oṃ Mukuṭine Namaḥ* I	ॐ मुकुटिने नमः ।
916.	*Oṃ Padmahastāya Namaḥ* I	ॐ पद्महस्ताय नमः ।
917.	*Oṃ Himāṃśubhṛte Namaḥ* I	ॐ हिमांशुभृते नमः ।
918.	*Oṃ Sitāya Namaḥ* I	ॐ सिताय नमः ।
919.	*Oṃ Prasannavadanāya Namaḥ* I	ॐ प्रसन्नवदनाय नमः ।
920.	*Oṃ Padmodaranibhānanāya Namaḥ* I	ॐ पद्मोदरनिभाननाय नमः ।
921.	*Oṃ Sāyaṃ Divā Divyavapuṣe Namaḥ* I	ॐ सायं दिवा दिव्यवपुषे नमः ।
922.	*Oṃ Anirdeśyāya Namaḥ* I	ॐ अनिर्देश्याय नमः ।
923.	*Oṃ Mahālayāya Namaḥ* I	ॐ महालयाय नमः ।
924.	*Oṃ Mahārathāya Namaḥ* I	ॐ महारथाय नमः ।
925.	*Oṃ Mahate Namaḥ* I	ॐ महते नमः ।
926.	*Oṃ Īśāya Namaḥ* I	ॐ ईशाय नमः ।
927.	*Oṃ Śeṣāya Namaḥ* I	ॐ शेषाय नमः ।
928.	*Oṃ Sattvarajastamase Namaḥ* I	ॐ सत्त्वरजस्तमसे नमः ।

929.	*Oṃ Dhṛtātapatrapratimāya Namaḥ* |	ॐ धृतातपत्रप्रतिमाय नमः ।
930.	*Oṃ Vimarṣine Namaḥ* |	ॐ विमर्षिने नमः ।
931.	*Oṃ Nirṇayāya Namaḥ* |	ॐ निर्णयाय नमः ।
932.	*Oṃ Sthitāya Namaḥ* |	ॐ स्थिताय नमः ।
933.	*Oṃ Ahiṃsakāya Namaḥ* |	ॐ अहिंसकाय नमः ।
934.	*Oṃ Śuddhamataye Namaḥ* |	ॐ शुद्धमतये नमः ।
935.	*Oṃ Advitīyāya Namaḥ* |	ॐ अद्वितीयाय नमः ।
936.	*Oṃ Vivardhanāya Namaḥ* |	ॐ विवर्धनाय नमः ।
937.	*Oṃ Sarvadāya Namaḥ* |	ॐ सर्वदाय नमः ।
938.	*Oṃ Dhanadāya Namaḥ* |	ॐ धनदाय नमः ।
939.	*Oṃ Mokṣāya Namaḥ* |	ॐ मोक्षाय नमः ।
940.	*Oṃ Vihāriṇe Namaḥ* |	ॐ विहारिणे नमः ।
941.	*Oṃ Bahudāyakāya Namaḥ* |	ॐ बहुदायकाय नमः ।
942.	*Oṃ Cārurātriharāya Namaḥ* |	ॐ चारुरात्रिहराय नमः ।
943.	*Oṃ Nāthāya Namaḥ* |	ॐ नाथाय नमः ।
944.	*Oṃ Bhagavate Namaḥ* |	ॐ भगवते नमः ।
945.	*Oṃ Sarvagāya Namaḥ* |	ॐ सर्वगाय नमः ।
946.	*Oṃ Avyayāya Namaḥ* |	ॐ अव्ययाय नमः ।
947.	*Oṃ Manoharavapave Namaḥ* |	ॐ मनोहरवपवे नमः ।
948.	*Oṃ Śubhrāya Namaḥ* |	ॐ शुभ्राय नमः ।
949.	*Oṃ Śobhanāya Namaḥ* |	ॐ शोभनाय नमः ।
950.	*Oṃ Suprabhāvanāya Namaḥ*	ॐ सुप्रभावनाय नमः ।
951.	*Oṃ Suprabhāvāya Namaḥ* |	ॐ सुप्रभावाय नमः ।
952.	*Oṃ Supratāpāya Namaḥ* |	ॐ सुप्रतापाय नमः ।
953.	*Oṃ Sunetrāya Namaḥ* |	ॐ सुनेत्राय नमः ।

954.	*Oṃ Digvidikpataye Namaḥ* I	ॐ दिग्विदिक्पतये नमः ।
955.	*Oṃ Rājñīpriyāya Namaḥ* I	ॐ राज्ञीप्रियाय नमः ।
956.	*Oṃ Śabdakarāya Namaḥ* I	ॐ शब्दकराय नमः ।
957.	*Oṃ Graheśāya Namaḥ* I	ॐ ग्रहेशाय नमः ।
958.	*Oṃ Timirāpahāya Namaḥ* I	ॐ तिमिरापहाय नमः ।
959.	*Oṃ Saiṃhikeyaripave Namaḥ* I	ॐ सैंहिकेयरिपवे नमः ।
960.	*Oṃ Devāya Namaḥ* I	ॐ देवाय नमः ।
961.	*Oṃ Varadāya Namaḥ* I	ॐ वरदाय नमः ।
962.	*Oṃ Varanāyakāya Namaḥ* I	ॐ वरनायकाय नमः ।
963.	*Oṃ Caturbhujāya Namaḥ* I	ॐ चतुर्भुजायनमः ।
964.	*Oṃ Mahāyogine Namaḥ* I	ॐ महायोगिने नमः ।
965.	*Oṃ Yogīśvarapataye Namaḥ*	ॐ योगीश्वरपतये नमः ।
966.	*Oṃ Anādirūpāya Namaḥ* I	ॐ अनादिरूपाय नमः ।
967.	*Oṃ Aditijāya Namaḥ* I	ॐ अदितिजाय नमः ।
968.	*Oṃ Ratnakāntaye Namaḥ* I	ॐ रत्नकान्तये नमः ।
969.	*Oṃ Prabhāmayāya Namaḥ* I	ॐ प्रभामयाय नमः ।
970.	*Oṃ Jagatpradīpāya Namaḥ* I	ॐ जगत्प्रदीपाय नमः ।
971.	*Oṃ Vistīrṇāya Namaḥ* I	ॐ विस्तीर्णाय नमः ।
972.	*Oṃ Mahāvistīrṇamaṇḍalāya Namaḥ* I	ॐ महाविस्तीर्णमण्डलाय नमः ।
973.	*Oṃ Ekacakrarathāya Namaḥ*	ॐ एकचक्ररथाय नमः ।
974.	*Oṃ Svarṇarathāya Namaḥ* I	ॐ स्वर्णरथाय नमः ।
975.	*Oṃ Svarṇaśarīradhṛṣe Namaḥ* I	ॐ स्वर्णशरीरधृषे नमः ।
976.	*Oṃ Nirālambāya Namaḥ* I	ॐ निरालम्बाय नमः ।
977.	*Oṃ Gaganagāya Namaḥ* I	ॐ गगनगाय नमः ।

978.	*Oṃ Dharma Karma Prabhāvakṛte Namaḥ* ।	ॐ धर्मकर्मप्रभावकृते नमः ।
979.	*Oṃ Dharmātmane Namaḥ* ।	ॐ धर्मात्मने नमः ।
980.	*Oṃ Karmaṇāṃ Sākṣiṇe Namaḥ* ।	ॐ कर्मणां साक्षिणे नमः ।
981.	*Oṃ Pratyakṣāya Namaḥ* ।	ॐ प्रत्यक्षाय नमः ।
982.	*Oṃ Parameśvarāya Namaḥ* ।	ॐ परमेश्वराय नमः ।
983.	*Oṃ Merusevine Namaḥ* ।	ॐ मेरुसेविने नमः ।
984.	*Oṃ Sumedhāvine Namaḥ* ।	ॐ सुमेधाविने नमः ।
985.	*Oṃ Merurakṣākarāya Namaḥ* ।	ॐ मेरुरक्षाकराय नमः ।
986.	*Oṃ Mahate Namaḥ* ।	ॐ महते नमः ।
987.	*Oṃ Ādhārabhūtāya Namaḥ* ।	ॐ आधारभूताय नमः ।
988.	*Oṃ Ratimate Namaḥ* ।	ॐ रतिमते नमः ।
989.	*Oṃ Dhanadhānyakṛte Namaḥ* ।	ॐ धनधान्यकृते नमः ।
990.	*Oṃ Pāpasantāpahartre Namaḥ* ।	ॐ पापसन्तापहर्त्रे नमः ।
991.	*Oṃ Manovāñchitadāyakāya Namaḥ* ।	ॐ मनोवाञ्छितदायकाय नमः ।
992.	*Oṃ Rogahartre Namaḥ* ।	ॐ रोगहर्त्रे नमः ।
993.	*Oṃ Rājyadāyine Namaḥ* ।	ॐ राज्यदायिने नमः ।
994.	*Oṃ Ramaṇīyaguṇāya Namaḥ* ।	ॐ रमणीयगुणाय नमः ।
995.	*Oṃ Anṛṇine Namaḥ* ।	ॐ अनृणिने नमः ।
996.	*Oṃ Kālatrayānantarūpāya Namaḥ* ।	ॐ कालत्रयानन्तरूपाय नमः ।
997.	*Oṃ Munivṛndanamaskṛtāya Namaḥ* ।	ॐ मुनिवृन्दनमस्कृताय नमः ।

998.	*Oṃ Sandhyārāgakarāya Namaḥ* I	ॐ सन्ध्यारागकराय नमः ।
999.	*Oṃ Siddhāya Namaḥ* I	ॐ सिद्धाय नमः ।
1000.	*Oṃ Sandhyā Vandana Vanditāya Namaḥ* I	ॐ सन्ध्यावन्दनवन्दिताय नमः ।
1001.	*Oṃ Sāmrājyadānaniratāya Namaḥ* I	ॐ साम्राज्यदाननिरताय नमः ।
1002.	*Oṃ Samārādhanatoṣavate Namaḥ* I	ॐ समाराधनतोषवते नमः ।
1003.	*Oṃ Bhakta Duḥkhaḥ Kṣayakarāya Namaḥ* I	ॐ भक्तदुःखक्षयकराय नमः ।
1004.	*Oṃ Bhavasāgaratārakāya Namaḥ* I	ॐ भवसागरतारकाय नमः ।
1005.	*Oṃ Bhayāpahartre Namaḥ* I	ॐ भयापहर्त्रे नमः ।
1006.	*Oṃ Bhagavate Namaḥ* I	ॐ भगवते नमः ।
1007.	*Oṃ Aprameyaparākramāya Namaḥ* I	ॐ अप्रमेयपराक्रमाय नमः ।
1008.	*Oṃ Manusvāmine Namaḥ* I	ॐ मनुस्वामिने नमः ।
1009.	*Oṃ Manupataye Namaḥ* I	ॐ मनुपतये नमः ।
1010.	*Oṃ Mānyāya Namaḥ* I	ॐ मान्याय नमः ।
1011.	*Oṃ Manvantarādhipāya Namaḥ* I	ॐ मन्वन्तराधिपाय नमः ।

Phalaśrutiḥ

Etatte Sarvamākhyātaṃ Yanmāṃ Tvaṃ Paripṛccasi I
Nāmnāṃ Sahasraṃ Savituḥ Pārāśaryo Yadāha Me II 1

Dhanyaṃ Yaśasyamāyuṣyaṃ Duḥkhaduḥsvapnanāśanam I
Bandhamokṣakaraṃ Caiva Bhānornāmānukīrtanāt II 2

Yastvidaṃ Śṛṇuyānnityaṃ Paṭhedvā Prayato Naraḥ |
Akṣayaṃ Sukhamannādyaṃ Bhavettasyopasādhitam || 3

Nṛpāgnitaskarabhayaṃ Vyādhito Na Bhayaṃ Bhavet |
Vijayī Ca Bhavennityamāśrayaṃ Paramāpnuyāt || 4

Kīrtimān Subhago Vidvān Sa Sukhī Priyadarśanaḥ |
Jīvedvarṣaśatāyuśca Sarvavyādhivivarjitaḥ || 5

Nāmnāṃ Sahasramidamaṃśumataḥ Paṭhedyaḥ
Prātaḥ Śucirniyamavān Susamṛddhiyuktaḥ |
Dūreṇa Taṃ Pariharanti Sadaiva Rogāḥ
Bhūtāḥ Suparṇamiva Sarvamahoragendrāḥ || 6

Iti Śrībhaviṣyapurāṇe Saptamakalpe Śrībhagavatsūryasya
Sahasranāmāvaliḥ Samāptā |

*****

फलश्रुतिः

एतत्ते सर्वमाख्यातं यन्मां त्वं परिपृच्छसि ।
नाम्नां सहस्रं सवितुः पाराशर्यो यदाह मे ॥ १

धन्यं यशस्यमायुष्यं दुःखदुःस्वप्ननाशनम् ।
बन्धमोक्षकरं चैव भानोर्नामानुकीर्तनात् ॥ २

यस्त्विदं शृणुयान्नित्यं पठेद्वा प्रयतो नरः ।
अक्षयं सुखमन्नाद्यं भवेत्तस्योपसाधितम् ॥ ३

नृपाग्नितस्करभयं व्याधितो न भयं भवेत् ।
विजयी च भवेन्नित्यमाश्रयं परमाप्नुयात् ॥ ४

कीर्तिमान् सुभगो विद्वान् स सुखी प्रियदर्शनः ।
जीवेद्वर्षशतायुश्च सर्वव्याधिविवर्जितः ॥ ५

नाम्नां सहस्रमिदमंशुमतः पठेद्यःप्रातः शुचिर्नियमवान् सुसमृद्धियुक्तः ।
दूरेण तं परिहरन्ति सदैव रोगाः भूताः सुपर्णमिव सर्वमहोरगेन्द्राः ॥ ६

इति श्रीभविष्यपुराणे सप्तमकल्पे श्रीभगवत्सूर्यस्य सहस्रनामावलिः समाप्ता ।

*****

About the Author

(http://Ramamurthy.jaagruti.co.in)

Dr. Ramamurthy is a versatile personality having experience and expertise in various areas of banking, related IT solutions, information security, IT audit, Vedas, Samskrutam and so on.

His thirst for continuous learning does not subside. Even at the age of late fifties, he did research on a unique topic "Information Technology and Samskrutam" and obtained Ph.D. – doctorate degree from University of Madras. He is into a project of developing a Samskrutam based compiler.

It is his passion to spread his knowledge and experience through conducting classes, training programs and writing books.

He has already published books as detailed below. Further books are in pipe-line.

#	Title	Remarks	Pages
		Indology Related	
1.	*Shrī Lalitā Sahasranāmam*	English Translation of Shrī *Bhāskararāya's Bhāśyam*	750
2.	Power of *Shrī Vidyā*	The Secrets Demystified – With Lucid English Rendering and Commentaries	80
3.	ஸ்ரீ வித்யையின் ஶக்தி	ஸ்ரீ வித்யா ரகசியங்கள்	100
4.	*Samatā* – **समता**	An Exposition of Similarities in *Lalitā Sahasranāma* with *Soundaryalaharī, Saptaśatī, Viśṇu Sahasranāma* and *Shrīmad Bhagavad Gīta*	172
5.	ஸமதா – **समता**	ஸ்ரீ லலிதா ஸஹஸ்ரநாமம் ஸௌந்தர்யலஹரீ, ஸப்தஶதீ, ஸ்ரீ விஷ்ணு ஸஹஸ்ரநாமம் மற்றும் ஸ்ரீமத் பகவத் கீதைகளில் ஒற்றுமையின் ஒரு வெளிப்பாடு	266
6.	*Advaita* In *Shākta*	Advaita Philosophy Discussed in Shakta Related Books	80
7.	*Shrī Lalitā Triśatī*	300 Divine Names of The Celestial Mother – **English** Translation of *Shrī Ādhi Śaṅkara's Bhāśyam*	193
8.	ஸ்ரீ லலிதா த்ரிஶதி	300 Divine Names of The Celestial Mother – Tamil Translation of *Shrī Ādi Śaṅkara's Bhāśyam*	234

#	Title	Remarks	Pages
9.	Secrets of *Mahāśakti*	Chandi Demystified	78
10.	*Daśa Mahā Vidyā*	Ten Cosmic Forms of The Divine Mother	60
11.	ஸ்ரீ வித்யா பேதங்கள்	ஸ்ரீவித்யா உபாசனையின் படிகள் - கோவை ஶதச் சண்டீ மலர்	51
12.	*Shrīvidya* Variances	Variances In Srividya Upasana	50
13.	ஸ்ரீ தேவீ ஸ்துதிகள்	பல முக்கிய அம்பாள் ஸ்தோத்ரங்கள்	133
14.	Śrī Devī Stutis – श्रीदेवी स्तुतिः	Various Important Stotras of Sri Devi	223
15.	ஷண்மத மந்த்ரங்கள்	பொள்ளாச்சி ஸ்ரீ ஸஹஸ்ரசண்டீ மஹாயாக நினைவு மலர்	145
16.	*Śanmata Mantras* – षण्मत मन्त्राः	Important Mantras Relating to Gods of Six Religions	87
17.	தேவதா மந்த்ரங்கள்	அக்கரைப்பட்டி ஸஹஸ்ரசண்டீ மஹாயாக நினைவு மலர்	32
18.	ஆதி ஶங்கரரும் ஷண்மதமும்	ஷண்மதங்களைப் பற்றிய ஒரு அறிமுகம்	32
19.	ஸ்ரீ ஷண்மத தேவதா அர்ச்சனை	ஸ்ரீ மஹா கும்பாபிஷேக மலர்	64
20.	*Vaidhīka* Wedding	Typical Wedding Process in English	56
21.	வைதீகத் திருமணம்	Typical Wedding Process in Tamil	57
22.	ஸ்ரீகுரு பாத பூஜா விதானம்	சித்தகிரி ஸஹஸ்ரசண்டீ மலர்	44
23.	குரு வார வழிபாடு		70
24.	ஸ்ரீவித்யா ஶடாம்னாய மந்த்ரங்கள்	சித்தகிரி ஸஹஸ்ரசண்டீ மலர்	60
25.	*Ekatā*	Oneness Among Shiva, *Viṣṇu* and Shakti	277
26.	ஏகதா - एकता	ஶிவபெருமான், விஷ்ணு மற்றும் ஶக்திக்குள் ஒற்றுமை	370
27.	*Vedas* – An Analytical Perspective	A Description of Veda, Vedanta, Vedanga, Jyotisha, Shastra, Etc.	240
28.	வேதங்கள் - ஒரு பகுப்பாய்வு	A Description of Veda, Vedanta, Vedanga, Jyotisha, Shastra, Etc.	280
29.	பரமாச்சார்யாள் நோக்கில் ஸ்ரீ லலிதாம்பிகா	The Explanation Given by Paramacharya on Some of The Names in Lalitā Sahasranama	175
30.	*Ṣaṇṇavati Tarpaṇa*	Repaying Debts to Ancestors	42
31.	ஷண்ணவதி தர்பணம்	முன்னோர் கடன் தீர்த்தல்	48
32.	*Shrī Mahā Pratyangirā Devī*	Holy Divine Mother in Ferocious Form	41
33.	ஸ்ரீ மஹா ப்ரத்யங்கிரா தேவீ	தெய்வீக அன்னையின் பயங்கர வடிவம்	51
34.	*Śrī Chakra Navāvarṇam*	Marvels of *Śrī Chakra*	115
35.	ஸ்ரீ சக்ர நவாவர்ணம்	ஸ்ரீ சக்ரத்தின் அதிசயங்கள்	130

#	Title	Remarks	Pages
36.	அம்பிகையின் (திரு) அவதாரங்கள்	ஸ்ரீ தேவியின் பல்வேறு அவதாரங்கள்	142
37.	Incarnations of Holy Mother	Different Incarnations of *Śrī Devī*	140
38.	ஸ்ரீ பிரணவானந்தர் - ஒரு சரிதம்	ஒரு அரிய ஸ்வாமிகளின் திவ்ய சரிதம்	121
39.	ஸன்யாஸம் - ஓர் அலசல்	ஹிந்து மத ஸன்யாஸ பேதங்கள் - ஒரு பகுப்பாய்வு	140
40.	Asceticism – An Analysis	A Study of Hindu *Sanyasam*	140
41.	ஶாந்தமும் ப்ரணவமும்	(ஸ்ரீ ஶாந்தானந்தரும் ஸ்ரீ ப்ரணவானந்தரும்) குரு சிஷ்யருக்கு உபதேசங்கள்	120
42.	ஸ்ரீ ஸஹஸ்ராக்ஷரீ வித்யா	2020 சாதுர்மாஸ்ய மலர்	84
43.	*Shakta Upanishats*	*Upanishats* About *Sri Devi*	385
44.	ஶாக்த உபநிஷதங்கள்	*Upanishats* About *Sri Devi*	400
45.	ஸ்ரீ தேவீ கீதை	Sri Devi Geeta	194
46.	*Śrī Devī Gīta*	Sri Devi Geeta	180
47.	*Śrī Gāyatrī Sahasranamam*	1,000 Divine Names of *Śrī Gāyatrī Mātā*	392
48.	ஸ்ரீ காயத்ரீ ஸஹஸ்ரநாமம்	ஸ்ரீ காயத்ரி மாதாவின் 1,000 திவ்ய நாமங்கள்	450
49.	ஸ்ரீ ஸௌந்தர்யலஹரீ - ஒரு உள் அறிவு	ஒரு உள்-அறிவு	250
50.	*Śrī Soundaryalaharī* – an Insight	An Insight	200
51.	ஸ்ரீ ஶிவானந்த^{3}லஹரீ- ஒரு உள் அறிவு	ஒரு உள்-அறிவு	176
52.	*Śrī Śivānandalaharī* – an Insight	An Insight	129
53.	*Śrī Vārāhī Devī*	Holy Divine Mother with A Hog Face	96
54.	ஸ்ரீ வாராஹீ தேவீ	பன்றி முகத்துடன் கூடிய புனிதத் தெய்வீக அன்னை	106
55.	Śrī Vijaya Bhairavar	A Terrifying, Sacred, Divine Form of Lord Shiva	164
56.	ஸ்ரீ விஜய பை$_{4}$ரவர்	ஶிவபெருமானின் ஒரு திகிலூட்டும் புனித தெய்வீக உருவம்	188
57.	ஸ்ரீ ப$_{4}$த்$_{3}$ர காளீ	ஸ்ரீ தேவியின் ஒரு திகிலூட்டும் புனித தெய்வீக உருவம் – 1st Devi of Dasha Maha Vidya	226
58.	*Śrī Bhadra Kālī*	A Startling, Sacred and Divine Form of *Śrī Devī* – 1st Devi of Dasha Maha Vidya	224
59.	திதி^{2} நித்யா தே^{3}விகள்	16 *Tithi Nitya Devis*	230
60.	*Tithi Nityā Devis*	16 *Tithi Nitya Devis*	186
61.	ஸ்ரீ தாரா – நீல ஸரஸ்வதீ	2nd Devi of Dasha Maha Vidya	182
62.	*Śrī Tārā Devī* – Blue *Saraswatī*	2nd Devi of Dasha Maha Vidya	174
63.	*Śrī Tripura Sundarī Devī*	3rd Devi of Dasha Maha Vidya	182
64.	ஸ்ரீ த்ரிபுர ஸுந்தரீ தேவீ	3rd Devi of Dasha Maha Vidya	192
65.	*Śrī Bhuvaneshwari Devī*	4th Devi of Dasha Maha Vidya	137

#	Title	Remarks	Pages
66.	ஸ்ரீ புவனேஶ்வரீ தேவீ	4th Devi of Dasha Maha Vidya	151
67.	*Śrī Tripura Bhairavi Devi*	5th Devi of Dasha Maha Vidya	132
68.	ஸ்ரீ த்ரிபுர பைரவீதேவீ	5th Devi of Dasha Maha Vidya	146
69.	*Śrī Kamalātmikā Devi*	6th Devi of Dasha Maha Vidya	138
70.	ஸ்ரீ சின்ன மஸ்தா தேவீ	6th Devi of Dasha Maha Vidya	164
71.	*Śrī Dhūmāvatī Devī*	7th Devi of Dasha Maha Vidya	141
72.	ஸ்ரீ தூ4மாவதீ தேவீ	7th Devi of Dasha Maha Vidya	166
73.	*Śrī Bhagalāmukhī Devī*	8th Devi of Dasha Maha Vidya	158
74.	ஸ்ரீ ப3க3லாமுகீ2 தேவீ	8th Devi of Dasha Maha Vidya	186
75.	*Śrī Mātangī Devī*	9th Devi of Dasha Maha Vidya	145
76.	ஸ்ரீ மாதங்கீ3 தே3வீ	9th Devi of Dasha Maha Vidya	171
77.	*Śrī Kamalātmikā Devī*	10th Devi of Dasha Maha Vidya	170
78.	ஸ்ரீ கமலாத்மிகா தே3வீ	10th Devi of Dasha Maha Vidya	226
79.	*Chaṇḍī Homa Vidhānam*	Process of Performing Chandi Homam	60
80.	சண்டீ ஹோம விதானம்	Process of Performing Chandi Homam	80
81.	ஸ்ரீ ருத்3ர ந்யாசம் & த்ரிஶதீ	300 Divine names of Lord Rudra and Japa Nyasam	224
82.	*Śrī Rudra Nyāsa & Triśatī*	300 Divine names of Lord Rudra and Japa Nyasam	160
83.	ஸ்ரீ ஸூர்ய ஸஹஸ்ர நாமம்	கருத்துக்களுடன் ஒரு விளக்கம்	404
84.	*Śrī Sūrya Sahasranāmam*	Explanation with Comments	320
	Applied Samskrutam Based		
85.	*Paribhāshā Stora*–S	An Exploration of *Lalitā Sahasranāmam*	96
86.	பரிபாஷா ஸ்தோத்ரங்கள்	ஸ்ரீ லலிதா ஸஹஸ்ரநாமம் - ஒரு ஆய்வு	135
87.	*Shrī Cakra*, An Esoteric Approach	Mathematical Construction to Draw *Shrī Cakra*	64
88.	ஸ்ரீ சக்கரம் வரையும் முறை	ஸ்ரீ சக்கரம் வரைய கணித கட்டுமானம்	84
89.	Number System in Samskrutam	An Overview of Mathematics Based on Samskrutam	123
90.	ஸமஸ்க்ருதத்தில் எண்ணியல்	ஸமஸ்க்ருதத்தில் பொதிந்துள்ள எண் கணிதம்	140
91.	*Vedic* Mathematics	30 Formulae Elucidated	146
92.	Vedic IT	Information Technology and Samskrutam	162
	IT Based		
93.	Orthogonal Array	A Statistical Tool for Software Testing	180

#	Title	Remarks	Pages
		Banking Based	
94.	Retail Banking	A Guide Book for Novice	213
95.	Corporate Banking	A Guide Book for Novice	232
96.	Dictionary of Financial Terms	A Guide Book for All – Demystifying Myriad Global Financial Terms	215
97.	GRC In BFS Industry	(**G**overnance, **R**isk Management and **C**ompliance by Banking & Finance Industry)	200

*****

www.ingramcontent.com/pod-product-compliance
Ingram Content Group UK Ltd.
Pitfield, Milton Keynes, MK11 3LW, UK
UKHW011514190726
13845UKWH00034B/1249

9 789334 137903